EPISTEMOLOGY: 50 PUZZLES, PARADOXES, AND THOUGHT EXPERIMENTS

In this new kind of entrée to contemporary epistemology, Kevin McCain presents fifty of the field's most important puzzles, paradoxes, and thought experiments. Assuming no familiarity with epistemology from the reader, McCain titles each case with a memorable name, describes the details of the case, explains the issue(s) to which the case is relevant, and assesses its significance. McCain also briefly reviews the key responses to the case that have been put forward, and provides a helpful list of suggested readings on the topic. Each entry is accessible, succinct, and self-contained. *Epistemology: 50 Puzzles, Paradoxes, and Thought Experiments* is a fantastic learning tool as well as a handy resource for anyone interested in epistemological issues.

Key Features:

- Though concise overall, offers broad coverage of the key areas of epistemology.
- Describes each imaginative case directly and in a memorable way, making the cases accessible and easy to remember.
- Provides a list of Suggested Readings for each case, divided into General Overviews, Seminal Presentations, and Other Important Discussions.

Kevin McCain is Associate Professor of Philosophy at the University of Alabama at Birmingham. His published works include *Evidentialism and Epistemic Justification* (2014), *The Nature of Scientific Knowledge: An Explanatory Approach* (2016), (with Ted Poston) *Best Explanations: New Essays on Inference to the Best Explanation* (2017), and (with Kostas Kampourakis) *Uncertainty: How It Makes Science Advance* (2019).

PUZZLES, PARADOXES, AND THOUGHT EXPERIMENTS IN PHILOSOPHY

Imaginative cases—or what might be called puzzles, paradoxes, and other thought experiments–play a central role in philosophy. This series offers students and researchers a wide range of such imaginative cases, with each volume devoted to fifty such cases in a major subfield of philosophy. Every book in the series includes: some initial background information on each case, a clear and detailed description of the case, and an explanation of the issue(s) to which the case is relevant. Key responses to the case and suggested readings lists are also included.

Recently Published Volumes:

EPISTEMOLOGY
KEVIN McCAIN

FREE WILL AND HUMAN AGENCY
GARRETT PENDERGRAFT

Forthcoming Volumes:

AESTHETICS
MICHEL-ANTOINE XHIGNESSE

PHILOSOPHY OF LANGUAGE
MICHAEL P. WOLF

BIOETHICS
SEAN AAS, COLLIN O'NEIL, AND CHIARA LEPORA

PHILOSOPHY OF MIND
TORIN ALTER, AMY KIND, AND CHASE B. WRENN

For a full list of published volumes in **Puzzles, Paradoxes, and Thought Experiments in Philosophy**, please visit www.routledge.com/Puzzles, Paradoxes, andThoughtExperimentsinPhilosophy/book-series/PPTEP

EPISTEMOLOGY: 50 PUZZLES, PARADOXES, AND THOUGHT EXPERIMENTS

Kevin McCain

Routledge
Taylor & Francis Group

NEW YORK AND LONDON

First published 2022
by Routledge
605 Third Avenue, New York, NY 10158

and by Routledge
2 Park Square, Milton Park, Abingdon, Oxon, OX14 4RN

Routledge is an imprint of the Taylor & Francis Group, an informa business

Library of Congress Cataloging-in-Publication Data
A catalog record for this title has been requested

ISBN: 978-0-367-63873-3 (hbk)
ISBN: 978-0-367-63872-6 (pbk)
ISBN: 978-1-003-12109-1 (ebk)

Typeset in Bembo
by codeMantra

CONTENTS

PREFACE

Welcome to the world of epistemology! This book brings together fifty of the most important and widely discussed puzzles, paradoxes, and thought experiments in epistemology. The entries are grouped around themes, but they can be read in any order. Additionally, there are cross-references throughout to help readers connect relevant points of contact between various entries. Each entry includes a brief discussion of the major responses to the puzzle, paradox, or thought experiment described so that readers can get a sense not only of the example itself but also of the positions on it that have emerged in the epistemological literature. The suggested readings that accompany each entry offer readers direction for diving more deeply into the issues surrounding entries that pique their interest.

Given the structure of this book, there is a variety of ways that it might be used in an epistemology or general philosophy course or even for individual study. One way would be to pair this book with an epistemology textbook so that students can explore the thought experiments and puzzles that motivate the general theories covered in the textbook. Another way would be to use this book as the sole primary text using the entries to spark engaging class discussions. Of course, there are many other ways that one might use this book in class or in one's own study. The entries in this book are accessible to the beginning epistemology student, and yet informative enough—especially with the suggested readings—to be a handy resource for researchers.

I have many people to thank for their help with this project. Andy Beck enthusiastically supported this project from the start, and he, like the entire team at Routledge, was a pleasure to work with at every stage of the process. Adam Carter and Jon Matheson pointed me to key literature for several of the entries. Maddie Burchfield, Peter Graham, Nikolas Pham, Parker Rose, Karthik Sadanand, Tanvee Sinha, and anonymous reviewers graciously provided very helpful feedback on an earlier draft of the book. Ted Poston is owed a special debt of gratitude for this project. He came up with the idea for this book and, when it turned out that he would not be in a position to be my coauthor, encouraged me to go solo. Finally, Molly, Kaison, and Wallace gave me the love and support needed to make any project worthwhile. Thank you all.

Of course, while I have endeavored to make sure that each and every claim I make in this book is accurate and I believe each of these claims, surely some errors remain. Any errors that remain are entirely my own and not attributable to any of the wonderful people mentioned in the previous paragraph. (If you think it is strange for me to admit that I think every claim I make in this book is true and at the same time say that there are some errors, see entry 49 on the Preface Paradox.)

PART I

NATURE OF KNOWLEDGE

GENERAL BACKGROUND: THE TRADITIONAL ACCOUNT OF KNOWLEDGE

The entries to follow begin with a bit of background information to help situate and make clear the particular puzzles, paradoxes, and thought experiments discussed. However, some general background on the traditional account of knowledge is helpful to have in hand for most all of the entries in this book. So, let's begin by taking a brief look at how knowledge has been understood for many years.

Epistemologists have distinguished between three primary kinds of knowledge: acquaintance knowledge, knowledge-how, and propositional knowledge. Although our focus for this background, and most of the book, is the last sort, it will be helpful to take a quick look at the other two as well.

Acquaintance knowledge is knowledge you have of people and things you are familiar with personally. For example, let's say that you have a dog, which your new acquaintance, Fred, has never seen. You tell Fred all sorts of facts about your dog. She is a Yorkshire Terrier. She is ten (human) years old. And so on. After you share this information about your dog, Fred will know a lot of facts *about* her. But, Fred doesn't know your dog. After all, Fred has never seen your dog or interacted with her in any way. You know your dog in a way that Fred does not. You have acquaintance knowledge of your dog; Fred doesn't.

Knowledge-how is different from acquaintance knowledge, and it at least seems to be different from knowledge of facts. Knowledge-how is the sort of knowledge common of abilities or skills. You *know how* to swim. You *know how* to throw a baseball. And so on. Knowing how to do something is different from having acquaintance knowledge, and it seems different from merely knowing facts. For instance, you might know all sorts of facts about how to swim and yet be in danger of drowning if you're ever thrown into deep water! Conversely, you might be an excellent swimmer but completely incapable of expressing your ability to swim in terms of facts about swimming. (Relatively recently, a debate has emerged concerning whether knowledge-how reduces to knowledge of facts, but we can set that aside for now—traditionally the two have been taken to be different.)

Propositional knowledge (which we will simply refer to as "knowledge" in the entries that follow) is knowledge of facts. This knowledge is called "propositional" because we mentally represent (think about) facts by way of thinking of *propositions*. In simplest terms propositions are what declarative sentences mean. Consider these three declarative sentences: "The dog is brown", "El perro es cafe", and "Der Hund ist braun". These three sentences are all declarative, but they are very different. They contain different words, and they are in different languages (English, Spanish, and German, respectively). However, they all *mean* the same thing. They all mean what we express with the English sentence "The dog is brown". How can they mean the same thing though? After all, the sentences look completely different, and if they were spoken out loud, they would sound completely different. The answer to this question is that although these declarative sentences are different in important ways, they express the same proposition (which represents the same fact, namely that the dog is brown). It is the fact represented by the proposition that you know when you have propositional knowledge (for simplicity, we will later simply speak of knowing a true proposition). This is why an English speaker, a Spanish speaker, and a German speaker might know that the same dog is brown, even though they would express this knowledge differently by using different sentences.

Now, let's take a closer look at the traditional account of propositional knowledge. This is sometimes referred to as the Justified True Belief (JTB) theory because it says that knowing that some proposition, p, just is having a justified true belief that p. Hence, in order for you to know that p, "the dog is brown" say, you must believe that p, p must be true, and your belief that p must be justified. It also says that any time you believe that p, p is true, and your belief that p is justified you know that p. It's worth briefly examining each of these three components of the traditional account of knowledge.

Belief. You might think that knowledge doesn't require belief because we sometimes say things that seem to suggest this. For example, if you were in an argument with someone who believes the Earth is flat, you might plausibly say: "I don't believe the Earth is spherical, I know it is!" It would be a mistake to take this as showing that you don't actually believe that the Earth spherical. Why? Because you behave the same way as someone who believes that the Earth is spherical does. You answer affirmatively if asked whether the shape of the Earth is a sphere. You are willing to use the proposition that the Earth is spherical in your reasoning, e.g. you reason that since the Earth is spherical, if someone were able to start walking in a straight line and do so long enough, she would end up where she started. So, the best explanation for why you might assert something like "I don't believe the Earth is spherical, I know it is!" is that you want to emphasize that this is not something that you *merely* believe. You are making it clear that this is something that you believe for good reasons, i.e. you have strong justification for accepting that the Earth is spherical. To make the general point clearer, think about your acquaintance Fred again, who not only doesn't believe the Earth is spherical, he actually believes that it is flat. Would we say that Fred knows that the Earth isn't flat? It seems not. Rather, it seems that we might say that he *should* know that the Earth isn't flat. Even if Fred is aware of all sorts of evidence for thinking that the Earth is spherical, it doesn't seem that he knows it isn't flat since he doesn't believe this. Hence, the traditional account of knowledge holds that belief is necessary for knowledge.

Truth. As with belief, there may be a temptation to think that knowledge doesn't really require truth. For example, when your team loses a big game that you thought you were going to win, you might say something like: "I just knew we were going to win." Superficially, it seems that you are saying that you have knowledge of something false—you had knowledge that the team would win, but it's false that the team would win. Is this the best way to understand what you are saying here though? It doesn't seem so. A much better explanation is that what you are really expressing is the fact that you were confident that the team would win or that you *thought you knew* that the team would win. In order to see this even more clearly, imagine that you and Fred, the flat earther, place a bet, the loser has to walk the other's dog. Fred bets that the Chicago Bears will win a particular football game, and you bet that they won't. Assume (unfortunately, for many years this has been a safe assumption!) that the Chicago Bears in fact lose the game. You come to collect on your bet, but Fred responds, "I know that they won, so you have to walk my dog." Would you think that Fred knows that the Chicago Bears won even though they didn't? Or would you think that Fred doesn't know what he's talking about and needs to get to walking your dog? Presumably, you'd conclude that Fred doesn't actually know that the Chicago Bears won regardless of how convinced he is that they did. Why not? Because it's not true. They didn't win, so Fred can't know that they did.

Justification. We've seen that knowledge requires true belief. Is that enough though? It seems not. Consider the following sort of situation: you and your new friend (talking about the JTB theory has led you to move from acquaintances to friends) Fred, the flat earther, are discussing another football game that neither of you watched. Neither of you has heard the game's final score, and you both know that the odds going into the game were even, i.e. it was predicted that the teams were equally likely to win. However, Fred decides to believe that the Detroit Lions won. You ask Fred why he thinks they won, and he responds: "No reason, I just really want them to win, so I believe that they did." Let's assume that in fact Fred, by pure luck, is correct because the Detroit Lions really did win the game. Does Fred *know* that the Detroit Lions won before you and he look up the score? Surely not. Fred has no reason to think that the Detroit Lions rather than their opponents won—he is simply believing because of wishful thinking. Not only does Fred fail to know that the Detroit Lions won, but it's also unreasonable for him to believe that they did. The rational thing for Fred to do is to suspend judgment about who won the game—he shouldn't believe the Detroit Lions won or believe that they lost. The rational thing is for Fred to not believe one way or other about the outcome of the game until he has some evidence about the score. Although Fred has a true belief about how the game went, he clearly doesn't know that the Detroit Lions won. Something more is needed for knowledge. This something more is justification. Roughly, justification amounts to having good reasons/evidence to believe something. Fred clearly lacks good reasons/evidence, so he fails to know. (For more discussion of justification, see *General Background: The Nature of Justification* pp. 113–119.)

We can put these insights together to get a precise formulation of the traditional account of knowledge:

Someone, S, knows that *p* if and only if: (1) S believes that *p*, (2) *p* is true, and (3) S's belief that *p* is justified.

PROMOTIONS AND TRAVELING FRIENDS (THE GETTIER PROBLEM)

Background: In order to appreciate one of the classic "Gettier cases", it is important to keep in mind a particular rule of logic, what is called "disjunction introduction". It is the inference rule that says that if p is true, then "p or q" is true. For example, if it is true that you have a dog, then it is also true that you have a dog or a cat. And, it is true that you have a dog or no pet; you have a dog or the moon is made of cheese; and so on. Hence, if it is true that you have a dog, then it is also true that you have a dog or (any claim whatsoever can be plugged in here).

EPISTEMOLOGICAL ISSUES: ANALYSIS OF KNOWLEDGE; GETTIER PROBLEM

Let's think about two people who are often referred to in philosophical examples, Smith and Jones. Smith and Jones work for the same company, and they are both vying for the same promotion. Smith can't help but do a bit of snooping concerning who got the promotion. As a result of his snooping, Smith comes to have excellent reasons for believing that Jones got the promotion, though it hasn't been officially announced yet. He overheard the boss saying that Jones got the promotion, he saw a letter congratulating Jones on the promotion, and he even saw the new plaque that will go on the coveted corner office that belongs to the person who got the promotion and it had "Jones" on it. On the basis of this information, Smith believes that Jones got the promotion. Smith also knows that Jones owns an Armani jacket. While sitting at his desk, Smith gets bored and starts thinking about facts concerning the person who got the promotion. He thinks to himself, "Jones got the promotion and Jones owns an Armani jacket," so "*the person* who got the promotion owns an Armani jacket."

So far the case of Smith and Jones is not all that interesting. However, let's consider a twist to the narrative. Imagine Smith also owns an Armani jacket. And despite all of the evidence, it is actually Smith who got the job—he misheard the boss, the letter congratulating Jones was for a different Jones and a different promotion, and the new plaque was for the other Jones and her new office. Does Smith *know* that the person who got the promotion owns an Armani jacket? It doesn't seem so. But, this appears to be a problem for the traditional account of knowledge. Smith justifiedly believes that Jones got the promotion, he knows that Jones owns an Armani jacket, and on the basis of his justified belief and knowledge he comes to believe that the person who got the promotion owns an Armani jacket. This belief is true because Smith owns such a jacket and he's the one who got the promotion. Smith believes it. And, Smith's belief is justified because it is the result of a simple logical inference from other things he justifiedly believes. Thus, it seems like this is a case of a justified true belief that doesn't amount to knowledge.

Let's consider another situation involving Smith and Jones as well as Smith's friend Brown. Smith has excellent reason to think that Jones owns a Ferrari. He's seen Jones driving a Ferrari. Jones has been telling everyone at the office that he owns a Ferrari. Being a bit of a snoop, Smith has noticed Jones looking at clubs for Ferrari owners on his computer. As a result of all of this information, Smith believes that Jones owns a Ferrari. Again, while sitting at his desk bored, Smith is thinking about his friend Brown. He knows that Brown is on vacation but has no idea where. Then, as often seems to be the case, Smith's thoughts turn to Jones and Jones' Ferrari. As he's sitting there, Smith decides to practice his logic skills to clear his head (it's a wonder he got the promotion given how he spends his time!). He thinks to himself "Jones owns a Ferrari," so "Jones owns a Ferrari or Brown is in Bucharest." Then he thinks "Jones owns a Ferrari," so "Jones owns a Ferrari or Brown is in Baltimore." Smith continues, "Jones owns a Ferrari," so "Jones owns a Ferrari or Brown is in Boston." Finally, he reasons "Jones owns a Ferrari," so "Jones owns a Ferrari or Brown is in Barcelona." Smith believes each of these propositions because he believes that Jones owns a Ferrari, and he knows that disjunction introduction is a legitimate rule of logic.

Now, let's add a twist to this situation as well. Let's assume that Jones doesn't actually own a Ferrari at all. Jones has been renting a Ferrari and doing everything possible to make it seem like he owns a Ferrari because he wants everyone at the office to think that he's doing great despite not getting the recent promotion. However, as luck would have it, Brown is actually on vacation in Barcelona. So, "Jones owns a Ferrari or Brown is in Barcelona" is true. Smith believes it, and his belief is justified. But, again, it seems that we have a situation where Smith's justified true belief doesn't amount to knowledge. Hence, it appears that the traditional account of knowledge fails.

Examples of the sort discussed in this entry are known as "Gettier" cases because Edmund Gettier was the first person to really emphasize that such cases pose a threat to the traditional account of knowledge (though other philosophers had discussed such cases prior to Gettier's discussion). Gettier cases, such as these, tend to follow a general pattern. In such cases, the subject has a justified belief, but as a result of bad luck their justification isn't tied to the truth of the proposition believed. However, as a matter of good luck, it turns out that what the subject believes is true. It is this correction of the bad luck by way of the later good luck that makes it so that there's always a twist to the stories depicted in Gettier cases.

Before considering responses to these cases, it is worth noting something extraordinary about this purported counterexample to the traditional account of knowledge: *almost all* epistemologists agree that it works. That is to say, almost all epistemologists think that the traditional account of knowledge is flawed. It is important to keep in mind though that what Gettier cases show is that justified true belief is not *sufficient* for knowledge. The cases do not show that justified true belief isn't *necessary* for knowledge. In other words, Gettier cases make it clear that someone might have a justified true belief while failing to have knowledge. However, they don't demonstrate that one can have knowledge without having a justified true belief. In fact, most epistemologists agree that justified true belief is necessary for knowledge. As a result, many of the responses to Gettier cases involve trying to solve the Gettier Problem, i.e. trying to determine what condition(s) must be added to justified true belief in order to have knowledge.

RESPONSES

One of the first responses to the Gettier Problem attempts to do away with justification as a requirement for knowledge altogether. The idea behind the causal theory of knowledge is that knowledge requires that one's true belief that p be causally connected in the appropriate way to the fact that p (Goldman 1967). In both of these cases, the fact that makes Smith's belief true isn't what is causing him to believe as he does. So, the causal theory of knowledge yields the correct result that Smith doesn't know in these cases.

Another early response is what is called the "no false reasons/evidence" approach (Clark 1963). Roughly, this says that in order for a justified true belief that p to count as knowledge, none of the justified beliefs that constitute one's evidence for p can be false. Smith fails to know on this account because in both cases he relies upon justified false beliefs (and so justified but false reasons) in his reasoning. A related response is that the strength of justification required for knowledge is incompatible with the falsity of the justified belief (Sutton 2007, Littlejohn 2012). This response denies Gettier's assumption that the amount of justification required for knowledge still allows for the possible falsity of the belief in question. The idea here is that you simply cannot have justified false beliefs, so Smith's beliefs about Jones getting the promotion and having a Ferrari wouldn't count as justified in the first place. Of course, this would mean that the conclusions he comes to believe based on these beliefs aren't justified either. So, again, Smith wouldn't count as knowing under this view.

Yet another early response appeals to the notion of "defeat" (Lehrer and Paxson 1969). Essentially, the idea behind this response to the Gettier Problem is that in addition to having a justified true belief it must also be the case that one's justification is not *defeated* in order for one to have knowledge. The relevant sense of "defeat" here concerns whether or not there are true propositions that if they were added to one's evidence would make it so that one no longer had justification. For example, there is a true proposition that if added to Smith's evidence would make it so that his belief that Jones owns a Ferrari or Brown is in Barcelona is unjustified. Specifically, the true proposition that Jones doesn't own a Ferrari would defeat Smith's justification. Since Smith's belief is defeasible in this way, this response rules it out as an instance of knowledge.

A different kind of response involves adding modal conditions such as sensitivity or safety to the traditional account of knowledge. S's belief that p is *sensitive* just in case if p were false, S wouldn't believe that p (Dretske 1969, Nozick 1981). S's belief that p is *safe* just in case in the closest worlds to this one ("closest worlds to this one" are ways that our universe could be different that are very similar to how the universe actually is) where S believes that p, p is true (Sosa 1999). Smith fails to satisfy either a sensitivity or safety condition in these cases, so again adding these sorts of conditions seems to spare the traditional account from having to say that Smith knows.

Finally, some respond to the Gettier Problem by claiming that it cannot be solved, and we should instead take knowledge to be unanalyzable (Williamson 2000). The thought here is that instead of trying to break knowledge down into components (such as justification, truth, and belief), we should take knowledge to be primitive and use it to understand other epistemic properties such as justification.

RECOMMENDED READING

GENERAL OVERVIEWS

The Analysis of Knowledge. *The Stanford Encyclopedia of Philosophy.* URL = https://plato.stanford.edu/archives/sum2018/entries/knowledge-analysis/

Gettier Problems. *Internet Encyclopedia of Philosophy.* URL = www.iep.utm.edu/gettier

SEMINAL PRESENTATION

Gettier, Edmund L. 1963. Is Justified True Belief Knowledge? *Analysis* 23: 121–123.

ADDITIONAL IMPORTANT DISCUSSIONS

Goldman, A. 1967. A Causal Theory of Knowing. *Journal of Philosophy* 64: 357–372.

Borges, R., de Almeida, C., and Klein, P. (eds) 2017. *Explaining Knowledge: New Essays on the Gettier Problem*. Oxford: Oxford University Press.

Clark, M. 1963. Knowledge and Grounds: A Comment on Mr. Gettier's Paper. *Analysis* 24: 46–48.

Dretske, F. 1969. *Seeing and Knowing*. Chicago, IL: University of Chicago Press.

Hetherington, S. (ed) 2018. *The Gettier Problem*. Cambridge: Cambridge University Press.

Lehrer, K. and Paxson, T. 1969. Knowledge: Undefeated Justified True Belief. *Journal of Philosophy* 66: 225–237.

Littlejohn, C. 2012. *Justification and the Truth-Connection*. Cambridge: Cambridge University Press.

Nozick, R. 1981. *Philosophical Explanations*. Cambridge, MA: Harvard University Press.

Pritchard, D. 2005. *Epistemic Luck*. New York: Oxford University Press.

Russell, B. 1948. *Human Knowledge: Its Scope and Limits*. New York: Simon and Schuster.

Shope, R.K. 1983. *The Analysis of Knowledge: A Decade of Research*. Princeton, NJ: Princeton University Press.

Sosa, E. 1999. How to Defeat Opposition to Moore. *Philosophical Perspectives* 33: 141–153.

Sutton, J. 2007. *Without Justification*. Cambridge, MA: MIT Press.

Williamson, T. 2000. *Knowledge and Its Limits*. Oxford: Oxford University Press.

Zagzebski, L. 1994. The Inescapability of the Gettier Problem. *Philosophical Quarterly* 44: 65–73.

2

A GRISLY DISCOVERY (CAUSAL THEORY OF KNOWLEDGE)

Background: One of the early responses to the Gettier Problem attempted to do away with the justification component of knowledge altogether by introducing a causal requirement on knowledge. There are various versions of causal theories of knowledge. However, the general idea is that a causal theory of knowledge replaces justification with an "appropriate" causal connection. One of the first and simplest versions of a causal theory of knowledge was put forward by Alvin Goldman. It says that S knows that p if and only if (1) S believes p, (2) p is true, and (3) the fact that p is appropriately causally connected with S's believing that p. One way that the fact that p could be causally connected with S's believing that p is for that fact to be a cause of her believing as she does. For example, the fact that there is a tree in the yard is part of the causal story for why S believes that there is a tree in the yard when she's gazing out a window overlooking the yard. Another way that the fact that p could be causally connected with S's believing that p is for her believing and the fact that p to have a common cause. An example of this might be S's belief that there is smoke coming out of the chimney because she is inside and sees the fire. In such a case, a common cause of her belief and the fact that smoke is coming out of the chimney is the fire in the fireplace. Unfortunately, it is very difficult to say precisely what counts as an "appropriate" causal connection and what doesn't. Fortunately for our purposes, we don't need an exact account of appropriateness in this sense.

EPISTEMOLOGICAL ISSUES: ANALYSIS OF KNOWLEDGE; CAUSAL THEORY OF KNOWLEDGE

Detective Skyrms has just arrived at the scene of a potential crime. Upon arriving, he immediately notices a body and the severed head that belongs to that body a few feet away. Skyrms, as would anyone else, immediately forms the true belief that the person is dead based upon what he sees.

As with the Gettier cases discussed in the previous entry though, the story here isn't quite so simple. Yes, the person is clearly dead. However, losing their head isn't what killed them. What actually happened was that the person was walking home from a party late at night when they heard a frightening sound. The person ran, tripped over a stone and fell to the ground. While lying there on the ground, the person became so frightened that they had a massive heart attack. Since there was no one around (the sound was simply the wind blowing through old chimes that had been left in some nearby trees), the person wasn't taken to the hospital. As a result, the person died of the heart attack. Unfortunately, the gruesome tale doesn't end there. A few hours later, after the person had been dead for quite some time, a deranged psychopath happened by the person's body and decided it would be fun to cut the head off. Of course, having just arrived on the scene, Skyrms isn't aware of all of these grisly details. He simply sees that the body and head are separated by a few feet and comes to believe that the person is dead.

Why does this example and its grisly details matter? Because it poses a significant problem for simple causal theories of knowledge. The reason is that in this case, it is clear that Skyrms knows that the person is dead. However, the fact that leads Skyrms to believe that the person is dead is that the person's head has been severed. But, the fact that the person's head has been severed isn't actually a cause of this person's death. So, the fact that the person died doesn't cause Skyrms' belief. Additionally, the fact that the person is dead isn't causally responsible for Skyrms' belief that their head has been severed. Hence, it seems that the fact the person is dead is neither a cause of Skyrms' belief that they are dead nor does it have a common cause with Skyrms' belief. As a result, the simple causal view that we discussed in the background yields the result that Skyrms doesn't really know that the person is dead. But, of course, he clearly does know. You don't have to be an ace detective like Skyrms to know that the person whose head has been completely severed from their body is dead.

Generally, this sort of example achieved its intended effect—showing that simple causal theories of knowledge are mistaken. This is something that even Alvin Goldman, who initially defended the simple sort of causal theory, accepts. However, this realization didn't lead to the complete abandonment of such theories. Instead, proponents of such views added various restrictions to the relevant causal processes.

RESPONSES

Some causal theorists responded to these sorts of examples by adding that if the fact that p is overdetermined (roughly, this means that there is more than one cause in play and any of those causes would ensure that p is true), an overdetermining cause can allow one to know that p. For example, in the above case, the person's death is overdetermined—the heart attack actually killed them, but even if it hadn't, having their head severed certainly would have done so (Swain 1972, 1978). Hence, on this sort of view, Skyrms counts as knowing that the person is dead because his belief is caused by an overdetermining cause of the fact that the person is dead.

A different revision to the causal account holds that one knows that p when one's belief that p is caused by the information that p (Dretske 1981). This would also seem to avoid the above problem, because the information that the person is dead is causing Skyrms' belief even though the cause of the person's death isn't. On this view, plausibly Skyrms knows that the person is dead, but he doesn't know the cause of the person's death.

Finally, the most prominent revision to simple causal theories came from Goldman (1976, 1979, 1986) himself when he developed his theory of reliabilism (see *General Background: The Nature of Justification* pp. 113–119). Reliabilism, which is a theory of justification, can be extended to an account of knowledge. Instead of requiring that the fact that p causes one's belief that p, reliabilism as it pertains to knowledge holds, roughly, that in order to know that p one's true belief that p must be caused by (be the output of) a reliable belief forming process (a process that tends to produce more true beliefs than false ones).

Reliabilism seems to be able to get the correct result in this case as well. Skyrms' belief that the person is dead seems to be reliable. After all, believing that someone is dead because you see that their head has been severed seems like a very reliable way of forming true beliefs about whether or not someone is dead.

RECOMMENDED READING

GENERAL OVERVIEW

The Analysis of Knowledge. *The Stanford Encyclopedia of Philosophy*. URL = https://plato.stanford.edu/archives/sum2018/entries/knowledge-analysis/

SEMINAL PRESENTATITONS

Goldman, A.I. 1967. A Causal Theory of Knowing. *Journal of Philosophy* 64: 357–372.
Skyrms, B. 1967. The Explication of "X knows that p". *Journal of Philosophy* 64: 373–389.

ADDITIONAL IMPORTANT DISCUSSIONS

Dretske, F. 1971. Conclusive Reasons. *Australasian Journal of Philosophy* 49: 1–22.
Dretske, F. 1981. *Knowledge and the Flow of Information*. Cambridge, MA: MIT Press.
Goldman, A. 1976. Discrimination and Perceptual Knowledge. *Journal of Philosophy* 73: 771–791.
Goldman, A. 1979. What Is Justified Belief? In G. Pappas (ed), *Justification and Knowledge*. Dordrecht: D. Reidel, 1–23.
Goldman, A. 1986. *Epistemology and Cognition*. Cambridge, MA: Harvard University Press.
Goldstick, D. 1972. A Contribution towards the Development of the Causal Theory of Knowledge. *Australasian Journal of Philosophy* 50: 238–248.
Hanson, P. 1978. Prospects for a Causal Theory of Knowledge. *Canadian Journal of Philosophy* 8: 457–473.
Swain, M. 1972. Knowledge, Causality, and Justification. *Journal of Philosophy* 69: 291–300.
Swain, M. 1978. Reasons, Causes, and Knowledge. *Journal of Philosophy* 75: 229–249.

3

A STRANGE COUNTY
(FAKE BARNS)

Background: Two of the earliest responses to the Gettier Problem were to opt for a causal account of knowledge or to accept the no false reasons/evidence response (see Promotions and Traveling Friends pp. 6–11 and A Grisly Discovery pp. 12–15). As has been common in the literature surrounding the Gettier Problem, soon after these responses were proposed new Gettier-style examples were put forward. These examples revealed that both the causal account of knowledge and the no false reasons/evidence response failed to solve the Gettier Problem. The problem with the causal account (aside from the counterexample described in the previous entry) is that it seems that there can be Gettier-style cases where the fact that p causes one's true belief in what seems to be the appropriate way, and yet one fails to know that p. The problem with the no false reasons/evidence response is that it relies on the subject making an explicit inference, i.e. reasoning from a justified false belief, but it is possible to construct Gettier-style examples where it doesn't seem that the subject is engaging in an inference at all. After this problem became clear, other responses were proposed. Many of these responses had the common feature of trying to restrict the reasoning or evidence that the subject is allowed to rely upon if knowledge is to be generated. However, a key feature of these sorts of responses is that they didn't put restrictions upon the environmental conditions in which the subject is found. It is this feature of fake barn scenarios like the one described in this entry that undermines the effectiveness of these modifications of the no false reasons/evidence response as well as the effectiveness of the causal theory of knowledge when it comes to solving the Gettier Problem.

EPISTEMOLOGICAL ISSUES: ANALYSIS OF KNOWLEDGE; GETTIER PROBLEM

In a rural portion of the U.S. Midwest there is a county that is known for its rolling hills and beautiful barns, let's call it "Barn County". In fact, Barn County's income is greatly supplemented by the many visitors who come to drive on the winding roads and gaze at the lovely barns. Unfortunately, being located in the Midwest severe storms and tornados are a genuine threat to Barn County. This year just a few weeks before tourist season was set to begin, a bad tornado ripped through the county and destroyed almost all of the barns. The citizens were rightly distraught—no one would want to visit Barn County without its barns! There wasn't enough time to rebuild the barns before tourist season, and half-built barns won't attract tourists. So, the people of Barn County came up with an idea. They would build barn façades before tourist season; that way people would still come to look at the barns and Barn County would have the revenue to rebuild its barns. These barn façades are like stage props—they are a single side of a barn propped up so that from the road (where tourists drive) they are indistinguishable from real barns. Of course, the citizens of Barn County are keeping this ruse a secret from everyone—we're the only people outside of Barn County to know this information. After all, barn enthusiasts have no interest in coming to see barn façades; they want the real thing.

Martha has decided to take a little vacation to celebrate a recent promotion. Being the barn lover that she is, Martha decides to take a trip to Barn County. Martha is blissfully unaware of the situation in Barn County. Martha is currently driving all over Barn County gazing at what she thinks are real barns. She says to herself (and believes) as she is looking at barn façades: "That's a lovely barn!" "There's another one!" "And, another!" In the midst of all these barn façades there happens to be one real barn—it is indistinguishable from the façades from Martha's vantage point. When she sees it along with the barn façades, she believes it is a lovely barn just as she believes of all the numerous fake barns that she sees.

It seems intuitive that Martha's belief about the real barn *and* her beliefs about the fake barns are justified. Martha knows what barns look like, she's looking at all of these façades and the real barn in good viewing conditions (the lighting is good, it's a clear day, etc.), and she has absolutely no reason to think that Barn County is full of barn façades. As a result, it seems perfectly reasonable for her to believe that each of these is a barn. This in itself isn't a problem because one can have justified false beliefs. But, consider when she looks at the real barn and believes that it is a barn her belief is not only justified, it's also true. Hence, when Martha sees the real barn it appears that she has a justified true belief. Nevertheless, it seems that Martha doesn't know that what she sees is a barn.

Importantly, this situation is different from the original sort of Gettier case because Martha isn't making an inference. She simply looks and forms the belief that what she sees is a barn. So, it can't be that Martha's justification for believing what she sees is a barn is based on false reasons/evidence. What is more, the problem doesn't seem to be one with Martha or her reasons at all. The problem seems to simply be the environment in which she unknowingly finds herself. The presence of the fake barns all around her seems to make it so that Martha doesn't know that she sees a barn when she is looking at the one real barn, even though her belief is justified and true. It appears that the Gettier Problem for the traditional account of knowledge not only arises when one relies upon justified false beliefs in one's reasoning, it also arises when one is in the wrong sort of environment.

The problem also seems to plague causal theories of knowledge. Martha's belief that she sees a barn is caused by the real barn in the way that such beliefs would normally be caused. So, it is a mystery how a causal theory of knowledge could yield the intuitive result that this true belief of Martha's doesn't amount to knowledge.

RESPONSES

A bit of history about the "fake barn" Gettier cases before discussing the philosophical issues. Often, the idea for these cases is credited to Alvin Goldman because of his widely known early discussion of such cases. However, Fred Dretske and Carl Ginet (Goldman actually credits Ginet with coming up with the examples) offered serious discussions of such examples before Goldman (in the case of Dretske, the discussion was in print several years before Goldman's presentation).

Now, let's discuss the cases themselves. Unlike the cases originally used to motivate the Gettier Problem, there is a sizeable number of epistemologists who deny the intuition at play here (empirical research (see Colaço et al. 2014) suggests that nonphilosophers may be inclined to deny this as well). They maintain that when Martha sees the one real barn she knows that it is a barn. One way this response has been motivated is by considering variations of the case where Martha is continually looking at the real barn while moving in and out of Barn County (roughly, one idea is to imagine that a river runs through Barn County and Martha is on a boat with a real barn on it that she looks at while she passes through the land filled with barn façades) (Gendler and Hawthorne 2005).

Many epistemologists deny that Martha knows that what she sees is a barn though. Some of the responses to the original Gettier cases are thought to solve the problem here as well. Most commonly, consideration of fake barn cases is used to motivate modal requirements on knowledge such as *safety* and *sensitivity*. Recall S's belief that *p* is *safe* just in case in the closest worlds to this one ("closest worlds to this one" are ways that our universe could be different that are very similar to how the universe actually is) where S believes that *p*, *p* is true. This is thought to not be satisfied in the fake barn cases because there are very close worlds in which Martha believes that she sees a barn, but she's wrong. There are so many barn façades around her that she could easily have looked at one of them and still believed that what she sees is a barn (Sosa 1999, 2007). When it comes to sensitivity, S's belief that *p* is *sensitive* just in case if *p* were false, S wouldn't believe that *p*. Again, it seems that Martha's belief fails to meet this requirement. Presumably, if it were false that what she sees is a barn, it would be because Martha is looking at one of the many barn façades. But if she were looking at a barn façade, Martha would believe that she is seeing a barn (Nozick 1981). Hence, requiring that modal conditions, such as safety or sensitivity, be satisfied in order to have knowledge seems to yield the correct result in fake barn cases.

RECOMMENDED READING

GENERAL OVERVIEWS

The Analysis of Knowledge. *The Stanford Encyclopedia of Philosophy*. URL = https://plato.stanford.edu/archives/sum2018/entries/knowledge-analysis/

Gettier Problems. *Internet Encyclopedia of Philosophy*. URL = www.iep.utm.edu/gettier

SEMINAL PRESENTATIONS

Dretske, F. 1969. *Seeing and Knowing*. Chicago, IL: University of Chicago Press.

Ginet, C. 1975. *Knowledge, Perception, and Memory*. Dordrecht: D. Reidel Publishing Company.

Goldman, A.I. 1976. Discrimination and Perceptual Knowledge. *Journal of Philosophy* 73: 771–791.

ADDITIONAL IMPORTANT DISCUSSIONS

Borges, R., de Almeida, C., and Klein, P. (eds) 2017. *Explaining Knowledge: New Essays on the Gettier Problem*. Oxford: Oxford University Press.

Colaço, D., Buckwalter, W., Stich, S., and Machery, E. 2014. Epistemic Intuitions in Fake-Barn Thought Experiments. *Episteme* 11: 199–212.

Gendler, T.S. and Hawthorne, J. 2005. The Real Guide to Fake Barns: A Catalogue of Gifts for Your Epistemic Enemies. *Philosophical Studies* 124: 331–352.

Hetherington, S. (ed) 2018. *The Gettier Problem*. Cambridge: Cambridge University Press.

Nozick, R. 1981. *Philosophical Explanations*. Cambridge, MA: Harvard University Press.

Pritchard, D. 2005. *Epistemic Luck*. New York: Oxford University Press.

Shope, R.K. 1983. *The Analysis of Knowledge: A Decade of Research*. Princeton, NJ: Princeton University Press.

Sosa, E. 1999. How to Defeat Opposition to Moore. *Philosophical Perspectives* 33: 141–153.

Sosa, E. 2007. *A Virtue Epistemology: Apt Belief and Reflective Knowledge*. Oxford: Oxford University Press.

4

RED BARNS AND BLUE FAÇADES (KRIPKE'S BARN)

Background: One sort of modal response to the Gettier Problem (in both its original form and the fake barn version) that initially seemed promising (and still has defenders) appeals to sensitivity. When Robert Nozick first developed his theory of knowledge, he provided motivations for a sensitivity requirement on knowledge that were independent of the Gettier Problem. This sort of independent motivation made (makes) adding a sensitivity requirement an appealing response to the Gettier Problem. Recall from the previous two entries that S's belief that p counts as sensitive just in case it is true that if p were false, S wouldn't believe that p. In the original Gettier cases (see Promotions and Traveling Friends pp. 6–11), Smith's belief that the person who got the promotion owns an Armani jacket and his belief concerning Jones owning a Ferrari or Brown being in Barcelona both fail to meet the sensitivity requirement. Since both beliefs rely upon other justified, but false, beliefs of Smith's, he would continue to believe that the person who got the promotion owns an Armani jacket and Jones owns a Ferrari or Brown is in Barcelona even if these beliefs were false. Similarly, when it comes to the fake barn case (see A Strange County pp. 16–20) Martha's justified true belief fails to be sensitive. After all, Martha would still believe that the object she sees is a barn if she were looking at a barn façade. Hence, Martha would believe that the object is a barn even if it weren't. Adding a sensitivity condition to the traditional account of knowledge seems to provide a solution to the original Gettier cases as well as fake barns.

EPISTEMOLOGICAL ISSUES: ANALYSIS OF KNOWLEDGE; GETTIER PROBLEM; SENSITIVITY

Let's consider a variation on *A Strange County* (see previous entry). It is still the case that a tornado has recently devastated the barns of Barn County. The citizens have still decided to put up barn façades so that tourists will come visit the county. The one difference in this version of the case is that due to the material that is used to make the fake barns, they are all painted blue—for some reason red paint eats through the cardboard that the citizens of Barn County use to make the barn façades. As a result, the one real barn left is painted red, but all of the numerous fake barns are painted blue.

Like the previous version of the case, Martha has decided to take a little vacation to celebrate her recent promotion. Being the barn lover that she is, Martha decides to take a trip to Barn County. Martha is blissfully unaware of the situation in Barn County—she has no idea that there are fake barns all throughout the county, nor does she know anything about the fact that only real barns are red. Martha is currently driving all over Barn County gazing at what she thinks are real barns. She says to herself (and believes) as she is looking at barn façades: "That's a lovely barn!" "There's another one!" "And, another!" Now, Martha happens to look at the one real barn. And thinks to herself, "What a lovely red barn!"

The sensitivity response to the Gettier Problem says that Martha's justified true belief that "that is a barn" fails to count as knowledge. Why? The reason is that this belief isn't sensitive to the truth of there actually being a barn present. After all, if Martha's belief were false (i.e. if she weren't actually seeing a barn), she would still believe it because she would be fooled by one of the barn façades. And Martha would still believe of the fake barn that it is a real barn. So, the sensitivity response yields the correct result that Martha doesn't know that the object she's looking at is a barn. But what about her more specific belief that "that is a *red* barn"? Here is where things get problematic for the sensitivity response. This belief seems to be sensitive. If it were false that "that is a red barn", Martha wouldn't believe "that is a red barn". Why not? Because all of the fake barns are blue. So, in cases where the object before Martha is not a red barn, it is because the object is a blue barn façade. In such cases, Martha wouldn't believe that it is a red barn; rather Martha would mistakenly believe that the object is a blue barn. As a result, Martha's belief that "that is a red barn" is sensitive to the truth of the object being a red barn. This means the sensitivity response yields a very counterintuitive result: Martha knows that the object is a *red barn*, but she doesn't know that it is a *barn*!

It strikes many epistemologists that this case succeeds as a counter-example to the idea that there is a sensitivity condition on knowledge. That is to say, they find it absurd to think that Martha can know that she's looking at a red barn but at the same time fail to know that she is looking at a barn. Consequently, many epistemologists take this sort of example to be a decisive reason to deny that the sensitivity response is successful and to deny that a sensitivity condition should be added to the traditional account of knowledge.

RESPONSES

One response to this case attempts to save the sensitivity condition by arguing that this example fails to constitute a genuine counterexample (Adams and Clarke 2005). The thought here is that it is important to recognize that Martha is using the fact that what she sees looks like a red barn to form her belief that there is a red barn. This "method" is one that only applies when there is what looks to be a red barn present. Hence, if the red barn wasn't there and Martha were to believe that what she sees is a barn, it would be because she was using some other method. As a result, according to this response, when Martha believes there is a red barn, she believes there is a barn in part because she is using the "red barn method". This method makes it so that Martha knows she is seeing something that is both red and a barn. While this response may save the sensitivity response from the problem of saying that Martha knows she sees a red barn but doesn't know that she sees a barn, we might worry that it makes the sensitivity response fail when it comes to fake barn cases (see *A Strange County* pp. 16–20). After all, it is plausible that Martha doesn't know that she's seeing a red barn in this case either, given all of the fake barns around her.

Another response is to admit that cases like this one show that the letter of the sensitivity response is incorrect but insist that it is nev-ertheless correct in spirit. This is the approach of most contemporary defenders of sensitivity conditions on knowledge—they modify the original sensitivity condition that we have been discussing in various ways in an attempt to avoid this and other problems (Black 2002, Roush 2005, Becker 2007, DeRose 2010, and Melchior 2019).

RECOMMENDED READING

GENERAL OVERVIEWS

The Analysis of Knowledge. *The Stanford Encyclopedia of Philosophy.* URL = https://plato.stanford.edu/archives/sum2018/entries/knowledge-analysis/
Gettier Problems. *Internet Encyclopedia of Philosophy.* URL = www.iep.utm.edu/gettier

SEMINAL PRESENTATION

Kripke, S. 2011. Nozick on Knowledge. In *Philosophical Troubles: Collected Papers*, Volume I (pp. 162–224). Oxford: Oxford University Press.

ADDITIONAL IMPORTANT DISCUSSIONS

Adams, F. and Clarke, M. 2005. Resurrecting the Tracking Theories. *Australasian Journal of Philosophy* 83: 207–221.
Becker, K. 2007. *Epistemology Modalized.* New York and London: Routledge.
Becker, K. and Black, T. (eds) 2017. *The Sensitivity Principle in Epistemology.* Cambridge: Cambridge University Press.
Black, T. 2002. A Moorean Response to Brain-In-A-Vat Skepticism. *Australasian Journal of Philosophy* 80: 148–163.
DeRose, K. 2010. Insensitivity Is Back, Baby! *Philosophical Perspectives* 24: 161–187.
Dretske, F. 2003. Skepticism: What Perception Teaches. In S. Luper (ed), *The Skeptics: Contemporary Essays.* Aldershot: Ashgate Publishing, 105–118.
Ichikawa, J.J. 2011. Quantifiers, Knowledge, and Counterfactuals. *Philosophy and Phenomenological Research* 82: 287–313.
Melchior, G. 2019. *Knowing and Checking: An Epistemological Investigation.* New York: Routledge.
Nozick, R. 1981. *Philosophical Explanations.* Cambridge, MA: Harvard University Press.
Pritchard, D. 2005. *Epistemic Luck.* New York: Oxford University Press.
Roush, S. 2005. *Tracking Truth: Knowledge, Evidence, and Science.* Oxford: Oxford University Press.
Sosa, E. 1999. How to Defeat Opposition to Moore. *Philosophical Perspectives* 33: 141–153.
Sosa, E. 2004. Replies. In J. Greco (ed), *Ernest Sosa: And His Critics.* Malden, MA: Blackwell Publishing, 275–326.

5

THE TOURIST (CREDIT VIEW OF KNOWLEDGE)

Background: Many virtue epistemologists embrace the idea that a necessary condition for knowledge is that the knower deserves credit for believing truly. So, for example, in order for S to know that there is a tree in the yard, she must in some sense deserve credit for truly believing that there is a tree in the yard. There are various ways that supporters of credit views of knowledge spell out the "deserving credit" condition. Rather than attempt a survey of them, it will be helpful to just consider one prominent version in order to get a good handle on what these views of knowledge are saying in general. According to some virtue reliabilists (these are theorists who claim that knowledge requires intellectual virtue but include a commitment to reliabilism in their account of intellectual virtues; for more on reliabilism see General Background: The Nature of Justification pp. 113–119), in order for S to deserve credit for the true belief that p, it has to be the case that believing the truth about p is intellectually valuable, S believes the truth about p, and S's believing this manifests S's reliable cognitive functioning. Credit theories of knowledge seem to be able to handle many Gettier cases because in various Gettier-style examples the subject believes truly, but it seems that their believing the truth isn't really creditable to them. Instead, in a Gettier case, credit theorists claim, it is a matter of luck that the person believes truly, and so their true belief shouldn't be credited to them.

EPISTEMOLOGICAL ISSUE: CREDIT VIEW OF KNOWLEDGE

Bob has recently arrived in New York City, which he is visiting for the very first time. He has just walked out of Grand Central Station onto 42nd Street. It's a beautiful day, so he thinks to himself that it'd be great to have a good look at the city. He's always wanted to see the Empire State Building, and he remembers that it has an observatory too, so he decides that's where he'll go. He reaches into his pocket to look up directions on his phone and realizes it's not there. Oh no! Bob suddenly remembers that he left his phone on the table at home before he went to the train station! Having no better options Bob looks around and walks up to the closest adult nearby and asks her for directions to the Empire State Building. The stranger happens to have lived in New York City all her life, and she not only knows Manhattan like the back of her hand, she is excellent at giving directions. She gives Bob great directions. She tells him that the Empire State Building is only about half a mile away from where they're standing. All he needs to do is walk down 42nd Street, take a left onto 5th Avenue, and in about eight blocks he'll be there. Bob forms a true belief about how to get to the Empire State Building immediately on the basis of the woman's testimony.

As examples in philosophy go, this one is pretty mundane. This case could easily happen because this sort of thing really does happen quite frequently—people ask strangers for directions when they're in an unfamiliar city. What makes the example of interest is that it seems that Bob knows the directions to the Empire State Building, but he's simply accepting what he's told from someone he doesn't know—he didn't even ask if she was from New York City! Thus, it doesn't seem that Bob really deserves credit for believing the truth about how to get to the Empire State Building. If this is correct, then credit views of knowledge are in serious trouble. This would be a case where someone has knowledge, but believing truly isn't something that can be credited to them.

RESPONSES

A response that doesn't involve abandoning the credit view of knowledge insists that Bob doesn't really have knowledge in this situation (Riggs 2009). The thinking here is that Bob just picked someone at random and accepted what he was told. This way of forming beliefs, the response goes, is too permissive to generate knowledge. Hence, while Bob doesn't deserve credit for believing truly, it isn't a problem for credit views of knowledge because Bob doesn't have knowledge.

Alternatively, another way of responding is to allow that Bob does have knowledge in this case but insist that he also deserves credit for believing truly. One way of fleshing out this sort of response is to maintain that testimonial knowledge requires both the testifier and the recipient of that testimony to be reliable (Riggs 2009). The former must be a reliable testifier and the latter must be reliable in receiving testimony. Hence, on this view of testimony, in order for Bob to gain knowledge from the stranger's testimony Bob must be reliable in separating good and bad testimony. As a result, the response contends Bob's believing truly in this case is to his credit.

A different response claims that credit for believing the truth can be shared (Greco 2010). The thought here is that the reason we tend to think that Bob doesn't deserve credit for believing the truth about how to get to the Empire State Building is that we are thinking about whether he alone deserves the credit. However, when we realize that credit can be shared between Bob and the woman who gives him directions, we realize that there isn't a problem for the credit view here because Bob deserves some of the credit for what he comes to know.

RECOMMENDED READING

SEMINAL PRESENTATIONS

Lackey, J. 2004. Review of DePaul, M. and Zagzebski, L., eds. (2003) *Intellectual Virtue: Perspectives from Ethics and Epistemology*. Oxford: Oxford University Press. *Notre Dame Philosophical Reviews*. URL = https://ndpr.nd.edu/news/intellectual-virtue-perspectives-from-ethics-and-epistemology/

Lackey, J. 2007. Why We Don't Deserve Credit for Everything We Know. *Synthese* 158: 345–361.

ADDITIONAL IMPORTANT DISCUSSIONS

Greco, J. 2003. Knowledge as Credit for True Belief. In M. DePaul and L. Zagzebski (eds), *Intellectual Virtue: Perspectives from Ethics and Epistemology*. Oxford: Oxford University Press, 111–134.

Greco, J. 2010. *Achieving Knowledge: A Virtue-Theoretic Account of Epistemic Norma-tivity*. Cambridge: Cambridge University Press.

Lackey, J. 2009. Knowledge and Credit. *Philosophical Studies* 142: 27–42.

Riggs, W. 2002. Reliability and the Value of Knowledge. *Philosophy and Phenome-nological Research* 64: 79–96.

Riggs, W. 2009. Two Problems of Easy Credit. *Synthese* 169: 201–216.

Sosa, E. 2003. The Place of Truth in Epistemology. In M. DePaul and L. Zagzebski (eds), *Intellectual Virtue: Perspectives from Ethics and Epistemology*. Oxford: Oxford University Press, 155–179.

Sosa, E. 2007. *A Virtue Epistemology: Apt Belief and Reflective Knowledge*. Oxford: Oxford University Press.

Sosa, E. 2009. Knowing Full Well: The Normativity of Beliefs as Performances. *Philosophical Studies* 142: 5–15.

Zagzebski, L. 1996. *Virtues of the Mind: An Inquiry into the Nature of Virtue and the Ethical Foundations of Knowledge*. Cambridge: Cambridge University Press.

Zagzebski, L. 2003. Intellectual Motivation and the Good of Truth. In M. DePaul and L. Zagzebski (eds), *Intellectual Virtue: Perspectives from Ethics and Epistemology*. Oxford: Oxford University Press, 135–154.

6

A HORRIBLE LIBRARY (KVANVIG'S COMANCHE CASE)

Background: Although it seems that understanding was perhaps the central epistemic concept in ancient philosophy, it largely fell by the wayside until very recently. Knowledge has been the primary focus of contemporary epistemologists. It is only since the late 1990s and early 2000s that understanding has again become the subject of serious investigation. One of the first debates to come out of this resurgence concerns whether understanding is really just a kind of knowledge or not, and consideration of fake barn-style Gettier cases helped kick off this debate.

EPISTEMOLOGICAL ISSUES: GETTIER PROBLEM; UNDERSTANDING

Jon has decided to learn about a particular historical figure, Alexander the Great, the old-fashioned way. Rather than look up information about Alexander the Great on the internet, Jon decides to read a history book about him at the local library. Unbeknownst to Jon, the library he visits is actually pretty horrible—it is full of books that are grossly inaccurate. There are many books about Alexander the Great in the library, but almost all of them are terribly unreliable. As luck would have it, Jon happens to randomly pick the one accurate book about Alexander the Great in the library. Jon reads the book and learns about Alexander's battle tactics, his tendency to grant a considerable amount of autonomy to the people he conquered, and so on. As a result of what Jon learns from the book, Jon is able to explain why Alexander was so successful in battle and how he was able to conquer so many places. If asked questions about Alexander or his victories in battle or his campaigns, Jon is able to readily give thoughtful and correct answers. Jon grasps how various features of Alexander's military strength along with his diplomatic strategies allowed him to maintain control of a vast region of the world. In fact, Jon is able to write essays on the topic that would convince accomplished historians that he has a firm understanding of Alexander and his successes.

Given Jon's grasp of various facts about Alexander and his ability to explain Alexander's successes, it seems that Jon *understands* why Alexander was successful. Nevertheless, it also seems that Jon doesn't *know* why Alexander was successful. Why not? The reason is that Jon is unknowingly in a fake barn-style Gettier case (see *A Strange County* pp. 16–20). The presence of all of the unreliable books that Jon could have easily consulted makes it so that Jon's justified true beliefs about Alexander are lucky in a way that seems incompatible with knowledge. Jon's coming to have justified true beliefs about Alexander is directly analogous to Martha's having a justified true belief that she is looking at a barn when she is surrounded by numerous barn façades. After all, Jon had no reason to suspect that he was in a horrible library, just as Martha had no reason to suspect that she was surrounded by barn façades. Jon had no reason to think that the book he picked was relevantly different than the other books about Alexander just as Martha had no reason to think that the barn she was looking at was different from the barn façades all around her. Further, Jon would have just as readily believed what the other books said about Alexander as he believed what the book he in fact read says. Again, this is just like Martha—she would have just as readily believed that a barn façade was a barn if she would've looked at one of them instead of the actual barn. Hence, it seems that Jon, in a way analogous to Martha, came to have justified true beliefs about Alexander by luck. So it seems that just as Martha's justified true belief about the barn fails to count as knowledge because of its lucky nature, Jon's true beliefs about Alexander, though justified, fail to count as knowledge.

Jon fails to have knowledge, but it seems that he does understand why Alexander was so successful. After all, Jon can accurately explain why Alexander was successful; he really does see how various facts about Alexander account for his success. What is more, Jon can express his grasp of these facts in such a way that experts on the subject would think that Jon truly understands. So, it seems that while Jon's ability to have knowledge has been undermined by all of the unreliable books he was surrounded by, his ability to come to understand wasn't. Thus, it appears that understanding is importantly different from knowledge.

RESPONSES

Although many epistemologists have followed Jonathan Kvanvig in arguing that understanding is compatible with forms of luck that undermine knowledge, not all have been persuaded by this sort of example. Some epistemologists respond by allowing that these cases really are ones where knowledge is absent, but they argue that there are similar cases where the kind of luck in play here also undermines understanding (Grimm 2006). The thought here is that knowledge and understanding are both susceptible to luck. So, they stand or fall together, as it were.

A different response to such cases is to argue (as we saw in the responses to *A Strange County* pp. 16–20) that the sort of situation described here isn't really a Gettier case at all. In other words, some argue that these fake barn-style cases don't undermine knowledge in general (Gendler and Hawthorne 2005). There have been some empirical studies that suggest that people don't generally have the intuition that the person in a fake barn-style case lacks knowledge (Colaço et al. 2014). And, there have also been studies that suggest that people are happy to attribute both knowledge and understanding in such cases (Wilkenfeld et al. 2016). Hence, some argue that this sort of case fails to show that understanding isn't reducible to knowledge because it isn't a case where one actually lacks knowledge.

RECOMMENDED READING

GENERAL OVERVIEWS

Understanding. *The Stanford Encyclopedia of Philosophy*.

Understanding in Epistemology. *Internet Encyclopedia of Philosophy*. URL = www. iep.utm.edu/understa/

Hannon, M. Forthcoming. Recent Work on Understanding. *American Philosophical Quarterly*.

SEMINAL PRESENTATION

Kvanvig, J.L. 2003. *The Value of Knowledge and the Pursuit of Understanding*. Cambridge: Cambridge University Press.

ADDITIONAL IMPORTANT DISCUSSIONS

Colaço, D., Buckwalter, W., Stich, S., and Machery, E. 2014. Epistemic Intuitions in Fake-Barn Thought Experiments. *Episteme* 11: 199–212.

Elgin, C. 2004. True Enough. *Philosophical Issues* 14: 113–131.

Elgin, C. 2007. Understanding and the Facts. *Philosophical Studies* 132: 33–42.

Gendler, T.S. and Hawthorne, J. 2005. The Real Guide to Fake Barns: A Catalogue of Gifts for Your Epistemic Enemies. *Philosophical Studies* 124: 331–352.

Grimm, S. 2006. Is Understanding a Species of Knowledge? *British Journal for the Philosophy of Science* 57: 515–535.

Hills, A. 2016. Understanding Why. *Nous* 50: 661–688.

Pritchard, D. 2009. Knowledge, Understanding and Epistemic Value. *Royal Institute of Philosophy Supplement* 64: 19–43.

Wilkenfeld, D.A., Plunkett, D., and Lombrozo, T. 2016. Depth and Deference: When and Why We Attribute Understanding. *Philosophical Studies* 173: 373–393.

Zagzebski, L. 1996. *Virtues of the Mind*. New York: Cambridge University Press.

Zagzebski, L. 2001. Recovering Understanding. In M. Steup (ed.), *Knowledge, Truth, and Duty: Essays on Epistemic Justification, Responsibility, and Virtue*. Oxford: Oxford University Press, 235–252.

7

THE QUIZ SHOW (KNOWLEDGE WITHOUT BELIEF)

Background: In the General Background to this part of the book, we explored the traditional account of knowledge. One of the things that we noted was that although it is widely thought that the traditional account of knowledge is ultimately flawed, it is just as widely (perhaps even more so) thought that the three components of the traditional account (justification, belief, and truth) are each necessary for knowledge. As with many things in philosophy, the consensus on this point is not universal. There are some who question whether various components of the traditional account of knowledge are really necessary. One of the more interesting challenges alleges that one can have knowledge without belief. More precisely, S can know that p, even though S does not believe that p is true.

EPISTEMOLOGICAL ISSUE: ANALYSIS OF KNOWLEDGE

Geoff is a smart guy and very studious. However, he is also prone to pretty severe stage fright and rather extreme test anxiety. Geoff signed a contract agreeing to be a game show contestant before he knew the nature of the show. Given his firm commitment to honoring contracts and his anxiety of what would happen if he is sued for breach of contract, Geoff has decided he will be on the show no matter what it is. Unfortunately, it just so happens that Geoff has been selected to be a contestant on a new game show—"The Quiz Show". The game for this show is straightforward. Contestants are given a quiz on a random subject, and the contestant who scores highest on the quiz wins the prize.

Geoff's day in the spotlight comes. He's on stage, and the show has just begun. Luckily, the wardrobe people are very good—they put him in clothes that won't show how badly he's sweating. Geoff is taking deep breaths to calm himself when the host announces that the quiz topic is World War II. This is an area of history that Geoff has studied quite extensively, so it should be a breeze for him. However, being on stage and having to take a test on top of that has made Geoff extremely nervous. As a result, his mind just goes blank. Not knowing what else to do, Geoff just quickly goes through the quiz putting in guesses for the dates of events. He doesn't believe these are correct— they're just guesses as far as he's concerned. But, Geoff figures it's best to at least complete the quiz.

When all is said and done, Geoff scores very well on the quiz. He gets almost every question correct! The odds that anyone could have gotten a score as high as Geoff's by simply guessing are tremendously low—so low in fact that no one believes Geoff when he says that he was guessing. They all insist that he knew the answers even though he claims he didn't believe that they were correct.

A.D. Woozley and Colin Radford put forward their seminal presentations of this kind of example in an attempt to illustrate that belief isn't necessary for knowledge. While certainly a minority position, they are not alone in thinking that these cases constitute another sort of counterexample to the traditional account of knowledge (Lewis 1996).

RESPONSES

Immediately after these cases were first put forward, there were philosophers who agreed with Woozley and Radford that one can know that p without believing that p. But, there were also others who simply denied that these cases are genuine counterexamples. Yet others argued that these sorts of cases simply aren't clear enough to be used to determine whether the traditional account of knowledge has a problem or not.

More recently, some have sought to use experimental methods to settle the dispute about cases of this kind. It has been argued that the data suggest that ordinary people (i.e. nonphilosophers) tend to agree that knowledge doesn't require belief and that this shows that this sort of case is successful as a counterexample to the traditional account of knowledge (Myers-Schulz and Schwitzgebel 2013).

However, others have argued that what the empirical data show is that there are really two different kinds of belief—thin and thick (Buckwalter et al. 2015). Thin belief that p doesn't require explicitly assenting to the truth of the p; instead, one just has to represent or store p in one's mind as information. Thick belief requires more than this bare minimum of storing as information. Those who claim that there is this distinction between thick and thin belief argue that thin belief is all that is required for knowledge, and they maintain that in the sort of case that we saw above thin belief is present. And so, they maintain that these cases fail to show that knowledge doesn't require belief.

A related response makes use of a much more widely accepted philosophical distinction—the distinction between occurrent (consciously before one's mind) and dispositional (stored in some sense) beliefs (Rose and Schaffer 2013). On this way of approaching the issue, it is true that Geoff doesn't occurrently believe the various answers to the quiz questions. Nevertheless, Geoff does dispositionally believe them, and it is dispositional belief that is required for knowledge. Hence, this response also maintains that this sort of case fails to show that knowledge doesn't require belief.

A final response seeks to employ the distinction between propositional justification (having good reasons to believe that p) and doxastic justification (believing that p for good reasons) in order to analyze what is going on in cases like "The Quiz Show" (see the background for *Saul the Superstitious Lawyer* pp. 42–47 for more on propositional justification vs. doxastic justification). The general idea with this response is that an analogous distinction applies to knowledge (Veber 2014). Once this distinction is extended to knowledge, we end up with two kinds of knowledge—propositional and doxastic—and only the latter requires belief. Thus, given this response, it is true that Geoff knows without belief because he only has propositional knowledge, and this kind of knowledge doesn't require belief. Yet, this doesn't show that the traditional account of knowledge is false because some knowledge (the doxastic variety) does require belief.

RECOMMENDED READING

SEMINAL PRESENTATIONS

Radford, C. 1966. Knowledge: By Examples. *Analysis* 27: 1–11.
Woozley, A.D. 1952. Knowing and Not Knowing. *Proceedings of the Aristotelian Society* 53: 151–172.

ADDITIONAL IMPORTANT DISCUSSIONS

Baumann, P. 2019. Knowledge Requires Belief—and It Doesn't? On Belief as Such and Belief Necessary for Knowledge. *Inquiry* 62: 151–167.
Buckwalter, W., Rose, D., and Turri, J. 2015. Belief through Thick and Thin. *Nous* 49: 748–775.
Farkas, K. 2015. Belief May Not Be a Necessary Condition for Knowledge. *Erkenntnis* 80: 185–200.
Lewis, D. 1996. Elusive Knowledge. *Australasian Journal of Philosophy* 74: 549–567.
Myers-Schulz, B. and Schwitzgebel, E. 2013. Knowing That P Without Believing That P. *Nous* 47: 371–384.
Radford, C. 1988. Radford Revisiting. *Philosophical Quarterly* 38: 496–499.
Rose, D. and Schaffer, J. 2013. Knowledge Entails Dispositional Belief. *Philosophical Studies* 166: 19–50.
Veber, M. 2014. Knowledge with and without Belief. *Metaphilosophy* 45: 120–132.

8

TRIP TO THE ZOO (DRETSKE'S ZEBRA/DISGUISED MULE)

Background: There are a variety of epistemic closure principles and a number of ways of formulating them. One of the most prominent varieties of a closure principle is the one that encapsulates the idea that knowledge is closed under known entailment. To say that knowledge is closed under known entailment is to say, roughly, that if S knows that p, and S knows that p entails q, then S is in a position to know that q. On its face this sort of principle is extremely plausible. After all, it seems perfectly reasonable to think that we can easily extend our knowledge by deducing things that we know are logically entailed by things we know to be true.

EPISTEMOLOGICAL ISSUES: ANALYSIS OF KNOWLEDGE; EPISTEMIC CLOSURE

Andrew and Ebony decide to take a nice relaxing trip to the zoo. They've been enjoying the sunshine and seeing the various animals. At this point they've come to one of their favorite animals—the zebra. The area for the zebras is fairly big, so the only zebra they can see is a good distance away. Fortunately, it's still easy to see, and Andrew and Ebony can enjoy watching it as it has a snack. While they are looking at the zebra, Ebony remarks, "What a great looking zebra!" Andrew, who has a habit of trying out things he's heard in his epistemology class on his friends, replies, "Are you sure it's a zebra?" Ebony, a bit dumbfounded, looks at Andrew and then gestures at the zebra. "Of course, I'm sure it's a zebra. I know what zebras look like, and it's right there in plain sight." Andrew says, "well, you know Ebony, that if someone wanted to, they could paint a mule to look like a zebra. And, if they were good at it, the mule would look just like a zebra from this distance." Ebony, starting to get a bit tired of this line of questioning, responds "Why on earth would someone paint a mule to look like a zebra and put it in the zebra pen at the zoo?" Andrew thinks for a few moments, and then he says:

> There could be a reason. Maybe the zebras are sick, and the zookeepers know that people want to see zebras when they come to the zoo. So, rather than risk upsetting visitors they decided to paint some mules to look like zebras.

After this, Andrew and Ebony gaze at the animal for a few minutes in silence. Andrew breaks the silence, "can you really be sure that that's a zebra rather than a cleverly disguised mule?" After rolling her eyes, Ebony says, "let's go see the lions."

This sort of case is interesting because it seems that accepting that knowledge is closed under known entailment (or simply "closure") may commit us to something strange. Let's get clear on what closure commits us to here. Ebony and Andrew (and we) know that the animal's being a zebra logically entails that it's not a cleverly disguised mule. So, if it's a zebra, it's not a mule; and if it's a mule, it's not a zebra. So far so good. However, now things may seem to get a little strange. If Ebony knows that the animal is a zebra, then it seems that (via closure) she is in a position to know that it is not a cleverly disguised mule. But, how could she know that? After all, Andrew is correct that if the mule were painted in a careful way to look like a zebra, neither he nor Ebony would be able to tell the difference between the mule and a real zebra. This makes it seem that Ebony can't know that the animal is not a cleverly disguised mule. However, if Ebony can't know that the animal isn't a cleverly disguised mule, then by closure she doesn't know that the animal is a zebra. But, this doesn't seem right either. After all, can't people know that they are looking at zebras when they see them at the zoo?

Fred Dretske originally presented this case as a counterexample to closure. The thought being that we seem forced to deny one of these three: Ebony knows that the animal is a zebra; Ebony doesn't know that the animal isn't a cleverly disguised mule; knowledge is closed under known entailment. Dretske argued that the best option was to deny the third claim, that is, deny closure. This wasn't simply because of this sort of case, though. Dretske's account of knowledge where (roughly) one knows p when p is true and S believes p for conclusive reasons, i.e. for reasons that wouldn't hold if p were false, entails that closure is false. (Note there are similarities between Dretske's view of knowledge and Robert Nozick's sensitivity account of knowledge, which also requires denying closure; see *A Strange County* pp. 16–20 and *Red Barns and Blue Façades* pp. 21–24.) Of course, one might wonder how we are to ever know by looking that an animal is a zebra on Dretske's view since it seems that our reason (how it looks) could obtain even if the animal is a cleverly disguised mule. For Dretske the answer is to adopt a relevant alternatives view of knowledge. Basically, the idea here is that in order for a reason to count as conclusive it has to rule out all *relevant* alternatives, and in many contexts the alternative that the animal is a cleverly disguised mule is simply not relevant.

RESPONSES

Most epistemologists do not follow Dretske in denying closure. Some argue that in this case, it is actually intuitive that Ebony really does know that the animal is not a cleverly disguised mule (Vogel 1990, Feldman 1995). The thought is that the very reasons that make it so that Ebony knows that what she sees is a zebra also make it so that she knows that she's not looking at a cleverly disguised mule. For instance, Ebony is aware of the fact that she's at the zoo where it is common to see zebras but not common to see mules; she has never heard of a zoo disguising mules; she has no reason to think that the zookeepers at this zoo are pranksters or dishonest, and so on. Hence, the very things that make it so that Ebony knows that she is seeing a zebra also make it so that she knows that she's not seeing a cleverly disguised mule. Thus, some respond that we can account for what is going on in this case without giving up any of the three intuitively plausible claims.

Another way that some epistemologists respond to this sort of case without denying closure is to claim that "knowledge" is context sensitive (see *Going to the Bank* pp. 48–52 for more on this). Very roughly, the idea here is that whether it is true to say of someone that they have knowledge varies with the context (Cohen 1988, DeRose 1995). So, we might think that it is true to say "Ebony knows that the animal is a zebra" when in a context where the possibility that the animal is a cleverly disguised mule isn't relevant, before Andrew raises the possibility, say. But, once the possibility that the animal is a cleverly disguised mule is raised, it's no longer true to say "Ebony knows that the animal is a zebra". This response allows us to accept that Ebony does know that she's looking at a zebra (in some contexts) and also to accept that Ebony doesn't know that she's not looking at a cleverly disguised mule (in some contexts) without giving up closure.

RECOMMENDED READING

GENERAL OVERVIEWS

Epistemic Closure. *The Stanford Encyclopedia of Philosophy*. URL = https://plato. stanford.edu/entries/closure-epistemic/#toc

Epistemic Closure Principles. *Internet Encyclopedia of Philosophy*. URL = https:// iep.utm.edu/epis-clo/#SH3e

SEMINAL PRESENTATION

Dretske, F. 1970. Epistemic Operators. *Journal of Philosophy* 67: 1007–1023.

ADDITIONAL IMPORTANT DISCUSSIONS

Alspector-Kelly, M. 2019. *Against Knowledge Closure.* Cambridge: Cambridge University Press.

Cohen, S. 1988. How to be a Fallibilist. *Philosophical Perspectives* 2: 91–123.

DeRose, K. 1995. Solving the Skeptical Problem. *Philosophical Review* 104: 1–52.

Dretske, F. 2005. The Case against Closure. In M. Steup and E. Sosa (eds), *Contemporary Debates in Epistemology*. Malden, MA: Blackwell Publishing, 13–26.

Dretske, F. 2005. Reply to Hawthorne. In M. Steup and E. Sosa (eds), *Contemporary Debates in Epistemology*. Malden, MA: Blackwell Publishing, 43–46.

Feldman, R. 1995. In Defence of Closure. *Philosophical Quarterly* 45: 487–494.

Hawthorne, J. 2005. The Case for Closure. In M. Steup and E. Sosa (eds), *Contemporary Debates in Epistemology*. Malden, MA: Blackwell Publishing, 26–43.

Nozick, R. 1981. *Philosophical Explanations*. Cambridge, MA: Harvard University Press.

Stine, G. 1971. Dretske on Knowing the Logical Consequences. *Journal of Philosophy* 68: 296–299.

Vogel, J. 1990. Are There Counter Examples to the Closure Principle? In M. Roth (ed), *Doubting: Contemporary Perspectives on Skepticism*. Dordrecht: Kluwer, 13–27.

9

SAUL THE SUPERSTITIOUS LAWYER (KNOWLEDGE AND BASING)

Background: To appreciate this thought experiment, we have to first think about the basing relation. It is common to distinguish between things you have justification for believing (what is called "propositional justification") and things you justifiedly believe (what is called "doxastic justification"). You can have justification for believing something even if you don't actually believe it. Hence, you don't automatically justifiedly believe everything that you have justification for believing. In fact, in some cases you might have justification for believing something and believe it, but still fail to justifiedly believe it! A very brief excursion into the realm of ethics might be helpful here.

When it comes to morality, we can distinguish between merely doing the right thing and doing the right thing for the right reasons. For example, if you help an elderly person across a busy street, you are doing the right thing. But, if you help this person across the street only so that you can rob this person, you did the right thing (helping the elderly person across the street) but for the wrong reason (rather than to help, it was to rob the person). The same sort of thing applies in epistemology. There's the right thing to believe (what you have justification for believing) and there's believing the right thing for the right reasons (justifiedly believing). In order to have justification for believing some claim, you have to have good reasons/evidence for thinking that the claim is true. In order to justifiedly believe some claim, you not only have to have good reasons for thinking the claim is true, but you also have to believe the claim because of those good reasons, i.e. you have to base your belief on those reasons. The relation that your belief has to bear to your justification for that belief to count as justified is known as the "basing relation".

Why is this so important? One reason is that most epistemologists agree that in order to have knowledge that some proposition, p, is true, you must justifiedly believe that p. That is to say, it is not enough that p is true, you believe p, and you have justification for believing p (and you satisfy whatever is needed to block Gettier cases; see Promotions and Traveling Friends pp. 6–11 and A Strange County pp. 16–20). Knowledge requires that your belief that p is actually based on your justification for p.

The most common view of the basing relation is that it is a causal or counterfactual dependence relation. On this understanding of the basing relation a person's belief that p is based on her evidence for p when having that evidence causes her to have the belief that p, or (assuming that causation isn't simply a matter of counterfactual dependence) the person's belief counterfactually depends upon her having evidence that supports believing that p. To say that someone's belief counterfactually depends upon her having some evidence means one or both of two things. First, it can mean that the person wouldn't have the belief that p if she didn't have the evidence she does. Second, it can mean that the person would have the belief that p if she does have the evidence. Simply put, the idea is that the person's belief that p is based upon her evidence when her having that evidence explains why she has the belief and/or if she were to lack the evidence she has, the lack of evidence would explain why she doesn't have the belief.

EPISTEMOLOGICAL ISSUE: BASING RELATION

Saul is a very competent, if a bit unscrupulous, lawyer, but he's also very superstitious. Usually, his superstitions don't make a difference to the performance of his duties as a lawyer. However, on this occasion they do.

Saul is defending a client who is on trial for four horrendous crimes. Saul knows for a fact that his client committed three of these crimes. This doesn't matter to Saul though; he's still going to mount the best defense he possibly can. After all, Saul always says that it's the prosecution's job to make sure the guilty are punished; it's Saul's job to win cases and make sure clients don't go to jail. He doesn't care whether his clients are innocent. In fact, he tends to believe that his clients are guilty. But, in the case of this particular client something interesting occurs. Saul already knows that the client committed three of the four crimes. However, one afternoon a few days before the trial is set, Saul reviews all of the evidence related to the fourth crime and realizes to his utter amazement that it provides conclusive support for thinking that his client is actually innocent of this crime. Nevertheless, Saul can't bring himself to believe that his client is innocent. He sees that the evidence provides very good reason for thinking that the client is innocent, and yet he still believes his client is guilty.

Later that evening, in an attempt to clear his head, Saul goes to visit a fortune-teller. The fortune-teller, who knows nothing about the evidence related to the trial and has absolutely no real fortune-telling powers, tells Saul that his client is innocent of the fourth crime. Saul has plenty of evidence for believing that fortune-tellers don't have real powers, but he is nevertheless very superstitious and continues to trust fortune-tellers. In this instance, once the fortune-teller tells him that the client is innocent of this crime, Saul immediately believes that his client is innocent. Does Saul now *know* that his client is innocent?

Let's get a little clearer about what's going on and the key question here. Before Saul reviews the evidence, he clearly doesn't know that his client is innocent because he has no reason to think this and has very good reason to think that his client is guilty (after all, the guy committed the other three crimes, and Saul pretty much never defends innocent people—he's unscrupulous, remember). Immediately after Saul reviews the evidence, it seems clear that he doesn't know that his client is innocent. He doesn't believe that his client is innocent, and knowledge requires belief (see *The Quiz Show* pp. 33–36 for a case that is designed to put pressure on this assumption). But, what about after he sees the fortune-teller? Now Saul believes that his client is innocent, the client actually is innocent of this crime, and

Saul has good reason for thinking he's innocent. What is more, Saul is not in the sort of situation that gives rise to the Gettier problem (see *Promotions and Traveling Friends* pp. 6–11 and *A Strange County* pp. 16–20 for more on what these situations are like). Does Saul now know that his client is innocent?

Importantly, if Saul does know that his client is innocent, then this case is a counterexample to the idea that the basing relation is a causal or counterfactual relation. Why is this? Well, Saul's belief that his client is innocent isn't caused by his having evidence for believing this. After all, he gains the evidence, but that doesn't cause him to believe the client is innocent. Instead, the claims of the fortune-teller are what cause Saul to believe that his client is innocent. Similarly, his belief doesn't counterfactually depend upon his evidence. He gets the evidence but doesn't form the belief that his client is innocent. Presumably, if he were to not have that evidence, it would make no difference to his believing that his client is innocent. Once the fortune-teller informs Saul that his client is innocent, he's going to believe that his client is innocent. If Saul were to somehow lose all his evidence for his client's innocence but still be told by the fortune-teller that his client is innocent, he'd still believe the client is innocent. All that seems to matter for Saul believing that his client is innocent is the fortune-teller telling him so. That all said, if Saul knows that his client is innocent (which would entail that he justifiedly believes that the client is innocent), then the basing relation cannot be a causal or counterfactual relation because his evidence doesn't bear the relevant sort of causal or counterfactual relation to his belief.

Keith Lehrer originally presented this sort of case in an attempt to provide a counterexample to causal/counterfactual views of the basing relation. According to Lehrer, Saul *does know* after he sees the fortune-teller. As we saw above, this is very important, *if* correct, because it shows that the basing relation cannot be a causal relation or a relation of counterfactual dependence. Lehrer takes this to be the lesson of this example and suggests that the basing relation is really a doxastic relation. The idea here, roughly, is that basing a belief that *p* on one's evidence requires that one have a belief to the effect that one's evidence provides sufficiently strong reasons to believe that *p*.

RESPONSES

The response favored by those who think the basing relation is a causal relation or a relation of counterfactual dependence is to simply deny that Saul knows (or even justifiedly believes that his client is innocent) (McCain 2012). This response holds that while Saul believes the right thing (that his client is innocent), he believes it for the wrong reasons (because the fortune-teller told him rather than because of his evidence).

Yet another response to this case is to accept, as Lehrer does, that Saul knows that his client is innocent, while maintaining that this doesn't show that causal and counterfactual dependence relations are irrelevant to basing (Korcz 2000). This response contends that the example of Saul shows that causal or counterfactual dependence relations aren't *necessary* for basing, but they are *sufficient*. In other words, the heart of this response is the idea that the example of Saul shows that one can justifiedly believe that *p*, even if one's evidence doesn't cause one's belief that *p* (or one's belief doesn't counterfactually depend upon one's evidence). Nevertheless, in cases where one's evidence *does cause* one's belief that *p* (or one's belief counterfactually depends upon one's evidence), one justifiedly believes that *p*. Hence, this sort of response tries to find a middle ground between the causal/counterfactual view of the basing relation and the doxastic view of the basing relation by allowing that justifiedly believing requires *either* what the causal/counterfactual view says *or* what the doxastic view says.

RECOMMENDED READING

GENERAL BACKGROUND ON BASING

Korcz, K.A. The Epistemic Basing Relation. In Edward N. Zalta (ed.), *The Stanford Encyclopedia of Philosophy* (Fall 2019 Edition). URL = https://plato.stanford.edu/archives/fall2019/entries/basing-epistemic/.

SEMINAL PRESENTATION

Lehrer, K. 1971. How Reasons Give us Knowledge, or the Case of the Gypsy Lawyer. *Journal of Philosophy* 68: 311–313.

ADDITIONAL IMPORTANT DISCUSSIONS

Carter, J.A. and Bondy, P. (eds) 2019. *Well-founded Belief: New Essays on the Epistemic Basing Relation*. New York: Routledge.

Korcz, K.A. 2000. The Causal-doxastic Theory of the Basing Relation. *Canadian Journal of Philosophy* 30: 525–550.

Kvanvig, J.L. 2003. Justification and Proper Basing. In E. Olsson (ed.), *The Epistemology of Keith Lehrer*. Dordrecht: Kluwer, 43–62.

McCain, K. 2012. The Interventionist Account of Causation and the Basing Relation. *Philosophical Studies* 159: 357–382.

Mittag, D. 2002. On the Causal-doxastic Theory of the Basing Relation. *Canadian Journal of Philosophy* 32: 543–559.

Neta, R. 2019. The Basing Relation. *Philosophical Review* 128: 179–217.

Tierney, H. and Smith, N.D. 2012. Keith Lehrer on the Basing Relation. *Philosophical Studies* 161: 27–36.

Wallbridge, K. 2018. The Peculiar Case of Lehrer's Lawyer. *Synthese* 195: 1615–1630.

10

GOING TO THE BANK (CONTEXTUALISM)

Background: A number of words in ordinary English are context-sensitive. Such words have different meanings (and so, sentences containing them have different requirements for counting as true) in different conversational contexts. For example, you may speak truly when you say "the dining room table is flat" in the context of discussing where to put a vase. However, if you're discussing where to conduct an extremely sensitive experiment, then "the dining room table is flat" doesn't seem true. "Flat" is context-sensitive—whether it is true to say of something that it is flat varies from one conversational context to another. Some have argued that "know" and related terms are also context-sensitive.

EPISTEMOLOGICAL ISSUES: CONTEXTUALISM

Let's image two scenarios. Here's the first one: Sally and her sister Sarah are on their way home Friday afternoon and trying to decide whether or not they should swing by the bank. Their grandmother sent them each a check for their birthday, and their bank's mobile deposit app isn't working. It's *not particularly important* to them to have the money in their account before next week, but they would prefer to have it sooner rather than later. However, if they could go the next day—on Saturday—that would be much more convenient than taking the time to go today. Sarah says, "Let's just go on home and go to the bank tomorrow. It'll be open. Jorge told me earlier today that he was there last Saturday, and he knows that it's open tomorrow." Sally responds, "OK, since Jorge knows that the bank is open tomorrow, let's just go home and deposit these checks tomorrow."

And here's the second scenario: Sally and her sister Sarah are on their way home Friday afternoon and trying to decide whether or not they should swing by the bank. Their grandmother sent them each a check for their birthday, and their bank's mobile deposit app isn't working. It's *extremely important* to them to have the money in their account before next week. If they don't get these checks deposited, they're not going to be able to pay their rent. However, if they could go the next day—on Saturday—that would be much more convenient than taking the time to go today. Sarah says, "Let's just go on home and go to the bank tomorrow. It'll be open. Jorge told me earlier today that he was there last Saturday, and he knows that it's open tomorrow." Sally responds:

> Are you sure? Jorge might have mixed up which day he was there last week. Plus, it's possible that the bank changed its hours and is closed on Saturdays now. Jorge doesn't really know that the bank is open tomorrow. Let's go to the bank now and get these checks deposited.

A key question about these two scenarios concerns whether Sally spoke truly when she claimed in one scenario that Jorge knows the bank is open on Saturday and in the other claimed that he doesn't know. What's particularly interesting about this question is that we might have the intuition that Sally spoke truly both times. In other words, Sally was correct in the first scenario when she said that Jorge knows the bank is open on Saturday, and she was correct in the second scenario when she said that Jorge doesn't know that the bank is open on Saturday. What's interesting about this? Nothing about Jorge is different in the two scenarios, nor is anything different about the bank! So, if Sally is correct in attributing knowledge to him in the first scenario and also correct in not attributing knowledge to him in the second scenario, it can't be because something about Jorge has changed from one scenario to the other. Instead, if Sally is correct in both situations, it has to be because of the differences in her own situation between these two scenarios. The fact that the stakes are low for Sally and Sarah would have to make it easier for Jorge to count as knowing that the bank is open on Saturday than when the stakes for them are high.

Keith DeRose first introduced this sort of bank case in an effort to demonstrate that the word "know" is context-sensitive. To get a firmer grip on this, think about another word that is clearly context-sensitive: "tall". It may be true to say of a two-year-old that he is tall when we are comparing him to other two-year-olds. However, when the context is the height of NBA players, it would also be true to say of the two-year-old that he isn't tall. Similarly, DeRose (and others) holds that whether it is correct to say that someone knows depends upon the context. Importantly, on this view, known as "contextualism", the relevant context is the context of the speaker (the person saying of someone that they know or don't know), not the context of the potential knower (if the knower is a different person from the speaker). Hence, contextualism says that what we should make of these cases is that Sally speaks correctly both times, because in the first scenario she is in a low-stakes context where it is correct to attribute knowledge to Jorge, and in the second scenario she is in a high-stakes context where it isn't correct to attribute knowledge to Jorge.

RESPONSES

There has been a considerable amount of empirical work on people's responses to pairs of cases like this. The goal has been to determine whether nonphilosophers think that attributions of knowledge vary with the stakes involved or not. The results are mixed. Some studies have seemed to vindicate the contextualist by suggesting that people are inclined to say that Sally is correct when she changes whether she attributes knowledge to Jorge depending upon her own situation (DeRose 2009). Other studies have seemed to suggest that actually what people track is whether the stakes are high or low for *Jorge* when it comes to attributing knowledge to him (Sripada and Stanley 2012). Still other studies have seemed to suggest that people are not inclined to change whether they think a knowledge attribution is correct because of raised or lowered stakes (Buckwalter and Schaffer 2015, Rose et al. 2019). These empirical results line up with the three major responses to these sorts of cases.

A response that denies contextualism but is similar, in that it maintains that the standards for whether it is correct to attribute knowledge to someone changes with the stakes involved, is what has come to be known as "subject sensitive invariantism" or "pragmatic encroachment" (Hawthorne 2004, Stanley 2005, Fantl and McGrath 2009). This response says that the relevant stakes are those of the potential knower. So, in the scenarios mentioned above, the pragmatic encroachment response says that whether it is true to say that Jorge knows/doesn't know that the bank is open depends upon the stakes for Jorge. If it is really important to Jorge that the bank be open on Saturday, then it is harder for him to have knowledge than if it isn't important to him.

The final response is what is sometimes called "classical invariantism" or "stable invariantism" (Conee 2014). This is the view that "know" isn't context-sensitive, and the requirements for knowledge do not change with the raising or lowering of stakes. On this response, if Jorge knows or fails to know in one of the scenarios, then he's in the same position in the other scenario. Additionally, this response claims that when Sally uses the word "know" it means exactly the same thing in both contexts—the requirements for correctly attributing knowledge don't change with the stakes. When it comes to what Sally says in these scenarios, stable invariantists might say that she is simply mistaken in one or the other scenario, or they may claim that she is correct in both but that is simply because in at least one of the scenarios she is speaking loosely, like when, for example, we say that "it's 3 o'clock" when in fact it's 3:05.

RECOMMENDED READING

GENERAL OVERVIEWS

Epistemic Contextualism. *The Stanford Encyclopedia of Philosophy*. URL = https:// plato.stanford.edu/entries/contextualism-epistemology/

Contextualism in Epistemology. *Internet Encyclopedia of Philosophy*. URL = https://iep.utm.edu/contextu/

SEMINAL PRESENTATION

DeRose, K. 1992. Contextualism and Knowledge Attributions. *Philosophy and Phenomenological Research* 52: 913–927.

ADDITIONAL IMPORTANT DISCUSSIONS

Buckwalter, W. and Schaffer, J. 2015. Knowledge, Stakes, and Mistakes. *Nous* 49: 201–234.

Cohen, S. 1988. How to be a Fallibilist. *Philosophical Perspectives* 2: 91–123.
Cohen, S. 1999. Contextualism, Skepticism, and the Structure of Reasons. *Philosophical Perspectives* 13: 57–89.

Conee, E. 2014. Contextualism Contested. In M. Steup, J. Turri, and E. Sosa (eds), *Contemporary Debates in Epistemology Second Edition*. Malden, MA: Blackwell Publishing, 60–69.

DeRose, K. 1995. Solving the Skeptical Problem. *Philosophical Review* 104: 1–52.

DeRose, K. 2009. *The Case for Contextualism*. New York: Oxford University Press.

Fantl, J. and McGrath, M. 2009. *Knowledge in an Uncertain World*. Oxford: Oxford University Press.

Hawthorne, J. 2004. *Knowledge and Lotteries*. New York: Oxford University Press.

Lewis, D. 1996. Elusive Knowledge. *Australasian Journal of Philosophy* 74: 549–567.

May, J., Sinnott-Armstrong, W., Hull, J.G., and Zimmerman, A. 2010. Practical Interests, Relevant Alternatives, and Knowledge Attributions: An Empirical Study. *Review of Philosophy and Psychology* 1: 265–273.

Pinillos, N.A. 2011. Some Recent Work in Experimental Epistemology. *Philosophy Compass* 6: 675–688.

Rose, D., et al. 2019. Nothing at Stake in Knowledge. *Nous* 53: 224–247.

Sripada, C. and Stanley, J. 2012. Empirical Tests of Interest-Relative Invariantism. *Episteme* 9: 3–26.

Stanley, J. 2005. *Knowledge and Practical Interests*. New York: Oxford University Press.

PART II

LIMITS OF KNOWLEDGE

GENERAL BACKGROUND: SKEPTICISM

Philosophical skepticism comes in many varieties. The primary feature shared by the various forms of skepticism is that they deny that we have knowledge in some domain. For example, a prominent form of skepticism denies that we know anything about the external world (the world outside of our own minds). Another commonality among kinds of skepticism is that they are usually motivated by appealing to thought experiments concerning possible skeptical scenarios such as that we are being deceived by a demon or that we are really just experiencing a computer simulation. Of course, these skeptical scenarios are often outlandish but that doesn't inhibit their functionality. All that is needed for a skeptical scenario to do its work is that the scenario be possible (in a very broad sense of "possible").

Discussions of skeptical scenarios and responses to skeptical arguments have been a central feature of epistemology for hundreds of years. This fact may give the false impression that most epistemologists are skeptics. Actually, most epistemologists think that the more famous forms of skepticism (such as skepticism about the world around us) are mistaken. Recognizing that most epistemologists are not skeptics, and yet epistemologists have spent (and continue to spend) a lot of time thinking about skepticism, prompts a question: Why? That is, why bother thinking about skeptical scenarios and skeptical arguments if almost no one actually accepts philosophical skepticism? There are a variety of reasons, two of which are worth mentioning here. One reason is that although *almost* no epistemologists are skeptics of this sort, some prominent epistemologists are. When well-informed experts sincerely hold a position, it is worth thinking carefully about it—even if the position is very unpopular. Another reason is that by thinking carefully about skeptical scenarios and the arguments they support, we can come to better understand both the nature of knowledge (and related things like justification and understanding) and the limits of our knowledge. It is especially important to keep this latter reason in mind as we explore the entries in this section. We can better appreciate the thought experiments that are coming if we keep in mind that many are designed to help us think about what it really takes to have knowledge and to challenge our common assumptions about the extent of our knowledge.

11

DESCARTES' DEMON (CARTESIAN/EXTERNAL WORLD SKEPTICISM)

Background: We commonly take ourselves to know a wide variety of things. Philosophical skeptics challenge whether we really have the knowledge that we think we have. It is important to keep in mind that generally skeptics do not claim that we fail to have knowledge because our beliefs are false. Rather, they typically maintain that our reasons/evidence for what we believe aren't good enough for us to really know.

EPISTEMOLOGICAL ISSUES: CARTESIAN/ EXTERNAL WORLD SKEPTICISM

Think about some of the things you know about the world around you. You're reading this book. Perhaps you're sitting in a chair. You have hands. And so on. Why do you believe these things? Presumably, you believe them on the basis of your experiences. You believe that you're reading this book, for instance, because it looks like you have a book in your hands. It feels like you have a book in your hands. And so on. So far, no problems.

But, have your experiences ever led you astray? For example, have you ever thought that you saw something but then as you moved closer realized that it wasn't what you thought? Or, are you familiar with any perceptual illusions such as the Müller-Lyer illusion:

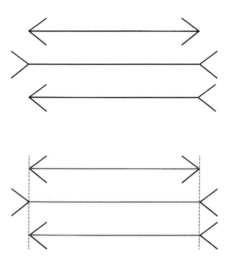

In the Müller-Lyer illusion, the lines appear to be different lengths, but they are actually the same. Our experiences aren't perfectly reliable, i.e. they sometimes lead us astray. Realization of this fact led Descartes to worry. If our experiences sometimes lead us astray, how can we tell when they are leading us astray and when they're not? It's not clear that we can. But, if we can't tell in general whether our experiences are leading us astray or not, then it seems possible that they always do.

Descartes considered the following sort of situation. Imagine that there is a being with god-like powers, and this being has malicious intentions. This particular being, a demon, has decided to spend its time and considerable resources tricking you into believing false things about the world around you. If this were the case, could you be tricked into thinking that you're reading a book when in fact there is no book at all? It seems so. Could you be tricked into thinking that you have hands when in fact you don't? It seems so. After all, couldn't the demon, with its god-like powers, cause you to have pretty much any sort of perceptual experience that it wanted? Presumably, you don't think that you are actually being deceived by a demon of the sort that Descartes described. But, why not? Things would look, feel, smell, sound, and taste exactly as they do now, whether things are as you take them to be or you are deceived by Descartes' demon. Since everything would seem the same, what grounds could you have for thinking that the world is as you normally think it is instead of that you are tricked by a demon? (Of course, nothing in particular hinges on the idea that it is a demon that is doing the deceiving here—the possibility that we are experiencing a computer simulation such as that depicted in the movie *The Matrix* or the possibility that we are simply brains in vats can do the same work as the demon that Descartes discusses.)

Now we face a serious problem. If you don't have grounds for thinking that the world is as you typically take it to be rather than that the world is one in which you are being deceived by a demon, it seems that you don't have good reasons to believe the things you normally do about the world around you. It appears that we face a very strong argument for skepticism here. To make the argument that Descartes' demon supports clearer, here is a simple formulation of it:

1) You don't know that you're not deceived by Descartes' demon.
2) If you don't know that you're not deceived by Descartes' demon, then you don't know anything about the world around you.
3) Therefore, you don't know anything about the world around you.

RESPONSES

One response to Descartes' demon is to simply accept skepticism. That is, one might grant that it is impossible for us to have reasons to think that we aren't being deceived by such a demon. And so, one might accept that because of this possibility, we lack knowledge of the world around us. The vast majority of epistemologists since Descartes have not opted for this response. Instead, most epistemologists have sought to find a flaw with the argument for skepticism yielded by this example.

One contemporary response to this issue is to embrace a reliabilist form of externalism (see *General Background: The Nature of Justification* pp. 113–119) (Greco 2008). The rough idea with this response is that you know things about the world around you so long as your beliefs are reliably produced (i.e. so long as the cognitive faculties that produce those beliefs tend to produce more true beliefs than false beliefs). On this response, the fact that you don't have reasons for thinking that you aren't deceived by a demon doesn't matter. Similarly, if your belief that you aren't deceived by a demon is reliably produced (and true), it'll amount to knowledge as well. So, according to this reliabilist response, premise (2) of the skeptical argument is false because it doesn't matter whether you know that you aren't deceived by a demon. All that matters is that your true beliefs are reliably produced. It may also be that premise (1) is false, given reliabilism. As long as you believe that you aren't deceived by a demon, it's true that you aren't deceived by a demon, and your belief is reliably produced, reliabilism will say that you know that you're not deceived.

Another externalist response is to accept a sensitivity account of knowledge of the sort discussed in earlier entries (see *A Strange County* pp. 16–20 and *Red Barns and Blue Façades* pp. 21–24) (Nozick 1981) or the somewhat similar relevant alternatives account of knowledge (see *Trip to the Zoo* pp. 37–41) (Dretske 1970, Stine 1976). Both of these accounts of knowledge incorporate a denial of closure, which would mean that (2) of the argument above is false. On both of these responses, it can be true that you don't know that you aren't deceived by a demon, but also true that you know things about the world around you.

Contextualism offers yet another response to this form of skepticism (see *Going to the Bank* pp. 48–52) (DeRose 1995, 2009, Lewis 1996, Cohen 1999). The contextualist claims that in ordinary contexts, it's true to say "S knows about the world around her" because the stakes are low (the reason for this is that skeptical alternatives aren't salient). It is also true to say "S doesn't know about the world around her" when you are in a skeptical context (i.e., a context where skeptical possibilities, such as that you are deceived by a demon, are made salient). On this response, the skeptical argument is invalid because it fails to take account of the differences between ordinary and skeptical contexts.

Another response is to meet the skeptic head-on and argue that your experiences actually do give you reasons to think that you aren't deceived by a demon and deny premise (1) on those grounds. One of the more popular ways of developing this response is to argue that your normal view of the world is the best explanation of your experiences being as they are (Vogel 1990, McCain 2014). Since this best explanation is considerably better than skeptical rivals, such as that you are deceived by a demon, you have sufficient grounds for thinking that you aren't deceived by a demon.

Yet another response is to adopt the Moorean approach (Moore 1939). The Moorean responds to this situation in roughly the following way. It's obvious that you know things about the world around you. This is so obvious, in fact, that you can be more sure that it is correct than you can that the skeptical argument yielded by consideration of Descartes' demon is sound. Hence, the Moorean says that since it is more obvious that you know things about the world around you than it is that the skeptical argument is sound, you should reject the skeptical argument. You don't need to know what is wrong with the argument; you just know that it is wrong.

A different response takes onboard Ludwig Wittgenstein's (1969) idea of "hinge propositions". Basically, this response holds that there are certain things that you are simply entitled to believe because of their role in your cognitive life (Wright 2004). One of the things you are entitled to believe in this sense is that you aren't deceived by Descartes' demon. So, this response maintains that you can know things about the world around you even if you don't have reasons to reject the possibility that you are deceived by a demon because you are entitled to believe that you aren't deceived in this way.

A final response involves arguing that the sort of scenario depicted isn't really a skeptical scenario at all (Chalmers 2010). The idea here is that even if you were to somehow discover that you are being tricked by a demon, this wouldn't make your ordinary beliefs about the world around you false. Rather, this discovery would allow you to learn about the fundamental nature of ordinary objects. You would learn that things like tables and chairs are very different than you thought—they aren't made of tiny particles, but instead they are patterns of stimulation that the demon gives you. In other words, learning that you are being affected by Descartes' demon would amount to learning metaphysics, or perhaps it would be something akin to learning fundamental physics.

RECOMMENDED READING

GENERAL OVERVIEWS

Skepticism. *The Stanford Encyclopedia of Philosophy*. URL = https://plato.stanford.edu/entries/skepticism/

Contemporary Skepticism. *Internet Encyclopedia of Philosophy*. URL = https://iep.utm.edu/skepcont/

SEMINAL PRESENTATION

Descartes, R. 1641/1931. *Meditations on First Philosophy*. In *Philosophical Works of Descartes (Volume 1)*, E. S. Haldane and G.R.T. Ross (eds/trans.). New York: Dover Publications.

ADDITIONAL IMPORTANT DISCUSSIONS

Beebe, J. 2017. Does Skepticism Presuppose Explanationism? In K. McCain and T. Poston (eds), *Best Explanations: New Essays on Inference to the Best Explanation*. Oxford: Oxford University Press, 173–187.

Chalmers, D. 2010. The Matrix as Metaphysics. In *The Character of Consciousness*. Oxford: Oxford University Press, 455–478.

Cohen, S. 1999. Contextualism, Skepticism, and the Structure of Reasons. *Philosophical Perspectives* 13: 57–89.

DeRose, K. 1995. Solving the Skeptical Problem. *Philosophical Review* 104: 1–52.

DeRose, K. 2009. *The Case for Contextualism*. New York: Oxford University Press.

Dretske, F. 1970. Epistemic Operators. *Journal of Philosophy* 67: 1007–1023.

Fumerton, R. 1995. *Metaepistemology and Skepticism*. Lanham, MD: Rowman & Littlefield.

Goldman, A.I. 1979. What Is Justified Belief? In G.S. Pappas (ed) *Justification and Knowledge: New Studies in Epistemology*. Dordrecht: Springer Netherlands, 1–23.

Greco, J. 2008. *Putting Skeptics in Their Place*. Cambridge: Cambridge University Press.

Lewis, D. 1996. Elusive Knowledge. *Australasian Journal of Philosophy* 74: 549–567.

McCain, K. 2014. *Evidentialism and Epistemic Justification*. New York: Routledge.

Moore, G.E. 1939. Proof of an External World. *Proceedings of the British Academy* 25: 273–300.

Nozick, R. 1981. *Philosophical Explanations*. Cambridge, MA: Harvard University Press.

Stine, G.C. 1976. Skepticism, Relevant Alternatives, and Deductive Closure. *Philosophical Studies* 29: 249–261.

Stroud, B. 1984. *The Significance of Philosophical Scepticism*. Oxford: Oxford University Press.

Vogel, J. 1990. Cartesian Skepticism and Inference to the Best Explanation. *Journal of Philosophy* 87: 658–666.

Williams, M. 1996. *Unnatural Doubts*. Princeton, NJ: Princeton University Press.

Wittgenstein, L. 1969. *On Certainty*. Oxford: Basil Blackwell.

Wright, C. 2004. Warrant for Nothing (and Foundations for Free)? *Aristotelian Society Supplementary Volume* 78: 167–212.

12

DESCARTES' DREAM (DREAMING SKEPTICISM)

Background: In the previous entry we saw one of Descartes' most famous skeptical scenarios. Here we will look at his other famous skeptical scenario. Although both scenarios are taken to pose a threat to our knowledge of the external world, some philosophers have argued that the way that do so is importantly different from one another.

EPISTEMOLOGICAL ISSUES: CARTESIAN/ EXTERNAL WORLD SKEPTICISM; DREAMING SKEPTICISM

Have you ever had a dream that seemed so real that while it was happening, you weren't aware that it was a dream? You may be familiar with this sort of dream—it seems so real that for a few moments when you wake up you are a bit disoriented. After such a dream, it takes you a few moments to figure out that you are now awake and what had seemed so real was actually a dream. Perhaps you've never had such a dream, but presumably you can still imagine what this would be like. If you've had such a dream (or even if you are just imagining having such a dream), Descartes asks us to consider: do you know that you aren't having such a dream right now? How can you be sure? Granted, you might think that a dream would be a tad more exciting than reading this epistemology book (though what could be more exciting than epistemology?!). But, couldn't a dream be realistic in the sense of not including you having unnatural abilities or doing anything spectacular? Is it possible (in the broad sense of the term)—however unlikely—that you could have a dream in which everything seems exactly the way it does when you are awake?

Descartes noticed that when it comes to beliefs about the external world, it could be that it seems to you that you are reading a book when in fact you are lying in your bed sleeping the night away. If things could look, feel, etc. the way they do now but you are actually dreaming, how can you know that you are awake rather than having a vivid dream? It seems that we face a skeptical challenge very similar to that posed by the possibility of massive deception (see *Descartes' Demon* pp. 55–60). After all, if you don't know that you're not asleep, then it seems you don't really know that things in the world around you are as you think they are.

At first, we might be tempted to think that this sort of dreaming skepticism is not only similar to the sort of skeptical challenge posed by a deceptive demon or being in a computer simulation, but that it is the exact same thing. However, there seems to be at least one very important difference. You have never met Descartes' demon, nor have you been in a computer simulation that is powerful enough to completely mimic your normal experiences. However, you have dreamed before! Hence, while you might think that the idea that you're being deceived by a demon or that you are in a computer simulation is ridiculous and so skepticism based on these possibilities should simply be ignored, it seems a bit harder to run this line of response to dreaming skepticism. It's not ridiculous to think that you might have a vivid dream that is hard to distinguish from reality—people (perhaps even you) have had, and continue to have, such dreams. Admittedly, it is a big move from this sort of dream to a dream that completely mimics waking life to the point where you can't tell whether you are awake right now. But, a skeptic might respond by asking how you know that you've ever been awake. Some people (again, perhaps you are one of these people) have dreams within dreams—instances where they are dreaming and seem to wake up but that is all part of a larger dream. Given this, why think that you are really awake now rather than dreaming? Why think that you haven't been dreaming your entire life?

If you can't be sure that you're awake, how can you know anything about the world around you? We might put this skeptical concern more formally:

1) You don't know that you're not dreaming.
2) If you don't know that you're not dreaming, then you don't know anything about the world around you.
3) Therefore, you don't know anything about the world around you.

RESPONSES

The argument for skepticism that the dreaming scenario helps generate is very similar to the argument of the previous entry (see *Descartes' Demon* pp. 55–60). It is perhaps unsurprising that many epistemologists treat the challenge posed by Descartes' dream as the same as the challenge posed by Descartes' demon. The general thought is that both possibilities threaten our knowledge of the world around us by offering a potential explanation of how we have all of the same experiences without actually interacting with the world around us in the way we think we do. Consequently, the same responses considered in the previous entry tend to be leveled at the skeptical argument arising from consideration of Descartes' dream.

Nevertheless, some insist that the threat posed by dreaming skepticism is importantly different from that posed by demon-style skepticism (Sosa 2007, Beebe 2017). The thought here is that when you are a victim of Descartes' demon, you might be tricked into thinking that there's a book in your hand right now even though there is no book. Descartes' demon and other skeptical scenarios depend upon some sort of deception—it seems that p is true (that you're holding a book, say), but p is false (you're not holding a book). The sort of skeptical challenge posed by the possibility of your dreaming seems different. After all, it could be that you in fact are holding a book in your hand while you are dreaming that you are. In this case, p seems true and *it is true*, and yet your ability to know has been undermined. Consideration of this difference between the two sorts of skeptical scenarios leads some to conclude that even if we can use the same responses to both sorts of skeptical arguments, the dreaming possibility teaches us something very important about how skeptical arguments work—they don't have to present a scenario where our beliefs are false in order to undermine our knowledge.

That all said, there is at least one very prominent response to dreaming skepticism that treats its differences from Descartes' demon as a key to settling the issue (Sosa 2007, Ichikawa 2008, 2009, 2018). There are two steps to this response. First, the response insists that dreams are like imaginings. It is because of this feature of dreams that we don't actually form beliefs about the content of our dreams while we are dreaming. Say, for example, you dream that you are holding a book. According to this response, you don't actually form a belief that you are holding a book. Instead, dreaming that you're holding a book is the same as it would be if you were to imagine holding a book when you're not. The second step is to rely upon the modal notion of safety. Recall from *Promotions and Traveling Friends* pp. 6–11 and *A Strange County* pp. 16–20 that S's belief that *p* is *safe* just in case in the closest worlds to this one where S believes that *p, p* is true. Since this response holds that we don't actually form beliefs in dreams, our beliefs are safe with respect to dream worlds. Let's consider this carefully by examining how this would work with your belief that you are holding a book. The thought is this, your belief that you are holding a book counts as safe because even if a dream world is close to the actual world, it is still the case that in the closest worlds where you *believe* that *p, p* is true. Why is this? Because the worlds in which you believe that *p* are worlds in which you are awake and perceiving the book. In dream worlds, you don't actually *believe* that *p*, so it can't be that you believe that *p* when *p* is false in those worlds. Since this response holds that all that is necessary for your belief to count as knowledge is that it is true and safe, it maintains that you can know things about the world around you regardless of the possibility that you may be dreaming.

RECOMMENDED READING

GENERAL OVERVIEWS

Dreams and Dreaming. *The Stanford Encyclopedia of Philosophy.* URL = https:// plato.stanford.edu/entries/dreams-dreaming/

Philosophy of Dreaming. *Internet Encyclopedia of Philosophy.* URL = https://iep. utm.edu/dreaming/#SH1b

SEMINAL PRESENTATION

Descartes, R. 1641/1931. *Meditations on First Philosophy*. In *Philosophical Works of Descartes (Volume 1)*, E. S. Haldane and G.R.T. Ross (eds/trans.). New York: Dover Publications.

ADDITIONAL IMPORTANT DISCUSSIONS

Ballantyne, N. and Evans, I. 2010. Sosa's dream. *Philosophical Studies* 148: 249–252.

Beebe, J. 2017. Does Skepticism Presuppose Explanationism? In K. McCain and T. Poston (eds), *Best Explanations: New Essays on Inference to the Best Explanation*. Oxford: Oxford University Press, 173–187.

Ichikawa, J.J. 2008. Sceptism and the Imagination Model of Dreaming. *Philosophical Quarterly* 58: 519–527.

Ichikawa, J.J. 2009. Dreaming and Imagination. *Mind and Language* 24: 103–121.

Ichikawa, J.J. 2018. Cartesian Epistemology without Cartesian Dreams? Commentary on Jennifer Windt's *Dreaming. Journal of Consciousness Studies* 25: 30–43.

Sosa, E. 2007. *A Virtue Epistemology: Apt Belief and Reflective Knowledge*. New York: Oxford University Press.

Stapleford, S. 2019. What's the Point of a Dreaming Argument? *Think* 52: 31–34.

Windt, J.M. 2015. *Dreaming: A Conceptual Framework for Philosophy of Mind and Empirical Research*. Cambridge, MA: MIT Press.

13

IS THE PAST REAL? (RUSSELL'S FIVE MINUTES OLD UNIVERSE)

Background: External world skepticism is perhaps the most widely discussed form of philosophical skepticism. However, some argue that skepticism about the sort of knowledge we typically take our memories to provide is an even harder problem to solve.

EPISTEMOLOGICAL ISSUES: SKEPTICISM ABOUT THE PAST; MEMORY SKEPTICISM

How old is the universe? Our current best science tells us that it is roughly 14 billion years old. But, how can we be sure? Let's consider two possibilities. First, the universe is as we think it is. Second, the universe and everything in it is exactly as it is right now, but instead of being 14 billion years old it popped into existence five minutes ago. Of course, you might immediately respond by pointing out that it doesn't seem like the universe is the sort of thing that could have simply popped into existence a few minutes ago. But, why not? There doesn't seem to be anything logically contradictory about the idea of the universe coming into existence a few minutes ago looking as if it were much older and filled with people, such as yourself, who have lots of false memories about a more distant past. How could you tell the difference between the five minutes old universe and the

14 billion years old universe? Your memories (and everyone else's) would be indistinguishable in the two scenarios. Any evidence that you could point to as reason for thinking that the universe is 14 billion years old would be present in both scenarios—it's just that in one scenario the evidence is genuine and in the other it is misleading. Given that the two situations are empirically indistinguishable, why should we think we're in one rather than the other?

The possibility of the five minutes old universe seems to generate a skeptical challenge that is similar in some ways to external world skepticism (see *Descartes' Demon* pp. 55–60 and *Descartes' Dream* pp. 61–65). Of course, there is one difference between these two kinds of skepticism that immediately stands out. The skeptical challenge here doesn't cast doubt on your knowledge of the world around you. After all, even if the universe is only five minutes old, it doesn't follow that your senses are deceiving you or that you are merely having a vivid dream. So, you could still know that you are reading this book right now, for example. However, the possibility that the universe is only five minutes old seems to cast doubt upon your knowledge of the past. If you can't be sure that the universe is as old as you think it is, it doesn't seem that you are in a position to know that what you believe about the past is true. Despite their differences, external world skepticism and skepticism about the past seem structurally similar. In both cases, the problem is that there is a skeptical scenario that seems indistinguishable from how the world actually is, and the possibility of this scenario seems to make it so that you can't have knowledge of the relevant sort (e.g., knowledge about the world around you or the past).

Consideration of this situation may also pose a challenge to whether you can trust your memory. If the universe were only five minutes old, all of your memories from more than five minutes ago would be false. That means that the vast majority of your memories would be false. If you can't be sure that the universe isn't only five minutes old, it seems that you can't be sure that your memories aren't false. This skepticism about the past may lead you to question whether you can trust your memory at all. After all, even setting aside the worry about the age of the universe, how can you establish that your memory is reliable? You may think that you could simply test your memory—think about something that you remember, that there's a soft drink in the refrigerator, say, and go check; if you're right, then you have evidence that your memory is reliable. Although this seems like a reasonable test, there's a serious problem—you'd be relying upon your memory the whole time! You have to use your memory to confirm that there being a soft drink in the refrigerator actually matches the memory that you are testing. Unfortunately, it doesn't seem that you can legitimately use your memory to determine that your memory is reliable. Imagine if you were going to buy a car and you wanted to know whether the salesperson was trustworthy. How convinced would you be if the salesperson said to you "look, you want to know whether I'm trustworthy? Just ask me. I'll tell you that I'm trustworthy." A salesperson telling you that they are trustworthy is not very good evidence for thinking they're trustworthy, is it? You might worry that using your memory to show that your memory is reliable amounts to the same thing.

Let's sum up. It seems that it is possible (in the broadest sense of the term) that the universe is only five minutes old, and it could be that a five minutes old universe is indistinguishable from how the universe actually is. Consideration of this possibility seems to generate two different skeptical challenges. The first is skepticism about the past, which challenges our knowledge of the past. The second is memory skepticism, which challenges whether our memory can give us knowledge at all. The difference between these two forms of skepticism can be seen if we consider a possibility where Russell's five-minutes-old universe hypothesis is true, but in this scenario our memory works fine. In such a case, memory would allow us to know things from less than five minutes ago. However, anything from more than five minutes ago would be false. Hence, it is at least possible to challenge our knowledge of the past while granting that the faculty of memory works well enough to give us knowledge.

RESPONSES

When it comes to the first skeptical challenge, skepticism about the past, it's structurally similar to external world skepticism. Consequently, it's not surprising that many of the sorts of responses that have been put forward in reply to external world skepticism have also been used to respond to it. We won't rehearse those responses again here (see *Descartes' Demon* pp. 55–60).

When it comes to skepticism about the reliability of memory, things appear to be different because the question of circularity takes center stage. Various responses have been given to this skeptical challenge. One variety of response attempts to respond to memory skepticism without relying on memory (Hasan forthcoming). The idea behind this general response is to use features of your current perceptual knowledge as evidence of the reliability of memory. For example, you might reason that the best explanation of its seeming to you that you remember something is that you actually remember it. Or, it may be that the best explanation of the apparent sensation you have of successfully predicting that it would seem to you now that you are reading this book is that you remember making that prediction a few moments ago.

Another response is to argue that not all forms of circularity are bad (Bergmann 2006). Very roughly, the idea here is that if you don't have positive reason to mistrust your memory, then there is nothing wrong with using it to establish the reliability of memory. Of course, it seems that in the face of the sort of skeptical challenge that we're discussing, the response would also have to claim that the mere possibility of the universe being only five minutes old doesn't give you sufficient reason to mistrust your memory.

A final sort of response to this skeptical challenge is to argue that memory skepticism of this sort is self-defeating (Rinard 2019). The general idea here is that this sort of skepticism would commit us to being skeptical of all complex reasoning, but it is irrational to be skeptical of complex reasoning ("complex reasoning" here is understood very broadly—i.e., even a simple argument with a couple of premises counts as complex reasoning in this sense). Simply put, the idea is that if we can't trust memory, then we cannot trust any complex reasoning. Why? Because we have to rely upon memory to engage in any complex reasoning. But, of course, it's irrational to be skeptical of complex reasoning because the only way that we could have reason to be skeptical of complex reasoning is if we engage in complex reasoning. If we can't trust complex reasoning, then we can't have grounds for doubting complex reasoning. In other words, if we are skeptical of complex reasoning, then we have no reason to be skeptical of complex reasoning! Since skepticism about complex reasoning is self-defeating, anything that commits us to being skeptical of complex reasoning is also self-defeating. According to this response, memory skepticism commits us to skepticism about complex reasoning. Hence, this response argues that we have grounds for denying memory skepticism because it is self-defeating (some argue that this response also applies to skepticism about the past).

RECOMMENDED READING

GENERAL OVERVIEWS

Epistemological Problems of Memory. *The Stanford Encyclopedia of Philosophy*. URL = https://plato.stanford.edu/entries/memory-episprob/

Epistemology of Memory. *Internet Encyclopedia of Philosophy*. URL = https://iep.utm.edu/epis-mem/

Moon, A. 2017. Skepticism and Memory. In S. Bernecker and K. Michaelian (eds), *The Routledge Handbook of Memory*. New York: Routledge, 335–347.

SEMINAL PRESENTATION

Russell, B. 1921. *The Analysis of Mind*. London: Allen and Unwin.

ADDITIONAL IMPORTANT DISCUSSIONS

Bergmann, M. 2006: *Justification without Awareness*. New York: Oxford University Press.

Bernecker, S. 2010. *Memory: A Philosophical Study*. Oxford: Oxford University Press.

Brandt, R. 1955. The Epistemological Status of Memory Beliefs. *Philosophical Review* 64: 78–95.

Frise, M. and McCain, K. Forthcoming. Forgetting Memory Skepticism. *Philosophy and Phenomenological Research*.

Fumerton, R. 1995. *Metaepistemology and Skepticism*. Lanham, MD: Rowman & Littlefield.

Harrod, R. 1942. Memory. *Mind* 51: 47–68.

Hasan, A. Forthcoming. The Reliability of Memory: An Argument from the Armchair. *Episteme*.

Rinard, S. 2019. Reasoning One's Way Out of Skepticism. In K. McCain and T. Poston (eds), *The Mystery of Skepticism: New Explorations*. Leiden: Brill, 240–264.

14

DESCARTES' APPLE SORTING PROBLEM (THE PROBLEM OF THE CRITERION)

Background: Many skeptical challenges rely upon the idea that our reasons/evidence could be misleading, but not all do. The problem of the criterion threatens our knowledge by questioning whether we can have good reasons/evidence at all.

EPISTEMOLOGICAL ISSUES: EPISTEMOLOGICAL METHODOLOGY; SKEPTICISM

Descartes asks us to consider trying to sort good apples from bad apples. A very important task—because as we all know, one bad apple can ruin the bunch! Of course, this is easy. You can sort good and bad apples, no problem. But imagine that you are completely unfamiliar with apples and that no one is around to tell you how to go about sorting them. You have a basket full of apples in front of you, and you are going to sort several more baskets full. How could you possibly sort the good apples from the bad? If you knew the answer to one of these questions, you'd be set: (a) which of the apples in this basket are good apples? (b) How can you tell which apples are good? If you knew the answer to (a), you could use that answer to come up with an answer to (b), and so proceed to sort the remaining apples. Or, if you knew the answer to (b), you could use that to answer (a). Unfortunately, you don't know the answer to either question. Even worse, it seems that before you can know the answer to (a) you have to *already know* the answer to (b), and before you can know the answer to (b) you have to *already know* the answer to (a). It appears that you are going to have a very tough time sorting these apples! This is essentially the problem of the criterion.

One prominent way of understanding the problem of the criterion is just the apple sorting problem applied to epistemological theorizing. It arises when we consider these two questions about knowledge:

(A) What do we know?
(B) How are we to decide whether something counts as knowledge or not?

The problem is, as it was with sorting apples, it seems that we need to know the answer to (A) before we can answer (B), but we need to know the answer to (B) before we can answer (A). It seems that we are stuck. We simply aren't in a position to determine what we actually know. Now, we might just *assume* an answer to (A) and use that to answer (B), or we might *assume* an answer to (B) and use that to answer (A). But, in either case, it seems like we would be begging the question against anyone who went the other way. That is, if you assume an answer to (A) and someone else assumes an answer to (B), neither of you would have any claim to having a better answer than the other one does when all is said and done. In light of this, we might worry that there is no way to legitimately answer either question. This, of course, would spell doom for a major project in epistemology—it would mean that we cannot know what is required for knowledge or even which of our beliefs count as knowledge.

Of course, even if this problem only arose for epistemologists trying to come up with a theory of knowledge, it would be significant. It is, however, much more threatening than that. Think about ethical reasoning. When we try to figure out the correct moral theory, we face a version of the problem of the criterion. After all, we are trying to answer these two questions:

(A★) Which actions are morally permissible?
(B★) How are we to decide whether something is morally permissible?

Again, it seems that we cannot answer (A★) without first having an answer to (B★), and vice versa. It is hard to see how we could ever go about determining the correct moral theory without running smack into this problem. We might worry that, as with the case of knowledge, we are left in a position where we cannot determine the correct theory of what makes actions morally permissible or even which actions are morally permissible.

Now, we might be tempted to think that both of these versions of the problem of the criterion arise because we are trying to work out philosophical theories. Hence, maybe we're safe as long as we don't go in for philosophical theorizing. So, philosophy is doomed from the start, but at least the rest of our intellectual lives are safe. Unfortunately, this take on things underestimates the reach of the problem of the criterion. In its most general form, the problem of the criterion can be understood in terms of these two questions:

(A★★) Which propositions are true?
(B★★) How can we tell which propositions are true?

All of the other forms of the problem of the criterion are just particular instances of this general schema. Thus, it shouldn't surprise us that, as with all the other versions of this problem, it seems that we need to know the answer to (A★★) before we can answer (B★★), but we need to know the answer to (B★★) before we can answer (A★★). Again, we might simply assume an answer to (A★★) or (B★★), and then use that answer to come up with an answer to the other question. But, as before, assuming either answer seems to be begging the question. So, we seem to be stuck. What makes this especially troubling is that in this general form, it applies to any proposition that we might consider. The problem of the criterion appears to have a very broad scope indeed.

RESPONSES

There are three classic responses to this problem: particularism, methodism, and skepticism (Chisholm 1973). Let's start with skepticism. The skeptic says that since we can't know the answer to (B★★) unless we first know the answer to (A★★) and we can't know the answer to (A★★) unless we first know the answer to (B★★), we can't know the answer to either question. So, the *skeptic* claims we can't even begin the project of trying to figure out which propositions are true. We are left with no good reason to think that any particular proposition is true and no good reason to think that any particular method for determining which propositions are true is reliable. The *particularist* assumes an answer to (A★★) and uses that to develop an answer to (B★★). In other words, the particularist starts by assuming that various propositions are true and looks at what these propositions have in common to come up with a method for determining whether other propositions are true. The *methodist* assumes an answer to (B★★) and uses that to answer (A★★). That is to say, the methodist starts by assuming that a particular method for determining which propositions are true is reliable and then uses that method to figure out whether particular propositions are true. Of course, we might worry that just *assuming* an answer to either question is no good! Some supporters of these responses acknowledge that we must make some assumption, but they claim that this doesn't mean that skepticism is correct—they claim that skepticism also has to start with mere assumptions. They point out that the skeptic must assume that we can't have an answer to either (A★★) or (B★★).

There is, however, an additional response that seeks to avoid *assuming* an answer to either question from the start. The *explanationist* proposes that we start with our intuitions about answers to (A★★) and (B★★) rather than taking answers to these questions for granted (DePaul 1988, Moser 1989, Conee 2004, McCain and Rowley 2014). Next, this response says to make modifications until we end up in a state of reflective equilibrium when it comes to our intuitions (roughly, the idea is to use our intuitions to come up with the best overall answer to both (A★★) and (B★★) without assuming an answer to either question from the start).

RECOMMENDED READING

GENERAL OVERVIEW

The Problem of the Criterion. *The Internet Encyclopedia of Philosophy.* URL = https://www.iep.utm.edu/criterio/

SEMINAL PRESENTATION

Sextus Empiricus. 1996. *The Skeptic Way: Sextus Empiricus's Outlines of Pyrrhonism*, (trans.) B. Mates. New York: Oxford University Press. (Particularly Book 2)

ADDITIONAL IMPORTANT DISCUSSIONS

Amico, R.P. 1993. *The Problem of the Criterion*. Lanham, MD: Rowman & Little-field Publishers, Inc.

Chisholm, R.M. 1973. *The Problem of the Criterion*. Milwaukee, WI: Marquette University Press.

Cling, A.D. 1994. Posing the Problem of the Criterion. *Philosophical Studies* 75: 261–292.

Conee, E. 2004. First Things First. In E. Conee and R. Feldman, *Evidentialism*. New York: Oxford University Press, 11–36.

DePaul, M. 1988. The Problem of the Criterion and Coherence Methods in Ethics. *Canadian Journal of Philosophy* 18: 67–86.

Fumerton, R. 2008. The Problem of the Criterion. In J. Greco (ed), *The Oxford Handbook of Skepticism*. Oxford: Oxford University Press, 34–52.

McCain, K. and Rowley, W. 2014. Pick Your Poison: Beg the Question or Embrace Circularity. *International Journal for the Study of Skepticism* 4: 125–140.

Moser, P.K. 1989. *Knowledge and Evidence*. Cambridge: Cambridge University Press.

Poston, T. 2011. Explanationist Plasticity & the Problem of the Criterion. *Philosophical Papers* 40: 395–419.

YOU'RE DEBASED!
(THE DEBASING DEMON)

Background: It is important to recall the general nature of the basing relation here (see background to Saul the Superstitious Lawyer pp. 42–47). The basic thought is that in order for someone to have a justified belief that p that person's belief that p must be based on the evidence/reasons that gives her justification for believing p.

The most common view of the basing relation is that it is a causal or counterfactual dependence relation. On this understanding of the basing relation, a person's belief that p is based on her evidence for p when her having that evidence causes her to have the belief that p or (assuming that causation isn't simply a matter of counterfactual dependence) the person's belief counterfactually depends upon her having evidence that supports believing that p. To say that someone's belief counterfactually depends upon her having some evidence means one or both of two things. First, it can mean that the person wouldn't have the belief that p if she didn't have the evidence she does. Second, it can mean that the person would have the belief that p if she does have the evidence. Simply put, the idea is that the person's belief that p is based upon her evidence when her having that evidence explains why she has the belief or if she were to lack the evidence she has, the lack of evidence would explain why she doesn't have the belief.

EPISTEMOLOGICAL ISSUES: BASING RELATION; SKEPTICISM

One of the newer thought experiments to hit the epistemological scene is the *Debasing Demon*. Unlike some other demons such as Descartes' demon (see *Descartes' Demon* pp. 55–60), the debasing demon doesn't trick you with illusions or anything of that sort. In fact, the debasing demon doesn't do anything to take away your good reasons for what you think, nor does it give you misleading evidence of any kind. Instead, the debasing demon makes it so that you don't believe what you do on the basis of the good reasons you have. In other words, the debasing demon makes it so that even if you have justification for believing various propositions, you don't justifiedly believe any of them.

The debasing demon can make it so that your beliefs aren't *based* on your reasons in one of two ways. One way is that the demon makes it so that, unbeknownst to you, some other mental states of yours cause you to believe as you do. For example, say that you read an article that has a very good argument for thinking that epistemology is the most important area of philosophy. As a result of this argument, you believe that epistemology is the most important area of philosophy. In a typical case, you justifiedly believe that epistemology is the most important area of philosophy—you believe this on the basis of good reasons. But, the debasing demon can ruin things for you. It can make it so that your current experience of reading this page, say, is in fact what is causing you to believe that epistemology is the most important area of philosophy. And, at the same time, the demon can make it so that the argument that you previously read is having no influence at all on your believing what you do. In such a situation, you are believing the right thing but for the wrong reasons. You have been debased. Another way the demon might debase you is by making it so that you don't hold your belief on the basis of any reason whatsoever, perhaps because it directly makes you have the belief. So, rather than making it so that some other mental state of yours causes you to believe that epistemology is the most important area of philosophy, the debasing demon causes you to have this belief by directly affecting your brain in an undetectable way. Again, you are debased!

Now, you might be thinking "this is ridiculous, there's no debasing demon!" Well, you're probably right. But, remember that often in epistemology in order for a thought experiment to be effective it doesn't have to be very likely—it just has to be *possible*. Is it possible (in the broadest sense of the term) that a debasing demon could exist? It seems so. Is it possible (in the broadest sense of the term) that right now you are the unwitting victim of a debasing demon? Again, it seems so. Well, since this seems possible, we might wonder whether any of our beliefs are actually justified. How do we know that we aren't debased? The possibility of the debasing demon casts doubt on whether any of our beliefs are justified. And, if our beliefs aren't justified, they don't qualify as knowledge. Hence, the debasing demon may threaten every bit of our (presumed) knowledge.

RESPONSES

There are two basic sorts of responses to the skeptical threat posed by the debasing demon. The most common is to allow that such a scenario is possible, i.e. there could be a debasing demon, and it could mess up the bases for your beliefs in the way just described, but argue that this doesn't lead to widespread skepticism. One version of this approach argues that in order for the possibility of a debasing demon to actually lead to skepticism, we would have to accept the very implausible principle that any time we know that p we also know that we know that p (Brueckner 2011). After all, the possibility of the debasing demon seems to threaten your knowledge that you are reading this book, say, indirectly by giving you a reason to doubt whether you know that you know that you are reading this book. It does this by giving you a reason to doubt whether you know that your belief about the book is properly based on your evidence. But, this response contends, this amounts to a threat to your knowledge that you are reading this book only if we accept that in order to know something you must also know that you know it. This principle (often called the "KK principle") has been widely criticized in other contexts. Hence, this response maintains that the possibility of the debasing demon doesn't really threaten your knowledge of things like the fact that you are reading this book. However, it does seem to allow that the debasing demon poses a genuine threat to your higher-order knowledge (e.g. your knowledge of whether you know that you are reading this book).

Another version of this first sort of approach meets the challenge of the debasing demon head-on. This response simply argues that we in fact have a lot of evidence that our beliefs are properly based upon our evidence (Conee 2015). So, even though a debasing demon is possible, we have good reason to think that we aren't its victims. Hence, this response contends that the possibility of the debasing demon doesn't seem to threaten any of our knowledge.

The second basic sort of response is to argue that although it may seem like there could be a demon that operates in exactly this sort of way, the debasing demon is in fact impossible (Bondy and Carter 2018). The idea here is that it is impossible for our beliefs to seem to us that they are held on the basis of good reasons when in fact they are not. If this is correct, then it appears that initial appearances notwithstanding the debasing demon is not actually a genuine possibility. Of course, this general approach to responding to the debasing demon seems to assume that something other than causal or counterfactual dependence is sufficient for basing.

RECOMMENDED READING

GENERAL BACKGROUND ON BASING

The Epistemic Basing Relation. *The Stanford Encyclopedia of Philosophy.* URL = https://plato.stanford.edu/archives/fall2019/entries/basing-epistemic/

SEMINAL PRESENTATION

Schaffer, J. 2010. The Debasing Demon. *Analysis* 70: 228–237.

ADDITIONAL IMPORTANT DISCUSSIONS

Ballantyne, N. and Evans, I. 2013. Schaffer's Demon. *Pacific Philosophical Quarterly* 94: 552–559.
Bondy, P. and Carter, J.A. 2018. The Basing Relation and the Impossibility of the Debasing Demon. *American Philosophical Quarterly* 55: 203–216.
Brueckner, A. 2011. Debasing Scepticism. *Analysis* 71: 295–297.
Conee, E. 2015. Debasing Skepticism Refuted. *Episteme* 12: 1–11.
Cunningham, J.J. Forthcoming. The Basis of Debasing Scepticism. *Erkenntnis.*

16

WINNING THE LOTTERY (LOTTERY SKEPTICISM)

Background: The far-fetched scenarios that many skeptical challenges rely upon give some the impression that they are easy to dismiss. Even if the strangeness of demon scenarios and five minutes old universes allows us to simply ignore the skeptical challenges that they raise, there are other skeptical challenges that are not so easily dismissed. Lottery skepticism raises challenges to our knowledge that don't rely on such scenarios at all. In fact, lottery skeptical challenges arise from consideration of things that we actually know occur in real life.

EPISTEMOLOGICAL ISSUE: LOTTERY SKEPTICISM

Imagine you've just purchased a lottery ticket for the Mega Millions Lottery. The odds of your winning are quite low (for example, the odds of winning the January 2018 drawing of this lottery were about 302.6 million to 1). Despite the low odds, do you *know* that you won't win? It doesn't seem so. After all, you know how bad the odds of winning the lottery are before you bought the ticket, so if the odds are such that you can know that you'll lose, why did you waste your money? It seems that rather than knowing that you won't win, you know that it is *extremely unlikely* that you'll win. This isn't very interesting to think about on its own. However, now consider something it seems (assuming that you aren't already rich) you do know—you won't be able to purchase a new Lamborghini Aventador S Roadster (if you're in the market for a car and curious, the MSRP for the 2020 model starts at $460,427). But, wait! If you were to win the lottery, you could afford to buy this car because you would have millions of dollars. We have a puzzle here. It seems you don't know that you won't win the lottery, but it also seems that you do know that you won't have the money to buy a new Lamborghini. And at the same time, you know that *if* you did win the lottery, you would have the money to buy a new Lamborghini. What are we to make of this?

While the lottery scenario we just discussed is interesting, you may not find it all that troublesome because you may never buy lottery tickets. However, we can't simply set this aside as a mere curiosity. There are skeptical arguments that arise from similar considerations, and these arguments threaten our knowledge of many of the things we ordinarily take ourselves to know. For example, it seems that you know where you'll be in a few hours. But, unfortunately, many people die suddenly and unexpectedly without any previous indication of illness. As morbid as it sounds, this can be understood as "winning" a bad lottery. The odds that you will die in this way in a few hours are (thankfully!) very low. Nevertheless, do you *know* that you won't "win" this lottery in the next few hours? It seems not. Yet, it seems that you know what you'll be doing in a few hours. But your knowing what you'll be doing in the next few hours entails that you know that you won't die suddenly and unexpectedly before then. Let's think of another, much less distressing but still unpleasant example. Assume that you drive a car to campus as many students do at many universities. After parking in the lot, you go to class. While in class, do you know where your car is? It seems that you do. After all, as long as you're not suffering from memory problems, you remember where you parked your car. But, cars are stolen every day and some cars are towed from parking lots even when they shouldn't be. Do you know that you haven't "won the lottery" of having your car stolen or inappropriately towed while you have been in class? It doesn't seem so. Doesn't your knowing where your car is entail that you know that it wasn't stolen or towed away though? Again, we have a case where it seems that you fail to know a lottery proposition, and yet it seems that you know an ordinary proposition that entails that you do know the lottery proposition. To make the skeptical challenge here explicit, consider this argument:

1) If you don't know the lottery proposition (that you'll lose the lottery; that you won't die unexpectedly; that your car wasn't stolen or towed; etc.), then you don't know the ordinary proposition (that you won't be able to afford a new Lamborghini; that you'll be doing a particular thing in a few hours; that your car is in the parking lot where you left it; etc.).
2) You don't know the lottery proposition.
3) Therefore, you don't know the ordinary proposition.

RESPONSES

There are a number of responses to these sorts of lottery cases (Hawthorne 2004). One response is to simply embrace the skeptical consequences. In other words, we might think that since you don't know the relevant lottery propositions, you don't know the corresponding ordinary propositions either. Of course, this would amount to a wide-ranging skepticism since a large number of the things we ordinarily think we know seem to entail knowing that we won't win various "lotteries". Which, of course, means that if you don't know that you won't win these lotteries, you don't know the corresponding ordinary propositions.

Another response goes the other direction. This response accepts that you do know the ordinary propositions, and it insists that you know the lottery propositions as well. According to this response, even if you buy a lottery ticket, you *know* that you are going to lose. Typically, those who opt for this sort of response attempt to offer some explanation of why it is that you buy a ticket even though you know that you are going to lose. For example, they may contend that perhaps you buy the ticket because it prompts you to enjoy imagining what it would be like if you were to have the money from the lottery.

There are various responses that lie between these first two. These other responses attempt to limit how widely one's knowledge is affected by such lottery cases. For instance, one proposal along these lines is that knowing that p requires an explanatory link between the fact that p and one's belief that p (Nelkin 2000, Goldman 2008).

On this account, it turns out that you don't know that you won't win the lottery or that you can't afford a Lamborghini, but it may turn out that you do know where your car is. The gist of this proposal is that there is no explanatory link between the fact of your losing the lottery, say, and your belief that you lost. The reason is that you would have the same reasons/evidence for believing that you will lose even if in fact you were to win. However, when it comes to your knowledge of where your car is, your car being in the parking lot does help explain your belief.

Another way of developing the middle-ground sort of approach advocates distinguishing between statistical evidence and nonstatistical evidence (Buchak 2014, Carter et al. 2016). The general idea here is that when your evidence, such as your knowledge of the lottery's odds, is purely statistical, it doesn't license you in believing outright. That is to say, it doesn't justify believing outright that you will lose. Instead, it only justifies believing that it is very likely that you will lose. However, when you have other sorts of evidence at play, you can (and should) outright believe. So, while you shouldn't believe (and don't know) that you won't win the lottery because your evidence for this is purely statistical, you should believe (and plausibly know) where your car is because you have nonstatistical evidence for this. Hence, it may be that these sorts of responses can be developed so that the "lotteries" that seem to threaten our ordinary beliefs don't really do so.

A different sort of response to the threat of lottery skepticism involves denying closure. The idea here is that you can know the ordinary propositions without knowing the corresponding lottery propositions, but this doesn't matter. Essentially, this response denies premise (1) of the argument above. You can know p and fail to know that q despite the fact that you know that p entails q (see *Trip to the Zoo* pp. 37–41).

As with other skeptical challenges, it is possible to appeal to contextualism or pragmatic encroachment here too (see *Going to the Bank* pp. 48–52) (Baumann 2004). So, some respond to these sorts of lottery cases by arguing that it is appropriate to say that "S knows that she can't afford a new Lamborghini" in ordinary contexts, but in contexts where the possibility of S's winning the lottery has been made salient, it isn't appropriate to say that "S knows that she can't afford a new Lamborghini." Others, embracing pragmatic encroachment, argue that you know that you can't afford a Lamborghini in ordinary situations, but when the stakes are raised by consideration of the possibility that you will win the lottery you no longer know that you can't afford one (Hawthorne 2004).

RECOMMENDED READING

SEMINAL PRESENTATIONS

Harman, G. 1973. *Thought*. Princeton, NJ: Princeton University Press.
Vogel, J. 1990. Are There Counterexamples to the Closure Principle? In M. Roth (ed), *Doubting: Contemporary Perspectives on Skepticism*. Dordrecht: Kluwer, 13–27.

ADDITIONAL IMPORTANT DISCUSSIONS

Baumann, P. 2004. Lotteries and Contexts. *Erkenntnis* 61: 415–428.
Buchak, L. 2014. Belief, Credence, and Norms. *Philosophical Studies* 169: 285–311.
Carter, J.A., Jarvis, B.W., and Rubin, K. 2016. Belief without Credence. *Synthese* 193: 2323–2351.
Goldman, A. 2008. Knowledge, Explanation, and Lotteries. *Nous* 42: 466–481.
Hawthorne, J. 2004. *Knowledge and Lotteries*. Oxford: Oxford University Press.
Mills, E. 2012. Lotteries, Quasi-Lotteries, and Sceptisim. *Australasian Journal of Philosophy* 90: 335–352.
Nelkin, D. 2000. Paradox, Knowledge, and Rationality. *Philosophical Review* 109: 373–409.
Smith, M. 2010. What Else Justification Could Be. *Nous* 44: 10–31.
Staffel, J. 2016. Beliefs, Buses and Lotteries: Why Rational Belief Can't Be Stably High Credence. *Philosophical Studies* 173: 1721–1734.

17

YOU ONLY BELIEVE THAT BECAUSE... (CONTINGENCY OF BELIEF)

Background: It may seem to be a truism that we believe some things simply because of where we were born, who our parents are, and so on. Consideration of the contingency of our beliefs may lead to skeptical challenges though. After all, if we would have believed differently simply by being born elsewhere, one might think that this tells us something important about the fragility of the reasons/evidence we have for our beliefs.

EPISTEMOLOGICAL ISSUE: THE PROBLEM OF CONTINGENCY OF BELIEF

Let's consider a few scenarios. Unlike many of the scenarios we have discussed (and will discuss later in this book), these scenarios are not at all outlandish. In fact, they are pretty common.

Scenario 1: Hannah is a Christian. She and her friend Horatio are having a discussion about religion. Horatio says, "even if Christianity is true, you can't know that it is." To this Hannah replies, "Why not?" Horatio answers, "You only believe Christianity because you were born and raised in the Bible Belt." (The term "Bible Belt" refers to a region of the southern U.S. where Protestant Christianity plays a strong role in politics and society at large.) "If," Horatio continues:

you had been born somewhere else you wouldn't be a Christian. For example, if you had been born and raised in Saudi Arabia, you'd be a Muslim. Or, if you had been born and raised in Japan, you likely wouldn't be religious at all.

"So? Maybe I'm just lucky," Hannah says. To which, Horatio responds:

That's my point! Even if you are right and Christianity is true, it's just a matter of luck that you believe it. It's not because of good evidence; it's because of where you happened to be born. You don't know it's true.

Scenario 2: Philosophers Abdul and Anna are talking about epistemology. In particular, they are arguing over internalism and externalism (see *General Background: The Nature of Justification* pp. 113–119). Finally, Abdul exclaims, "You're only an internalist because you studied at the University of Rochester! If you had went to a different school, you'd be an externalist like me." Anna responds, "Well, you're only an externalist because you were at Rutgers! If you had went to a different school, then you'd be an internalist like me."

Scenario 3: Pedro and Penelope are discussing politics. It turns out that Pedro is a Republican and Penelope is a Democrat. Perhaps unsurprisingly they are getting a bit frustrated with each other's take on a particular issue. They both realize that things would be much simpler if the other just had the "right" political view. So, they try to convince each other—Pedro works to convince Penelope that Republicans have the better platform and Penelope works to convince Pedro that things are the other way around. After quite a while of trying and getting nowhere, Penelope says, "Look, the only reason that you are a Republican is that you grew up in Alabama and your parents are Republicans." Pedro replies, "Well, you're only a Democrat because you grew up in Illinois and your parents are Democrats."

Scenarios like these are familiar. The rationality of a person's beliefs is challenged on the grounds that they wouldn't have those beliefs if they would've been born in a different place or time or to a different sort of family. The heart of the criticism here is that irrelevant influences are at least partly responsible for the person believing as they do. Although this sort of criticism is perhaps most often raised in the context of challenging someone's religious, political, or philosophical views, if we stop and think about it something similar could be said about a great number of our beliefs. Hence, if this sort of criticism really challenges the knowledge or justification that one has in the three domains described in the above scenarios, it would seem to also challenge beliefs in other domains. Thus, while the concern about irrelevant influences doesn't lead to as widespread of a skeptical threat as some of the possibilities discussed in earlier entries, it does seem to be fairly wide-ranging and worthy of careful consideration.

Although it can be difficult to spell out exactly how to best understand the skeptical challenge that arises when someone presses the "you only believe that because…" objection, the key point is that the challenge casts doubt on the connection that the belief(s) in question bears to the truth. Learning that something like where you were born affects what you believe may give you a good reason to doubt that your beliefs are sufficiently responsive to evidence to count as justified or known. In other words, when a person's belief that p is challenged on the grounds that they only believe that p because of some influences that aren't sufficiently connected to the truth, it seems that this challenge gives the person reason to doubt that the evidence they have for p is good enough to warrant believing it.

RESPONSES

One way of understanding the challenge posed by "you only believe that because…" is as giving one reasons to think that one's belief(s) isn't formed in a way that is sensitive or safe. Recall saying that S's belief that p is sensitive amounts to claiming that if p were false, S wouldn't believe that p. When it comes to safety, S's belief that p is safe just in case in the closest worlds to this one where S believes that p, p is true. So, this challenge might be understood as giving one reasons to think that one would have the same belief even if that belief were false (i.e. that the belief isn't sensitive to the truth). Another way to understand the challenge is as alleging that one's belief isn't safe because there are nearby worlds (perhaps even this world!) where S believes p but p is false. Given these understandings of the challenge, it is possible to respond by arguing that sensitivity and safety aren't necessary for knowledge or justification (Bogardus 2013). If these modal conditions aren't really required for knowledge, then pointing out that one's belief fails to meet either of these conditions doesn't really threaten one's justification for that belief or threaten whether such a belief can count as knowledge.

A different approach to this general challenge is to embrace what is known as "permissivism" (Schoenfield 2014). It is perhaps easiest to understand permissivism by contrasting it with what is known as "uniqueness". Uniqueness is the idea that for any particular set of evidence that evidence makes only one doxastic attitude (e.g. believing, disbelieving, or suspending judgment) toward p rational. For example, if E is the evidence in question and E makes believing p rational, then uniqueness says that any doxastic attitude toward p other than belief, when all the evidence one has is E, is irrational. Permissivism is the denial of uniqueness. It says that it is possible for the same body of evidence to support more than one doxastic attitude toward the same proposition. Hence, according to permissivism, even though E makes believing p rational, it might also make suspending judgment about p or believing not p rational too. How does this help with the issue at hand though? One way that accepting permissivism might help here is that one could plausibly acknowledge that if one were born somewhere else, one wouldn't believe that p, but insist that this doesn't make believing that p irrational. After all, if permissivism is true, then it could be that even given the same evidence, more than one doxastic attitude toward p can be rational. So, it might be that one's belief that p is rational, and also true that if one were born somewhere else that believing not p would be rational without this fact undermining the rationality of one's belief that p because the evidence can support either believing or not believing.

A final sort of response involves distinguishing between various situations where the challenge that "you only believe that because…" arises. One might think that only some of these cases really pose a threat to one's knowledge/justification (Vavova 2018). For example, one might think that only to the extent that one faces this challenge and has *independent* reason to think that one is mistaken about the belief in question should one be worried about the belief that p. Another way of developing this sort of response is to argue that some beliefs are what might be called "epistemically self-promoting" (Moon 2021). The idea here is that some beliefs can themselves provide good reason to think that one's having those beliefs is the result of a reliable process. This sort of response has recently been offered in support of particular religious beliefs. The gist is that some religious beliefs provide grounds for thinking that one's having those religious beliefs is the result of a reliable belief forming process. Hence, these beliefs are self-promoting—they give reason to think that one who has the beliefs formed them in a reliable way. The thought is that this might allow one to rebut the doubt that "you only believe that because…" is supposed to raise.

RECOMMENDED READING

SEMINAL PRESENTATIONS

Descartes, R. 1649/1999. *Discourse on Method and Related Writings*. D.M. Clarke (trans). London: Penguin.

Mill, J.S. 1859/2002. *On Liberty*. New York: Dover Publications.

ADDITIONAL IMPORTANT DISCUSSIONS

Ballantyne, N. 2018. Is Epistemic Permissivism Intuitive? *American Philosophical Quarterly* 55: 365–378.

Bogardus, T. 2013. The Problem of Contingency for Religious Belief. *Faith and Philosophy* 30: 371–392.

Hick, J. 1997. The Epistemological Challenge of Religious Pluralism. *Faith and Philosophy* 14: 277–286.

Kitcher, P. 2011. Challenges for Secularism. In G. Levine (ed), *The Joy of Secularism: 11 Essays for How We Live Now*. Princeton, NJ: Princeton University Press, 24–56.

Moon, A. 2021. Circular and Question-begging Responses to Religious Disagreement and Debunking Arguments. *Philosophical Studies* 178: 785–809.

Plantinga, A. 1997. Ad Hick. *Faith and Philosophy* 14: 295–298.

Schoenfield, M. 2014. Permission to Believe: Why Permissivism Is True and What it Tells us about Irrelevant Influences on Belief. *Nous* 48: 193–218.

Vavova, K. 2018. Irrelevant Influences. *Philosophy and Phenomenological Research* 96: 134–152.

White, R. 2010. You Just Believe That Because… *Philosophical Perspectives* 24: 573–615.

18

HOT OR COLD?
(ANTI-LUMINOSITY)

Background: It was a common assumption throughout much of the history of philosophy that we have special access to the contents of our own minds. This assumption is quite common in nonphilosophical contexts as well. We naturally tend to think that we have special access to our own thoughts and sensations. This access seems special in at least two ways. The first is simply that we have access to our mental states that no one else has. For instance, no one else can literally feel your pain; only you can feel your pain. The second way our access to the contents of our mental seems special is that it is apparently luminous. The luminosity of our mental states means that when we are in a particular mental state we are always in a position to know that we are in that mental state. For example, when you are in pain, you are in a position to know that you are in pain; when you feel cold, you are in a position to know that you feel cold; and so on. There are various reasons why the luminosity of our mental states in particular has been thought to be very important. One of the most prominent reasons, at least since the time of Descartes, is that this feature of our cognitive lives is thought to give us a starting point in responding to skepticism. Perhaps we can be tricked concerning the world around us, as the skeptic alleges, but, the thought goes, at least we can't be tricked about the contents of our own minds. Since our mental states are luminous, we can use our knowledge of them as a foundation from which we can build our response to the skeptic.

EPISTEMOLOGICAL ISSUE: LUMINOSITY OF MENTAL STATES

Barry has been working out early in the morning. When he finishes his workout at 6 am he feels hot and is considering his feeling. Barry is in a unique situation though. He has been asked to participate in a trial for a new relaxation room at the gym. This room allows one to very gradually cool off during a specific amount of time. Since Barry is part of the trial, he has agreed to stay in the room until noon. Throughout his time in the room, how warm he feels continually changes by the minutest amount every millisecond. By the end of his time in the room, Barry no longer feels hot—in fact, he feels downright cold! So, at the beginning of the process Barry feels hot and knows it, and at the end of the process Barry feels cold and knows it.

Is Barry in a position to know whether he is hot at every point throughout this process? It doesn't seem so. After all, the changes from millisecond to millisecond are extremely small. Plausibly, there will be a point at which Barry transitions from feeling hot to not feeling hot, but the difference between the two will be imperceptible. The changes that Barry experiences are happening every millisecond. Given this, there will be a point at which Barry is at the bare minimum of feeling hot one moment and the very next millisecond he has transitioned to as close to feeling hot as he can be without actually feeling hot. It seems that at this transition Barry won't be able to tell the difference. The same seems true when we consider Barry's transition from feeling comfortable (the stage after feeling hot) to feeling cold. There will be a point at which Barry has reached the limit for feeling comfortable and the next millisecond a minute change will make it so that Barry feels cold.

Why does this matter? Well, if Barry's mental states are luminous, then at any point he is in a particular state, such as feeling hot or cold, he is in a position to know that he is in that state. However, many epistemologists accept that in order for someone to know that p in a particular circumstance, C, it has to be the case that in every situation that is sufficiently similar to C, the person wouldn't falsely believe that p. Keeping this—along with the conditions Barry is experiencing in the relaxation room—in mind seems to spell trouble for the idea that our mental states are luminous. When Barry reaches the borderline for feeling hot and feeling comfortable (not hot) the change from one to the other will be so minute that it seems that Barry could easily mistake the two. But this means that Barry might falsely believe that he feels hot in a situation that is similar to the situation he is in when he is just barely hot. If so, then it seems that Barry isn't really in a position to know that he is hot when he is just barely hot. Once Barry approaches the borderline between being hot and being comfortable, it seems that he won't be in a position to know whether he is hot or not. This, however, means that whether or not he is hot is not luminous to him. Thus, it appears that our mental states are not really as luminous as we might have thought. Hence, Timothy Williamson contended, when first presenting this sort of argument, the philosophical tradition and our commonsense thinking about luminosity are mistaken.

RESPONSES

One response to this sort of situation is to concede that Williamson is correct that there are borderline cases where our mental states are not luminous, but insist that in clear cases they still are luminous (Reed 2006). For example, this sort of response accepts that Barry isn't in a position to know whether he feels hot or not once he is near the borderline between feeling hot and feeling comfortable. However, it holds that when Barry is *not* near a borderline, his mental states are luminous to him. So, when Barry is more than just barely feeling hot, he is in a position to know that he feels hot.

A different response seeks to limit the reach of Williamson's argument in another way. According to this response, some mental states are "self-presenting," in the sense that the mental state is identical to the belief that the mental state exists (or perhaps is itself part of the content of the belief that the state exists). The idea here is that feeling hot and believing that one feels hot are in fact the same mental state. If this is so, then one cannot easily mistake that one feels hot when one does. This response at most mitigates Williamson's argument to some degree because intuitively many (perhaps most) of our mental states are not self-presenting in this sense.

Yet another response involves arguing that safety from error isn't really necessary for knowledge (Vogel 2010). That is to say, this way of responding argues that it is possible to know that p in a particular circumstance, C, even if it is not the case that in every situation that is sufficiently similar to C, one wouldn't falsely believe that p. Without this safety from error requirement, Barry's case fails to show that our mental states (even at the borders) aren't luminous.

A final response is to maintain that, contrary to Williamson's claims, the anti-luminosity argument undergirded by cases like those of Barry employs the same sort of reasoning as the Sorites Paradox (this is the sort of paradox where it seems that a single grain of sand can't by itself make the difference between having a heap of sand and not having a heap of sand, but it is clear that if we add enough single grains of sand, eventually we end up with a heap of sand) (Cohen 2010). This response contends that just as the Sorites Paradox in its various forms improperly exploits the vagueness of terms such as "heap", the considerations in favor of anti-luminosity exploit vagueness in terms like "knows" and "feels hot".

RECOMMENDED READING

SEMINAL PRESENTATIONS

Williamson, T. 1996. Cognitive Homelessness. *Journal of Philosophy* 93: 554–573.
Williamson, T. 2000. *Knowledge and Its Limits*. Oxford: Oxford University Press.

ADDITIONAL IMPORTANT DISCUSSIONS

Berker, S. 2008. Luminosity Regained. *Philosopher's Imprint* 8: 1–22.
Brueckner, A. and Fiocco, M.O. 2002. Williamson's Anti-luminosity Argument. *Philosophical Studies* 110: 285–293.
Cohen, S. 2010. Luminosity, Reliability, and the Sorites. *Philosophy and Phenomenological Research* 81: 718–730.
Conee, E. 2005. The Comforts of Home. *Philosophy and Phenomenological Research* 70: 444–451.
Reed, B. 2006. Shelter for the Cognitively Homeless. *Synthese* 148: 303–308.
Srinivasan, A. 2015. Are We Luminous? *Philosophy and Phenomenological Research* 90: 294–319.
Vogel, J. 2010. Luminosity and Indiscriminability. *Philosophical Perspectives* 24: 547–572.
Weatherson, B. 2004. Luminous Margins. *Australasian Journal of Philosophy* 82: 373–383.
Zardini, E. 2013. Luminosity and Determinacy. *Philosophical Studies* 165: 765–786.

19

A CUT-RATE EYE EXAM (BOOTSTRAPPING/EASY KNOWLEDGE)

Background: Some theories of knowledge are what we might call "basic knowledge structure" theories. Basic knowledge structure theories allow that one can have basic knowledge in the sense that a source can give one knowledge without one having to first know that that source is reliable. For example, a basic knowledge structure theory might say that perception is a basic source of knowledge. This would mean that one can gain knowledge from perception (one's senses—vision, hearing, etc.) without first knowing that one's perceptual faculties are reliable. Or similarly, a basic knowledge structure theory might say that one can know things by relying on memory without first having to know that memory is reliable. The reasoning that motivates such theories is that it seems that we would be stuck with an infinite regress if we were to insist that one must first know that a faculty is reliable before we can gain knowledge from that faculty. After all, if this is true of all faculties, how would we possibly come to have knowledge that any of them are reliable? In order to avoid such a regress, and the skeptical consequences of it, many accept some version of a basic knowledge structure theory.

EPISTEMOLOGICAL ISSUES: BOOTSTRAPPING; PROBLEM OF EASY KNOWLEDGE

Stew wants to check to see if his color vision is reliable, but he doesn't want to spend the money to go see an optometrist. Luckily, while browsing the internet, an ad for the "Basic Knowledge Theory Vision Test" (BKTV test), a very inexpensive home vision test, pops up. Stew orders the test and a few days later it arrives in the mail. The BKTV test is quite simple. It consists of a large stack of color cards (the cards are simply a single color; they have no writing on them nor any other identifying marks), and one completes the test by simply looking at the cards. That's it. Stew sits down and takes his vision test. It goes like this:

> Stew looks at the first card, and it looks red to him. So, he knows that it's red. Stew thinks to himself "The card's red, and it looks red. Got it right! I'm off to a good start." He looks at the next card, which looks blue. Again, Stew thinks "The card is blue, and it looks blue. Two for two!" He continues in this fashion for quite some time. Each time he looks at a card and sees that it looks a particular color, so he concludes each time that he has gotten it correct because he has basic knowledge of the color of the card (from looking at it) and he knows via introspection that the card looks that color to him. After going through a very large number of cards, Stew finally stops and thinks, "I sure am glad I purchased this home vision test. Now I know that my color vision is reliable! And, I didn't have to waste the money to actually go to the eye doctor."

What should we think about this color vision test? Does Stew really now know that his color vision is reliable? It seems clear that he hasn't gained a bit of support for thinking that his color vision is reliable. However, basic knowledge structure theories seem committed to claiming that he did. Here's why. Assume that unbeknownst to him, Stew's color vision really is reliable and the cards really look the way that he thinks. So, when a card looks red to him it's because it's red, when it looks blue it's because the card is blue, and so on. According to basic knowledge structure theories, Stew can know that a card is red because it looks red (he doesn't need to know that his color vision is reliable in order to know this). As a result, when Stew looks at the first card, he knows it's red. Basic knowledge structure theories also allow that Stew can know about how things look to him via introspection without first knowing that introspection is reliable. Hence, when Stew thinks about it, he knows that the card looks red to him. From these two items of knowledge, Stew can easily deduce that he was correct with respect to the first card: it looks red to Stew and it is red, so Stew got it right. The same applies to all of the other cards. Now, after going through enough cards, Stew has a sufficient amount of evidence for coming to know that his color vision is reliable. Thus, it seems that basic knowledge structure theories are committed to claiming that Stew can come to know that his color vision is reliable in this sort of way. However, intuitively this sort of "bootstrapping" process can't allow one to come to know that one's vision (or any other cognitive faculty) is reliable.

The sort of case described in this entry was first put forward as an objection to reliabilist theories of justification/knowledge (see *General Background: The Nature of Justification* pp. 113–119). These theories say roughly that one only needs to have reliable faculties in order to have knowledge from those faculties. In other words, one doesn't have to have any reason to think that one's faculties are reliable in order to gain knowledge from those faculties. So, one initial response to these sorts of cases was that they show that reliabilism is false (Fumerton 1995, Vogel 2000). However, it was later shown that reliabilism isn't the only theory targeted—any basic knowledge structure theory faces this problem.

RESPONSES

One response to this sort of situation is to argue that the problem here is that the process is "rule-circular" (it uses a rule/faculty to support the use of that very rule/faculty), and that rule-circularity cannot produce knowledge or justification (Vogel 2008). A version of this response doesn't prohibit the use of rule-circular methods in general, but rather claims that such methods can only be legitimately used when one isn't already doubtful about the rule/faculty being tested (Bergmann 2004). Consequently, this sort of response says that the problem in Stew's case isn't that he is using his vision to show that his vision is reliable. Instead, the problem lies in the fact that Stew has reason to doubt that his vision is reliable, and yet he is still using it to establish that his vision is reliable.

A different sort of response argues that the problem here is that such bootstrapping processes fail to track the truth (Roush 2005). The processes aren't really sensitive to the truth of whether Stew's vision is reliable or not. After all, Stew would end up with the same belief that his color vision is reliable by using this test even if his vision was actually horribly unreliable. It is because of this feature that it may be claimed that this process doesn't give Stew any evidence concerning the reliability of his vision.

A somewhat related response is to argue that the problem here is that Stew is using a "no-lose" method (Titelbaum 2010). In other words, Stew is gathering information about his color vision in such a way that he cannot get any evidence that goes against its reliability. This response insists that such methods cannot produce knowledge/justification.

A different sort of response holds that the way to respond to this sort of case is to insist that one cannot combine basic knowledge (that a particular card is red) with reflective knowledge (that the card looks red) (McCain and Moretti forthcoming). The idea here is that although Stew might know the card is red and that it looks red to him, he cannot use these two items of knowledge as evidence for thinking that his vision is reliable.

Yet another sort of response to this kind of case argues that the problem lies in the fact that the reasoning that Stew employs assumes "cumulative transitivity" (Weisberg 2010). Cumulative transitivity is the idea that if p supports believing q, and "p and q" supports believing r, then p supports believing r. However, this response points out that cumulative transitivity fails in cases where the support provided isn't absolutely certain, such as in these cases. To see the failure of cumulative transitivity, consider this sort of situation. The fact that Stew did well on his term paper supports thinking that he has a firm grasp of the material. Stew's doing well on the term paper and having a firm grasp of the material supports thinking that he didn't plagiarize the paper. However, the mere fact that he did well on the paper doesn't, on its own, support thinking that Stew didn't plagiarize. Stew's doing well on the BKTV test is analogous to his doing well on the term paper—it doesn't support, on its own, that Stew's color vision is reliable.

RECOMMENDED READING

GENERAL OVERVIEW

Weisberg, J. 2012. The Bootstrapping Problem. *Philosophy Compass* 7: 597–610.

SEMINAL PRESENTATIONS

Fumerton, R. 1995. *Metaepistemology and Skepticism*. Lanham, MD: Rowman & Littlefield.

Cohen, S. 2002. Basic Knowledge and the Problem of Easy Knowledge. *Philosophy and Phenomenological Research* 65: 309–329.

Vogel, J. 2000. Reliabilism Leveled. *Journal of Philosophy* 97: 602–623.

ADDITIONAL IMPORTANT DISCUSSIONS

Bergmann, M. 2004. Epistemic Circularity: Malignant and Benign. *Philosophy and Phenomenological Research* 69: 709–727.

Cohen, S. 2010. Bootstrapping, Defeasible Reasoning, and *A Priori* Justification. *Philosophical Perspectives* 24: 141–159.

Douven, I. and Kelp, C. 2013. Proper Bootstrapping. *Synthese* 190: 171–185.

McCain, K. and Moretti, L. Forthcoming. *Appearance and Explanation: Phenomenal Explanationism in Epistemology*. Oxford: Oxford University Press.

Roush, S. 2005. *Tracking Truth: Knowledge, Evidence, and Science*. New York: Oxford University Press.

Titelbaum, M. 2010. Tell Me You Love Me: Bootstrapping, Externalism, and No-Lose Epistemology. *Philosophical Studies* 149: 119–134.

Vogel, J. 2008. Epistemic Bootstrapping. *Journal of Philosophy* 105: 518–539.

Weisberg, J. 2010. Bootstrapping in General. *Philosophy and Phenomenological Research* 81: 525–548.

20

OFF TO THE RACES! (DISJUNCTION OBJECTION TO IBE)

Background: Inference to the best explanation (IBE) is a common method of reasoning in both science and our ordinary lives. The general idea with IBE is that when we are confronted with a set of facts in need of explaining, it is reasonable to believe that the best explanation of the facts is true. This method lies at the heart of Darwin's argument in support of evolution, it led to the discovery of Neptune, and it is involved in a number of other important scientific achievements. Perhaps its most familiar and explicit use comes from depictions of detective work. The detective considers all of the evidence and concludes that a particular person is guilty because their guilt best explains all of the evidence. We do something similar when we conclude, for example, that the dog ate the sandwich that was on the table because the plate that was on the table is on the floor, there are crumbs but no sandwich on the floor, you didn't eat the sandwich, and only you and the dog are home. This sort of reasoning is common and commonly accepted as good reasoning, i.e. as providing justification/knowledge. Hence, most agree that it is reasonable to believe that the best explanation of some facts is true. In other words, when p is the best explanation of the facts among all of the rival explanations, it is reasonable to believe that p is true. Of course, for this to make sense we have to recognize that "explanation" in the sense that matters for IBE refers to "potential explanation" (something that, if true, would explain the relevant facts). After all, in order for there to be rival explanations (explanations that are contrary to each other in the sense that at most one of them is true), it has to be that these rival explanations are potential explanations because at most one of these explanations is a genuine explanation if we are referring to the actual (i.e. true) explanation of the facts. Consequently, IBE is the idea that we should accept that the best potential explanation of a relevant set of facts is the actual explanation of those facts.

EPISTEMOLOGICAL ISSUES: INFERENCE TO THE BEST EXPLANATION; DISJUNCTION OBJECTION

Bas is at the Kentucky Derby. He's considering whether or not to place a bet on the big race. He starts thinking through his options. Of the 20 horses in the race, Lucky III is favored to win. He's from champion stock; the previous two Lucky's both won major races and Lucky III looks every bit as strong and as fast as them. However, Bas realizes that the other 19 horses are all top thoroughbreds as well. While he's trying to decide what to do, he goes to have a snack. Absorbed in his deliberations, Bas doesn't realize that the race has begun. In fact, Bas isn't even watching when he hears a loud cheer as the race ends! When Bas hears the crowd cheering, he realizes that the race is over, but he didn't place his bet or even see who won. The announcer hasn't declared the winner yet either.

Now we come to the relevant question: what should Bas think about the outcome of the race? Particularly, should Bas think that Lucky III won? Intuitively, the answer is "no." Even though Lucky III was the favorite to win the race, there were 19 other top horses in the race, and though Lucky III's odds are some of the best in history 2–5 (as of the writing of this, 2–5 odds are the shortest odds that a horse has been given for winning the Kentucky derby), it's still likely that Lucky III didn't win. After all, 2–5 odds mean that it is predicted that Lucky III would win two out of seven times in this race, i.e. less than 30% of the time. Hence, despite being heavily the favorite to win the race, the probability of Lucky III winning is significantly lower than 50%. As a result, it seems clear that Bas shouldn't believe that Lucky III won. Instead, he should think that the winner was in the group of the other 19 horses. However, it isn't clear that inference to the best explanation (IBE) can yield this result.

Let's think about the situation in a bit more detail. The facts that need to be explained are that the race was won and the various qualities of the horses racing. Which potential explanation best explains these facts? It seems that "Lucky III won" is the best explanation. Lucky III was the favorite to win because he has qualities that make him superior to the each of the other horses when it comes to racing. Another way to look at it is this: if we were to compare each of the other 19 horses with Lucky III, that Lucky III won would be a better explanation than that the other horse won. For example, that Lucky III won is a better explanation than that horse 1 won, it's a better explanation than that horse 2 won, and so on. Hence, it seems that Lucky III's winning is the best explanation of the evidence, and yet it seems that it would be unreasonable for Bas to infer that Lucky III won the race. It appears that IBE yields the wrong result by licensing an inference to a conclusion that is likely false.

This sort of case was originally presented independently by Richard Fumerton and Bas Van Fraassen to show that, contrary to what we might have thought and to our ordinary reasoning practices, IBE is not a legitimate way to reason. Hence, the cases where science has relied upon instances of IBE and achieved great success were either just matters of luck or else really some other method of reasoning was being used and the causes of the achievements have simply been misdescribed.

RESPONSES

One way of responding to this problem is to insist that one can be justified in believing a proposition even if that proposition isn't likely to be true (Smith 2016). Thus, one might argue that contrary to our initial intuition in this case, Bas really should believe that Lucky III won even though it's likely that he is mistaken. On this response, IBE doesn't have a problem even if it licenses inferring things that aren't likely to be true because believing such things can still be justified.

By far, the most common, non-skeptical response to this problem though doesn't require denying that one can be justified in believing a proposition only if the proposition is likely to be true. Rather, the most common sort of response involves restricting IBE in an important way (Musgrave 1988, Lipton 2004, McCain 2016). As we described it above (and as it is often described in ordinary life—and sometimes in the philosophical literature), IBE says that we can infer that p when p explains the relevant facts in a way that makes p a better explanation of those facts than the available rival explanations. If we construe IBE in this way though, it leads to the problem depicted in the horserace example. However, several philosophers have argued that the way to block this sort of problem is to recognize that IBE needs to be restricted to cases where the best explanation is "good enough." The general idea here is that it's not enough that p explains the relevant facts better than each of the available rival explanations—in order for it to be reasonable to believe that p, it has to also be true that p is in its own right a sufficiently good explanation of the facts. One way that this sort of restriction to sufficiently good explanations might be spelled out is to insist that p must have a minimum probability of being true in order to be inferred, which presumably "Lucky III won" doesn't have for Bas in the above case (McCain and Poston 2019). Another way of spelling this idea out is that the best explanation is "good enough" when we are justified in believing that this explanation is better than any other explanation that could be formulated (Dellsén forthcoming). The gist here is that in order to legitimately infer that p because p is the best explanation of some relevant set of facts, it has to be the case that it is reasonable for us to believe that any other explanations we might be able to come up with will be inferior to p. In the horserace case, it's plausible that we can come up with a better explanation, namely that some horse out of the group of the other 19 horses won the race.

RECOMMENDED READING

GENERAL OVERVIEW

Abduction. *Stanford Encyclopedia of Philosophy*. URL = https://plato.stanford.edu/entries/abduction/

SEMINAL PRESENTATIONS

Fumerton, R. 1995. *Metaepistemology and Skepticism*. Lanham, MD: Rowman & Littlefield.

McCain, K. and Poston, T. 2019. Dispelling the Disjunction Objection to Explanatory Inference. *Philosopher's Imprint* 19: 1–8.

van Fraassen, B. 1989. *Laws and Symmetry*. Oxford: Oxford University Press.

ADDITIONAL IMPORTANT DISCUSSIONS

Dellsén, F. Forthcoming. Explanatory Consolidation: From 'Best' to 'Good Enough'. *Philosophy and Phenomenological Research*.

Lipton, P. 2004. *Inference to the Best Explanation 2nd Edition*. New York: Routledge.

McCain, K. 2016. *The Nature of Scientific Knowledge: An Explanatory Approach*. Cham: Springer.

Musgrave, A. 1988. The Ultimate Argument for Scientific Realism. In R. Nola (ed), *Relativism and Realism in Science*. Dordrecht: Kluwer, 229–252.

Nozick, R. 1993. *The Nature of Rationality*. Princeton, NJ: Princeton University Press.

Smith, M. 2016. *Between Probability and Certainty: What Justifies Belief*. New York: Oxford University Press.

21

TO TRANSFORM OR NOT TO TRANSFORM? (TRANSFORMATIVE EXPERIENCE)

Background: According to decision theory, when you are trying to determine the rational action to take, you need to consider both the odds of certain outcomes and their values. Here's a simple case. How can you determine whether it's rational for you to take an umbrella with you on a particular day? Look at how likely rain is and the value of the various outcomes, and then calculate which of the options gives you the best expected outcome. Let's say that this is how you value the possible outcomes (the higher the number the more you value the outcome):

	Rains	Doesn't Rain
Take Umbrella	2	−2
Don't Take Umbrella	−10	2

Should you take an umbrella? Well, it depends upon what the odds of rain are. Let's assume that there's a 50% chance of rain. Decision theory tells us that you can calculate whether it's rational for you to take the umbrella or not given your values and the chances of the various outcomes. Here's how the calculations go:

Take Umbrella: Rains (2 × .5 = 1); Doesn't Rain (−2 × .5 = −1)
Don't Take Umbrella: Rains (−10 × .5 = −5); Doesn't Rain (2 × .5 = 1)

Now simply add up the expected values for each. Take Umbrella: 0; Don't Take Umbrella: −4. Clearly in this case, the rational choice is to take an umbrella because the expected value of not taking one is much lower than the expected value of taking one. The purpose of this brief background is primarily to highlight that according to standard decision theory, you need two critical items of information in order to calculate what it's rational to do in a given situation: you need information about how likely various outcomes are and you need information about what your values are.

EPISTEMOLOGICAL ISSUES: TRANSFORMATIVE EXPERIENCE; RATIONAL DECISION THEORY

Laurie is thinking about whether she should become a parent or not. At this point, she's not worried about settling on a particular method of becoming a parent—natural birth, adoption, etc.—but rather she is simply considering whether to become a parent at all. Laurie knows decision theory, so she decides to work out the calculations to help her gain some clarity (this is a philosopher's version of a pros and cons list!). She starts with thinking about her choice: try to become a parent or don't try to become a parent. And the two possible outcomes: become a parent or not become a parent.

	Become a parent	*Don't become a parent*
Try to become a parent	A	B
Don't try to become a parent	C	D

So, Laurie realizes that there are four possibilities: A, B, C, D.

Now all she has to do is figure out how much she values each of these possibilities and how likely they are to occur. Unfortunately, Laurie hits a snag here. She realizes that she has no idea what it's like for *her* to be a parent. She's never been a parent before, and there's nothing in her life that really gives her a good sense of what it's like to be a parent. She realizes that this is something that she could only really know about if she were already a parent. So, she has no way to determine how valuable A or C is to her. To make things even more difficult, she realizes that what she values would likely change if she were to become a parent. She knows that people's views of parenthood often change when they become parents—some change so that after becoming a parent they really like it, but others change so that they really dislike being a parent. So, Laurie realizes that becoming a parent would be a transformative experience—it would change her not just in terms of becoming a parent, but also in terms of changing how she values things. Hence, something that she highly values now might be something that she doesn't value much at all after becoming a parent, and vice versa. But, this means that even if Laurie could somehow figure out how valuable A and C are to her now, she can't know what their values for her would be after she became a parent. It seems that in this sort of choice, where the choice leads to a transformation of this kind, Laurie can only get the information that she needs to make the rational decision *after* the choice has been made. How in the world is she going to rationally make this decision?

When L.A. Paul brought this sort of case to light, she proposed that we acknowledge that Laurie is in a position where she simply can't tell what she should do using decision theory. According to this response, this limitation of decision theory doesn't mean that it isn't helpful here though. Rather, this response suggests that what Laurie really needs to do is apply decision theory to a different choice: discovering what it is like to become a parent or not discovering this. It seems that Laurie can know how valuable it is to discover something like this before she knows what it is like to become a parent. So, she can make use of the tools of decision theory when it comes to this choice and that can help her to rationally decide whether or not to try to become a parent.

RESPONSES

A different way of responding to this challenge for decision theory involves arguing that the problem lies in the fact that the possible outcomes in this case are being represented in a way that is too coarse-grained (Pettigrew 2015, 2016). This response suggests that rather than simply considering the outcome "try to become a parent and succeed," say, Laurie should consider various values for success in her calculations. For example, the possibilities should include things like *try to become a parent and succeed and success becomes very valuable, try to become a parent and succeed and success becomes slightly valuable, try to become a parent and succeed and success becomes slightly disvaluable*, and so on. Once Laurie has an appropriately fine-grained representation of the outcomes, this response contends that standard decision theory will work just fine.

Another response to this challenge is to argue that standard decision theory has the resources to respond to this sort of challenge because it could appeal to a "master utility function" (Chang 2015). Essentially, the idea here is that rather than going off of what your actual values are for any particular outcomes, the way to make decisions is to decide based on the values your ideal self (the version of you that has all the relevant information and is perfectly rational) would have. So, Laurie's decision is rational when it corresponds to what her ideal self would choose. Of course, we might worry how in the world Laurie is supposed to know what her ideal self would choose though.

Yet another way to respond is to insist that Laurie actually can come to have evidence about what it's like to be a parent before becoming one herself (Harman 2015). While she cannot know this in the sense of actually having the experience (since she hasn't had it yet), she can reasonably estimate the value to her of becoming a parent by learning from the testimony of others, observing how people who are parents seem when it comes to their satisfaction with being parents, and inferring how she would value this change based on how similar sorts of experiences have been for her.

A final sort of response appeals to the reasonableness of trust (Compaijen 2018). The idea here is that in a situation like Laurie's, it can be reasonable for her to trust that her current desires will be fulfilled when making this sort of transformative choice. And, so the response goes, since it is reasonable for her to trust this, she can make a reasonable decision in this sort of situation by deciding based on her current values.

RECOMMENDED READING

SEMINAL PRESENTATIONS

Paul, L.A. 2014. *Transformative Experience*. Oxford: Oxford University Press.

Paul, L.A. 2015. What You Can't Expect When You're Expecting. *Res Philosophica* 92: 1–24.

Ullman-Margalit, E. 2006. Big Decisions: Opting, Converting, Drifting. *Royal Institute of Philosophy Supplement* 58: 157–172.

ADDITIONAL IMPORTANT DISCUSSIONS

Bykvist, K. 2006. Prudence for Changing Selves. *Utilitas* 18: 264–283.

Chang, R. 2015. Transformative Choices. *Res Philosophica* 92: 237–282.

Compaijen, R. 2018. Transformative Choice, Practical Reasons and Trust. *International Journal of Philosophical Studies* 26: 275–292.

Dougherty, T., Horowitz, S., and Sliwa, P. 2015. Expecting the Unexpected. *Res Philosophica* 92: 301–321.

Harman, E. 2015. Transformative Experience and Reliance on Moral Testimony. *Res Philosophica* 92: 323–339.

Pettigrew, R. 2015. Transformative Experience and Decision Theory. *Philosophy and Phenomenological Research* 91: 766–774.

Pettigrew, R. 2016. Book Review of L. A. Paul's *Transformative Experience*. *Mind* 125: 927–935.

22

MARY SEES AN APPLE (KNOWLEDGE ARGUMENT AGAINST PHYSICALISM)

Background: One of the major debates in philosophy of mind is that between physicalism and dualism. Physicalism is roughly the view that the universe is entirely physical. A consequence of physicalism is that the mind is entirely physical too. In other words, physicalism holds that there is no immaterial soul that thinks or any nonphysical mental properties. The various forms of dualism deny physicalism. Substance dualism contends that there are actually two distinct kinds of substances: physical and nonphysical. This is a view that Descartes famously defended where you are composed of a body and a mind, and although the two interact, they are distinct kinds of things. The other primary form of dualism is property dualism wherein there is only one kind of substance, but there are two different kinds of properties: physical and nonphysical. Hence, property dualism contends that when it comes to the mind, there is only one substance, the brain, but the brain has both physical and nonphysical properties. Given that this book is an epistemology book, it is natural to wonder why we are discussing this bit of philosophy of mind here. The reason is that one of the main arguments against physicalism (and so for dualism) is what is known as the "Knowledge Argument." The Knowledge Argument centers around whether or not there is more to be known than merely the physical facts about the universe. One of its key points is the claim that if one knows only physical facts, one's knowledge is limited in an important way—this is so even if one knows all the physical facts there are to know.

EPISTEMOLOGICAL ISSUES: THE KNOWLEDGE ARGUMENT; DUALISM VS. PHYSICALISM

Mary is a naturally brilliant person, and she has devoted her life to the pursuit of scientific knowledge. In fact, Mary has become one of the premier neuroscientists in the world. And when it comes to her specialty, color vision, no one is even close to as knowledgeable as Mary. She knows all the physical facts about color vision. Mary knows things that other neuroscientists only dream of knowing. When she finally gets around to publishing all that she knows, the study of color vision will be complete. She literally knows all the physical facts there are to know about color vision. So, when it comes to seeing red, say, Mary has the full scientific story.

That all said, Mary has had a very peculiar life until now. She has lived her entire life in a black and white room. Everything that she has ever seen in the room around her, her food, her TV, her computer screen, etc. has been black, white, or shades of gray. Mary has never in her life actually seen colors even though she isn't colorblind; in fact, Mary has no vision problems at all. She knows all about seeing red, but she's never actually experienced seeing red. However, all of that is about to change because she is about to be released from her black and white room.

Mary leaves her room and for the first time she lays her eyes on a bright, ripe, red apple. Now she knows what it's like to see red! But, if she only now knows what it's like to see red, that means that she didn't know this before seeing the apple. However, if Mary didn't know what it is like to see red, that means that although she knew all of the physical facts about seeing red, she didn't know all there is to know about seeing red. Hence, it seems that there are facts beyond the physical facts. If this assessment of Mary and her new experience with seeing red is true, then physicalism seems to be in trouble because there appear to be things in the universe that are not physical—such as the sort of thing that Mary experiences for the first time when she sees red.

RESPONSES

Some physicalists respond to this example by questioning whether the thought experiment involving Mary is really even possible.

For example, some point out that it isn't clear that one can actually learn all of the physical facts in the way that Mary would have to in the black and white room.

It is more common, however, for physicalists to accept that the scenario depicted above is possible, but argue that it fails to pose a genuine problem for physicalism. A popular response of this sort involves arguing that Mary doesn't actually learn new *facts* when she sees the red apple for the first time. There are two primary ways of developing this sort of response. One says that rather than propositional knowledge (i.e. knowledge of facts), Mary gains knowledge-how. She develops new abilities, such as the ability to determine whether something is red by looking at it (Lewis 1988, Nemirow 2007). The other primary way of developing this response insists that Mary neither gains propositional knowledge nor knowledge-how, but instead Mary gains acquaintance knowledge when she sees the red apple (Conee 1994). She is now acquainted with redness.

Perhaps the most prominent physicalist response to this scenario though is to allow that Mary does in fact gain new propositional knowledge when she sees the red apple for the first time. Nevertheless, this response contends that Mary's gaining this new knowledge isn't a problem for physicalism because although Mary comes to have new knowledge, it isn't knowledge of a *new* fact (Horgan 1984, Tye 1995). The thought is that Mary comes to possess a new phenomenal concept when she sees the apple—she now has the phenomenal concept of "red". Her possession of this new concept allows her to form new beliefs and know things using that concept. However, the response insists that the things she comes to know aren't new facts about color or color vision. Rather, the idea is that Mary is learning the same facts in a new way now that she sees red.

RECOMMENDED READING

GENERAL OVERVIEWS

Qualia: The Knowledge Argument, *Stanford Encyclopedia of Philosophy*. URL = https://plato.stanford.edu/entries/qualia-knowledge/

The Knowledge Argument against Physicalism. *Internet Encyclopedia of Philosophy*. URL = https://iep.utm.edu/know-arg/

SEMINAL PRESENTATIONS

Jackson, F. 1982. Epiphenomenal Qualia. *Philosophical Quarterly* 32: 127–136.
Jackson, F. 1986. What Mary Didn't Know. *Journal of Philosophy* 83: 291–295.

ADDITIONAL IMPORTANT DISCUSSIONS

Alter, T. 1998. A Limited Defense of the Knowledge Argument. *Philosophical Studies* 90: 35–56.

Chalmers, D. 1996. *The Conscious Mind: In Search of a Fundamental Theory.* Oxford: Oxford University Press.

Conee, E. 1994. Phenomenal Knowledge. *Australasian Journal of Philosophy* 72: 136–150.

Fumerton, R. 2013. *Knowledge, Thought, and the Case for Dualism.* Cambridge: Cambridge University Press.

Horgan, T. 1984. Jackson on Physical Information and Qualia. *Philosophical Quarterly* 32: 127–136.

Lewis, D. 1988. What Experience Teaches. *Proceedings of the Russellian Society* 13: 29–57.

Ludlow, P., Nagasawa, Y., and Stoljar, D. (eds). 2004. *There's Something About Mary: Essays on Phenomenal Consciousness and Frank Jackson's Knowledge Argument.* Cambridge, MA: MIT Press.

Nagel, T. 1974. What Is it Like to be a Bat? *Philosophical Review* 83: 435–450.

Nemirow, L. 2007. So This Is What It's Like: A Defense of the Ability Hypothesis. In T. Alter and S. Walter (eds), *Phenomenal Concepts and Phenomenal Knowledge: New Essays on Consciousness and Physicalism.* Oxford: Oxford University Press, 32–51.

Tye, M. 1995. *Ten Problems of Consciousness.* Cambridge, MA: MIT Press.

PART III

JUSTIFICATION

GENERAL BACKGROUND: THE NATURE OF JUSTIFICATION

In order to get a handle on the nature of justification, it is helpful to draw some important distinctions. To begin, there are multiple senses of the term "justification". Two of the primary ways we might use this term is in reference to either epistemic justification or pragmatic justification. These different kinds of justification are similar in that they have both been traditionally understood in terms of having good reasons. However, what counts as a "good reason" is very different when it comes to these different sorts of justification. The sorts of good reasons that matter for epistemic justification are reasons that indicate the truth of a particular proposition. For example, a visual experience as of a cat on the mat can provide epistemic justification for believing that there is a cat on the mat. A natural way of understanding this is that visual experience provides epistemic justification because it is a good reason for thinking that there is a cat on the mat. Put another way, this sort of visual experience is indicative of the truth of the proposition that there is a cat on the mat.

In order to see how the sort of good reasons that provide epistemic justification differ from those that provide pragmatic justification, let's consider an example. Walt has recently been diagnosed with an illness that he knows has an extremely low survival rate. In light of his knowledge of the low survival rate, Walt has a good reason that can make it epistemically justified for him to believe that he is unlikely to recover. Nevertheless, it may be that if Walt were to believe that he will recover, he would be able to better manage his suffering and be happier. In such a case, believing that he will recover is not epistemically justified for Walt. Nevertheless, this belief might be pragmatically justified. Good pragmatic reasons for belief do not need to be indicative of the truth; instead, they are simply reasons that make believing beneficial for the person. Hence, in this case Walt has pragmatic justification for believing that he will recover (believing is beneficial to him), but unfortunately, he lacks epistemic justification for believing that he will recover. Throughout our discussions, we are concerned with epistemic justification, the sort of justification that is connected to truth and is necessary for knowledge.

Another distinction that we will explore here is that between having justification for a belief and justifying a belief. The former, having justification, is a state of a person. Either a person has justification for believing something or they don't. Justifying a belief isn't a state of a person, but rather it is an action. Justifying a belief involves explaining to someone (possibly one's own self) the evidence or reasons that one has in support of a particular proposition.

Although having justification and justifying a belief are very different, it isn't hard to see why they are sometimes confused. If one fails in the attempt to justify a belief to someone, that may mean that one didn't have justification to begin with and still lacks it. That is to say, sometimes attempting to justify a belief leads to the realization that one doesn't have good reason to believe. There are also times when things work out the other way though. It is possible to realize that one has more reason to believe something than one originally thought as one goes through the process of justifying the belief.

Once we realize that justifying can help reveal whether we have good reasons to believe as we do, it can be easy to mistake justifying for having justification. But, we must avoid the mistake of thinking that one's belief isn't justified unless one can justify it. For one thing, someone can be justified in believing something even if they cannot justify that belief. For instance, young children have a number of justified beliefs (they may recognize various colors, what their favorite stuffed animal is, etc.). Yet, young children are apt to lack the sort of cognitive development needed to adequately justify their beliefs to someone else. For another thing, the act of attempting to justify a belief might itself generate new justification for believing something. It is possible that Kari believes that p despite lacking sufficient justification, but while attempting to justify her belief that p, she comes up with what are in fact very good reasons to believe that p. Prior to her attempt at justifying her belief that p, Kari didn't have sufficient justification to believe that p. Nevertheless, her act of justifying her belief actually generated justification for her to believe that p. Throughout our discussions, we are concerned with justification rather than the act of justifying because it is the former that is necessary for knowledge and of most interest to epistemologists.

TWO DEBATES

Before concluding our general discussion of the nature of justification, it is important to get a handle on two of the central debates concerning the nature of justification. The first concerns the structure of justification and the second is the internalism/externalism debate. Let's start with the former.

The debate about the structure of justification has its origins in the writings of ancient philosophers like Aristotle and Sextus Empiricus. In order to appreciate this debate, it is helpful to think about the challenge that gives rise to it, what is known as the "regress of reasons." The regress of reasons is pretty much what it sounds like; it is a regress that we face when we attempt to give reasons for the things that we believe. One way to think about this challenge is in terms of a series of "why" questions. Let's assume that you justifiedly believe that the University of Alabama won the most recent College Football Playoff National Championship. Why do you believe this? Perhaps because you read that they won on the CNN app on your phone. Why do you believe what the CNN app says? A plausible response is that CNN is a reliable source for this sort of information. Why do you think that CNN is a reliable source of information? Of course, this process can just keep going. The regress of reasons is just that it seems that for anything we believe we could ask for reasons in support of it, and we could ask for reasons in support of those reasons, and we could ask for reasons in support of the reasons that support our reasons, and so on. The regress of reasons is a challenge because the unending nature of this search for reasons seems to suggest that we can't have the support for our reasons that is necessary for justification.

The various positions concerning the structure of justification are simply attempts to solve the regress of reasons. By far, the two most prominent (non-skeptical) responses to this challenge are *foundationalism* and *coherentism*. There are numerous ways of filling in the details of each of these responses to the regress of reasons, but for our purposes it will be enough to just go over the general form that these two responses take. We will fill in some of the details later when looking at particular entries. That said, let's begin by taking a look at foundationalism.

The basic idea behind foundationalism is that the regress of reasons stops. According to foundationalists, the structure of justification is like the structure of a building. A building has many parts that all rest upon a foundation—so too with justification. All of our justification rests upon basic beliefs. These are justified beliefs that aren't themselves justified by some other beliefs. How then are they justified? Most foundationalists claim that basic beliefs get their justification by being based on experience. Importantly, experience isn't itself something that can be justified or unjustified. Consequently, it doesn't make sense to ask for a justifying reason for one's experience. Hence, foundationalists claim that the regress of reasons reaches a stopping point. If your belief that the University of Alabama won the most recent College Football Playoff National Championship is justified, then the foundationalist says that if we trace your reasons back far enough, we'll eventually come to a basic belief—a belief that is justified by experience. Once we hit this basic belief, we are at the foundation and there is nowhere else to go and no more questions to ask about your reasons for the belief. Such basic beliefs are the foundation upon which all of our other justified beliefs ultimately rest.

Coherentism offers a very different picture of the structure of justification. Coherentists contend that there is an assumption about the structure of justification implicit in the regress of reasons— the assumption that justification is a linear process. In other words, the regress of reasons assumes that justification is like a chain where the belief that q justifies the belief that p, the belief that *p* justifies the belief that *o*, the belief that *o* justifies the belief that *n*, and so on. According to coherentists, this assumption gives rise to the regress of reasons, and it is mistaken. Instead of thinking that justification is linear in this way, coherentists contend that justification is a holistic matter. Thus, rather than being analogous to a building like the foundationalists claim, coherentists insist that the structure of justification is like a web where beliefs are all connected to each other by various strands. On the coherentist picture, a belief is justified because of its connection to other beliefs in the web of beliefs. So, your belief that the University of Alabama won the most recent College Football Playoff National Championship is justified because it is connected to your other beliefs in such a way that the set of those beliefs is coherent. There are various ways that coherentists might spell out what it means for beliefs to be coherent with one another. One of the most promising ways of doing this is in terms of explanatory relations. The general idea is that coherence is a matter of beliefs explaining or being explained by one another. For instance, the truth of "the University of Alabama won the most recent College Football Playoff National Championship" explains why CNN reported that they did, CNN's record of reliable information when it comes to things of this sort explains why you trust the report, and so on.

Now let's turn to the second debate. The debate between internalists and externalists about the nature of epistemic justification is one of the major developments to come out of discussion of the Gettier Problem in contemporary epistemology. It's an unfortunate historical accident that there are a number of debates in philosophy that use the terms "internalism" and "externalism"; so it is especially important to get clear on exactly what this debate concerns. The internalism/externalism debate in epistemology concerns the nature of justification. Sometimes people speak of internalist and externalist views of knowledge, but this is misleading. All views of knowledge are external, in the sense that they hold that at least some of the requirements for knowledge exist outside of the knower's mental life. For instance, all parties to the internalism/externalism debate can agree that truth is a requirement for knowledge that doesn't simply depend upon the mind of the knower. Truth is external because what is true and what is false is determined by how the universe is, not by what we think about how the universe is.

The internalism/externalism debate is about justification, not knowledge. However, we need to draw a further distinction here because as we saw in the background to Saul the Superstitious Lawyer (pp. 42–47) there are at least two important senses of "justification". One concerns what one has justification for believing and the other concerns what one justifiedly believes. The former sort of justification is often called "propositional justification" because it is the justification one has in support of the truth of a particular proposition. Recall that one can have justification for believing something even if one doesn't actually believe it. The other sort of justification, when one justifiedly believes something, is often called "doxastic justification" because it concerns whether one's actual belief (a kind of doxastic attitude) is justified. The distinction between propositional justification and doxastic justification is important to keep in mind because most internalists think that something beyond what is internal to a subject's mental life is required for a belief to be based on one's reasons such as the belief being appropriately caused by one's reasons. As a result, even most internalists accept that doxastic justification is partly an external matter. Hence, really when we talk about internalists in epistemology, we are talking about people who maintain that propositional justification is internal. That said, since externalist theories are often formulated in terms of doxastic justification, we can treat the debate as concerning whether or not there are requirements outside of having particular mental states that determine whether someone justifiedly believes that p, aside from whatever is required to satisfy the basing relation.

Now that we have gotten sufficiently clear on the focus of the internalism/externalism debate, let's take a look at the opposing sides. All versions of internalism are committed to mentalism, and most forms of externalism are committed to the denial of mentalism (for our purposes, we can set aside the complication of getting into the details of externalist views that accept mentalism). Mentalism is the idea that any two individuals that are exactly alike mentally are exactly alike in terms of the propositional justification that they have. In other words, mentalism says that there can't be a difference in terms of propositional justification without a difference in terms of mental states. So, if Earl and Rich differ in terms of their propositional justification, say Rich is justified in believing that p and Earl isn't, then there must be some mental difference between Earl and Rich. And assuming that Earl and Rich both satisfy the requirements of the basing relation, internalists insist that it can't be that one of them justifiedly believes that p, but the other's belief that p is unjustified unless there is some mental difference between them. Externalism in all of its many varieties denies mentalism. In other words, externalist views of epistemic justification contend that Earl and Rich can be mental duplicates, i.e. exactly alike in terms of all of their memories, experiences, ways of thinking, and so on, and both satisfy the conditions necessary for the basing relation, and yet Rich justifiedly believes that p and Earl does not.

In order to help illustrate the differences between internalism and externalism, it will be helpful to look at a prominent version of each. Evidentialism is a prominent form of internalism that says that a person's justification at a particular time depends solely upon the evidence that the person has at that time. Evidentialists understand "evidence" quite broadly so that it includes a person's memories, sensations, experiences, and so on. Hence, an evidentialist would say that Rich has propositional justification for believing that p, if and only if the evidence that Rich has on the whole supports thinking that p is true. That is to say, Rich has to have more reason for thinking that p is true than he does for thinking that p is false. And, assuming that Rich's belief that p is appropriately based on his evidence in support of p, evidentialism yields the result that Rich's belief is justified.

On the externalist side, a prominent theory is reliabilism. The general idea of reliabilism is that beliefs are justified if and only if they are produced by reliable belief-forming processes. On reliabilism, what matters is whether Rich's belief is formed by a belief-forming process that tends to produce more true beliefs than false beliefs. Let's think once more of Earl and Rich. Evidentialism says that since they are mental duplicates, they have the same evidence. Thus, evidentialism says that if Rich's belief that p is justified, then so is Earl's, and vice versa. Reliabilism yields a different result. It could be that Rich, but not Earl, is in an environment where his belief-forming process is reliable. As a result, it could be that Rich's belief that p is justified because it's reliable, but Earl's isn't because his belief is unreliable. There have been several examples put forward as challenges to both internalism and externalism. Let's take a look at some of the most prominent.

23

THE UNFORTUNATE TWIN (NEW EVIL DEMON PROBLEM)

Background: There are two important things to remember for understanding this case. The first is the difference between internalism and externalism (see General Background: The Nature of Justification pp. 113–119). Most importantly, it is key to recall that externalist theories of justification claim that you can be justified in believing that p, even if you have no evidence or mentally accessible reason for p at all. The second thing to keep in mind is the nature of Cartesian skepticism. This is the sort of skepticism covered in Descartes' Demon (pp. 55–60). The idea here being that it is possible that one could be deceived by a demon or be a brain in a vat and yet have all of the sorts of experiences that we normally have.

EPISTEMOLOGICAL ISSUES: EPISTEMIC JUSTIFICATION: EXTERNALISM VS. INTERNALISM; NEW EVIL DEMON PROBLEM

Like any normal adult, Jenny has many justified beliefs (i.e. beliefs that she holds rationally/for good reasons). For example, Jenny believes that her phone number is 867-5309 for good reasons—she has memories that this is her number. Right now, she justifiedly believes that she is reading this book because the sort of experiences she is having right now provide good reasons to believe that she is reading a book (her experiences are very similar to your current experiences). And so on. As we noted, Jenny, like most of us, believes a lot of things for good reasons. So, she has a lot of justified beliefs. This fact is not really surprising or on its own all that interesting.

Now, let's think about someone who is very similar to Jenny. No, not just similar. Let's think of someone who is mentally *exactly* like Jenny. This person has all of the same beliefs that Jenny has and all of the same reasons for those beliefs too. For instance, this person believes that they are reading this book because they are having an experience that is indistinguishable from Jenny's current experience; they also believe that their phone number is 867-5309 because they have memories that are indistinguishable from Jenny's memories of her phone number. To make the point even clearer, this person is an *exact* mental duplicate of Jenny. But, unlike Jenny, who is a normal adult in a normal situation, this person is the victim in some sort of skeptical scenario. Perhaps they are being deceived by Descartes' Demon (see *Descartes' Demon* pp. 55–60) or they are a brain in a vat, or they are in the *Matrix*. Let's call this mental duplicate of Jenny in this situation "Denny". Denny has all of the same beliefs, as Jenny, thinks the same way that Jenny does, has the same experiences as Jenny, has the same memories, and so on. As we said, Denny is exactly like Jenny mentally, but in a skeptical scenario rather than in the real world.

An interesting question arises when we think about this possibility: what should we say about Denny's beliefs? Denny has all of the same beliefs as Jenny and they hold these beliefs for the same reasons that Jenny holds her beliefs, but many of Denny's beliefs are false. For example, Jenny and Denny both think that they are reading this book, but while Jenny really is reading it, Denny is being tricked into thinking this. Denny doesn't even have a book. Denny may not even have eyes to see the book or ears to hear the words of the book if someone were to read it to them. So, Denny's beliefs are false, whereas Jenny's are true.

But what about justification? Jenny and Denny believe all the same things for the same reasons. It seems that if Jenny is reasonable in believing as she does, so is Denny. After all, Jenny doesn't have any special information that Denny lacks. Denny thinks that they are reading about a crazy possibility where someone exactly like Jenny is in a skeptical scenario, and they are having the same thoughts and questions as Jenny when they think about this possibility. Given that Jenny should believe that she is reading this book, shouldn't Denny believe the same thing? After all, Denny has the same reasons for thinking this that Jenny does. On what grounds would it make sense to say that Jenny should believe that she's reading this book but Denny shouldn't? It can't simply be because Denny is wrong and Jenny's not. Otherwise, that would mean that we can never have justified false beliefs, but surely sometimes we can reasonably believe something despite being mistaken. That seems to be exactly what is going on with Denny. Thus, it seems that Jenny and Denny are both justified in believing the same things even though only one of them has true beliefs.

This possible situation is known as the *New Evil Demon Problem*. It is "new" because it's not quite the same as Descartes' original demon problem (see *Descartes' Demon* pp. 55–60). In fact, unlike Descartes' Demon, the New Evil Demon Problem isn't even used to argue for skepticism. But then, why is it a problem and why is it important? The answers to these questions go hand in hand. The New Evil Demon Problem is important because it is thought to teach us a valuable lesson about the nature of justification: we can have justified beliefs regardless of the external environment in which we find ourselves. It's considered a problem because this valuable lesson seems to be at odds with externalist theories of justification. Recall, such theories claim that what one is justified in believing is not simply a matter of the experiences, memories, and so on that one has. Instead, externalist theories of justification claim that epistemic justification is the result of beliefs being produced in the right way. Consequently, such theories seem committed to claiming that Denny's beliefs are all unjustified while Jenny's are justified, despite the fact that they have the same beliefs because of the same apparent memories, experiences, and so on. Why is this? Well, the environments that Jenny and Denny are in are very different, although they don't realize this. Jenny's environment is hospitable to her forming true beliefs, so the processes that lead to her beliefs are reliable. Unfortunately, Denny's belief-forming processes (which are the same as Jenny's) aren't reliable in the environment in which Denny is stuck. So, on externalist theories, Jenny's beliefs are justified and Denny's aren't, even though they have the same reasons for holding those beliefs. This doesn't seem right though. It seems that Jenny and

Denny are either both justified or both unjustified. Hence, the New Evil Demon Problem appears to pose a serious problem for externalist theories of epistemic justification.

RESPONSES

Externalists about epistemic justification are inclined to opt for various responses to this problem. One such response is to simply deny that Denny really is justified and claim that we are mistaken when we think so. Given the intuitive pull of the New Evil Demon Problem, it's unsurprising that this response is not very popular.

A more popular externalist response involves claiming that externalism can actually yield the intuitive result that Jenny and Denny are alike when it comes to justification. One way of doing this is to argue that we should judge Denny not by whether their beliefs are reliably produced in their own environment, but rather by whether their beliefs would be reliably produced if Denny were in the actual world (Sosa 1991, Comesaña 2002). When we judge in this way, Denny's beliefs are just as reliably produced as Jenny's are because they are produced by the same belief-forming processes and they are evaluated relative to their reliability in the actual world.

Another response that has become popular more recently is to argue that there are different sorts of justification at play when we think about this sort of case (Goldman 1988). In particular, some who take this response argue that while Denny's beliefs aren't justified, they are excusable or blameless. The idea here is that our intuitions about the New Evil Demon Problem are muddled because we tend to run together justification and excusability/blamelessness. We would excuse Denny for believing as they do, but that doesn't mean that Denny's beliefs are justified.

RECOMMENDED READING

GENERAL OVERVIEWS

The New Evil Demon Problem. *Internet Encyclopedia of Philosophy*. URL = https://www.iep.utm.edu/evil-new/
Reliabilist Epistemology. Stanford Encyclopedia of Philosophy. URL = https://plato.stanford.edu/entries/reliabilism/#RepRefMod

SEMINAL PRESENTATIONS

Cohen, S. 1984. Justification and Truth. *Philosophical Studies* 46: 279–296.
Cohen, S. and K. Lehrer. 1983. Justification, Truth, and Coherence. *Synthese* 55: 191–207.

ADDITIONAL IMPORTANT DISCUSSIONS

Comesaña, J. 2002. The Diagonal and the Demon. *Philosophical Studies* 110: 249–266.
Goldman, A. 1986. *Epistemology and Cognition*. Cambridge, MA: Harvard University Press.
Goldman, A. 1988. Strong and Weak Justification. *Philosophical Perspectives* 2: 51–69.
Sosa, E. 1991. *Knowledge in Perspective*. New York: Cambridge University Press.
Sutton, J. 2005. Stick To What You Know. *Nous* 39: 359–396.
Dutant, J (ed). Forthcoming. *The New Evil Demon: New Essays on Knowledge, Justification. and Rationality*. Oxford: Oxford University Press.

24

PSYCHIC POWERS (CLAIRVOYANCE CASES)

Background: One of the simplest externalist theories of epistemic justification is what we might call "simple process reliabilism". Simple process reliabilism says that S's belief that p is justified if and only if the belief is produced by a reliable belief-forming process. The key point here is again (see The Unfortunate Twin pp. 120–124) that on this account S doesn't need to have any evidence or reasons at all in support of p in order to be justified in believing that p. All that matters is that S's belief is produced in the right way.

EPISTEMOLOGICAL ISSUES: EPISTEMIC JUSTIFICATION: EXTERNALISM VS. INTERNALISM; CLAIRVOYANCE CASES

Ms. Cleo is a mostly normal adult except for one big thing—she's psychic. That's right, she really has psychic powers. In particular, she is a reliable clairvoyant. Her faculty of clairvoyance tends to produce way more true beliefs than false beliefs. Ms. Cleo has no idea that she has this psychic power though. In other words, she doesn't believe that she's psychic, she has no memory of using this power in the past and being correct, and so on. Hence, she has no reason at all to think that she is psychic. However, unlike most everyone else, Ms. Cleo is also woefully uninformed about how unlikely it is for anyone to have psychic powers. As a result, Ms. Cleo doesn't have any reason to think that she, or anyone else, can't have psychic powers. Thus, Ms. Cleo has no reason one way or the other about her psychic powers. One day, a belief pops into her mind—"the current mayor of New York City is visiting Los Angeles right now". Ms. Cleo has no evidence whatsoever for or against this. Nonetheless, the belief is reliably produced—it is the output of her reliable clairvoyant faculty.

Why is this case important? It matters because intuitively Ms. Cleo shouldn't believe that the current mayor of New York City is visiting Los Angeles right now. It seems that her belief is entirely unreasonable. Yet, Ms. Cleo's belief is reliable. Consequently, this case illustrates a failure of simple reliabilism (or any reliabilist view that holds that reliability is sufficient for justification). Ms. Cleo has a belief that is reliable but unjustified.

RESPONSES

Most everyone (opponents and proponents of reliabilism) agrees that this sort of case shows that simple reliabilism fails. Opponents of reliabilism take this to be yet another reason to reject reliabilist theories in general. Proponents of reliabilism seek to block such cases as counting as justified without giving up on reliabilism completely.

One response that reliabilists make to this sort of problem proposes that reliabilism be supplemented with a condition that requires that one's belief not be defeated in order to be justified (Goldman 1986). Roughly, the way that this response handles cases like that of Ms. Cleo is to argue that although her belief is produced by a reliable belief-forming process, it is not justified because she has available to her other reliable belief-forming processes that if she were to have used them she wouldn't believe that the current mayor of New York City is visiting Los Angeles right now. For instance, if she were to use the belief-forming process that leads her to not believe things that simply pop into her mind, she wouldn't have a belief about the current mayor of New York City's whereabouts.

Another response argues that the problem here is that Ms. Cleo has no evidence for the belief about the mayor's location. So, this response insists that reliabilism should incorporate an evidentialist component (Comesaña 2010). The general idea is that justification for believing p is like evidentialists claim, a matter of having evidence in support of p, but like reliabilists claim justification requires reliability. This response maintains that whether something counts as evidence for p depends upon whether it is a reliable indicator that p is true, i.e. when someone has that item of evidence, most of the time p is true. On this response, Ms. Cleo fails to have justification because she lacks sufficient evidence where "evidence" is understood in reliabilist terms.

Yet another response involves arguing that although Ms. Cleo's belief is reliable, it is not formed in the correct way to count as justified. One way of developing this sort of response is to argue that only belief-forming processes that are sufficiently "primal" can justify simply by being reliable (Lyons 2009). The rough idea here is that the process must be "inferentially opaque" (i.e. the person cannot introspectively access the process leading to the belief) and the process has to develop as a result of learning and innate constraints. Another way of fleshing out this sort of response is to argue that in addition to reliability, a process must be "properly functioning" in order to yield justified beliefs (Bergmann 2006, Ghijsen 2016). The thinking here is that a belief-forming process must either be designed (e.g. by God) to produce true beliefs of a particular kind or it must be reliable because it has developed by way of natural selection to produce true beliefs of a particular kind in a particular environment. This response holds that Ms. Cleo's belief, though reliable, is not justified because it results from a process that does not properly function in the relevant sense.

Yet another response maintains that Ms. Cleo's belief, though reliable, isn't justified because it doesn't manifest her cognitive virtues (Breyer and Greco 2008). The idea here is that in order for a belief-forming process to yield justified beliefs, that process has to be integrated with the person's character as a cognitive agent. Since Ms. Cleo is oblivious to her psychic powers and has no recollection of being accurate about this sort of thing, her clairvoyance faculty isn't sufficiently part of her character as a cognitive agent to deliver justified beliefs.

RECOMMENDED READING

GENERAL OVERVIEWS

Internalist vs. Externalist Conceptions of Epistemic Justification. *Stanford Encyclopedia of Philosophy.* URL = https://plato.stanford.edu/entries/justep-intext/#toc

Internalism and Externalism in Epistemology. *Internet Encyclopedia of Philosophy.* URL = https://iep.utm.edu/int-ext/#SSH2c.i

SEMINAL PRESENTATION

BonJour, L. 1980. Externalist Theories of Empirical Knowledge. *Midwest Studies in Philosophy* 5: 53–73.

ADDITIONAL IMPORTANT DISCUSSIONS

Bergmann, M. 2006. *Justification without Awareness.* New York: Oxford University Press.

Breyer, D. and Greco, J. 2008. Cognitive Integration and the Ownership of Belief: Response to Bernecker. *Philosophy and Phenomenological Research* 76: 73–184.

Comesaña, J. 2010. Evidentialist Reliabilism. *Nous* 44: 571–600.

Ghijsen, H. 2016. Norman and Truetemp Revisited Reliabilistically: A Proper Functionalist Account of Clairvoyance. *Episteme* 13: 89–110.

Goldman, A. 1986. *Epistemology and Cognition.* Cambridge, MA: Harvard University Press.

Graham, P. 2012. Epistemic Entitlement. *Nous* 46: 449–482.

Lehrer, K. 1990. *Theory of Knowledge.* Boulder, CO: Westview Press.

Lyons, J. 2009. *Perception and Basic Beliefs: Modules, Zombies, and the Problem of the External World.* Oxford: Oxford University Press.

Moon, A. 2018. How To Use Cognitive Faculties You Never Knew You Had. *Philosophical Quarterly* 99: 251–275.

25

AVOCADOS ARE HEALTHY, BUT I FORGOT WHY (FORGOTTEN EVIDENCE)

Background: Recall that a prominent form of internalism, evidentialism, claims that what a person is justified in believing at any particular time depends upon the evidence that the person has at that time (General Background: The Nature of Justification pp. 113–119). The idea that one's justification is dependent upon evidence or reasons that one has at a particular time isn't simply a feature of evidentialism though. This is a widespread commitment of most forms of internalism. And, some forms of externalism are committed to this claim as well. After all, there are some forms of externalism that require that one have evidence in order to have justification (see the responses section of Psychic Powers pp. 125–128). On all of these views of justification, it seems that if one doesn't have evidence for believing that p at a particular time, then if S believes that p at that time, the belief is unjustified.

EPISTEMOLOGICAL ISSUES: EPISTEMIC JUSTIFICATION: EXTERNALISM VS. INTERNALISM; FORGOTTEN EVIDENCE

We're going to consider two people: Belle and Bill. Let's start with Belle. Belle is a very careful person. She only trusts sources of information that she knows to be reliable, she doesn't believe things simply because she wants them to be true, and so on. That said, she is just like all of us. She's not infallible; sometimes she makes mistakes and sometimes she forgets things. Several months ago, Belle researched the health benefits of eating avocados. As per usual, Belle only consulted reliable sources of information when she learned that avocados have good fats, dietary fiber, and several vitamins. So, when Belle formed her belief that avocados are a healthy food to eat, she did so on the basis of good evidence. As a result, Belle formed a justified belief that avocados are a healthy food to eat. Now, several months later, Belle still believes that avocados are a healthy food to eat. However, she doesn't remember how she came to form this belief. That is to say, Belle has forgotten all of her evidence for this belief, but she still believes that avocados are a healthy food to eat.

Bill tends to be less careful about what he believes. At least sometimes Bill believes things without sufficiently good evidence. Several months ago, Bill formed the belief that avocados are a healthy food to eat. His evidence for this? The fact that he thinks avocados taste good. That's it. Bill didn't do any research into the health benefits of avocados, he didn't ask anyone who might know about this, etc. Bill simply formed the belief that avocados are healthy because he likes them. Clearly, Bill's belief that avocados are healthy wasn't justified. Now, however, many months later Bill has forgotten all about how he came to have the belief that avocados are healthy. Nevertheless, Bill still believes that avocados are a healthy food to eat.

We can easily see that Belle and Bill formed their beliefs very differently. Belle had good evidence for her belief and Bill didn't for his. So when they each initially formed their beliefs, Belle's was justified and Bill's was unjustified. But what are we to say about Belle's and Bill's beliefs now when they each bring this belief to mind? Now they have both forgotten their evidence for their beliefs. Nevertheless, it seems intuitive that Belle's belief is still justified (what we should say about Bill's belief is a bit less clear). After all, there are many things that we know that we have forgotten our original evidence for believing. Consider, you likely believe that George Washington was the first President of the United States; however, there's a very good chance that you don't remember learning this or the evidence you had for initially believing it. Nonetheless, you are justified (in fact, you know) that George Washington was the first President of the United States. Thus, it seems that at least some beliefs, such as yours about Washington and Belle's about avocados, are justified, even though the initial evidence in support of them has been forgotten. But how can this fact be squared with evidentialism or internalism more generally?

RESPONSES

Some internalists attempt to respond to these sorts of cases by claiming that one's present mental states are not what matter for determining justification; instead, what matters is the evidence that one had when originally forming a belief (Huemer 1999). If the belief is justified when initially formed, then it will be justified later (assuming that one hasn't gained new evidence that undermines the belief). And, if the belief is unjustified when initially formed, it will be unjustified later (assuming that the person hasn't gained new evidence in support of the belief). This sort of response appears to yield intuitive results. There is perhaps a problem though. It seems that this sort of response might fit the letter of internalism, but it doesn't seem to be in the right spirit. Many think that it runs counter to internalism to make justification depend upon things that are outside of the person's current mental states.

A different sort of internalist response is to accept a version of coherentism (Poston 2014). Coherentism is roughly the view that a belief is justified when it coheres sufficiently well with one's other beliefs. So, coherentists would say of Belle that her belief is justified now because, although she has forgotten her initial evidence for this belief, she has lots of evidence in terms of how well the belief coheres with other things she believes (such as that she wouldn't form a belief for no reason; that fruits and vegetables tend to be healthy; etc.). When it comes to Bill's belief, what coherentism says will depend upon further details concerning Bill's other beliefs. So, it may turn out on this response that Bill's belief is justified too. It will all come down to how well his belief about avocados coheres with the rest of his beliefs.

A different sort of internalist response says that beliefs in cases of forgotten evidence can be justified by a seeming to recollect (Conee and Feldman 2001, 2011, McCain 2015). The idea here is that Belle's belief about avocados is justified now because when the belief comes to her mind, it seems to her that she is remembering this as something that is true or even something that she knows to be true rather than something that is just coming to her mind. According to this response, there is something importantly different about the phenomenology of seeming to remember something and the phenomenology of simply considering something or forming a belief for the first time. It may be that the same is true of Bill when his belief about avocados comes to mind, so this response allows that Bill's belief might be justified as well.

A final sort of response is to adopt what is called "epistemic conservatism" (McGrath 2007, Smithies 2019). Epistemic conservatism is the idea that having a belief confers some positive epistemic status on the content of the belief. More simply put, epistemic conservatism holds that beliefs are innocent until proven guilty. So when it comes to Belle's belief now, epistemic conservatism says that her belief is justified until she has reasons to think it isn't true or was in fact unreliably formed. The same is true of Bill's belief now according to epistemic conservatism.

RECOMMENDED READING

GENERAL OVERVIEWS

Memory. *Stanford Encyclopedia of Philosophy*. URL = https://plato.stanford.edu/entries/memory/

Epistemology of Memory. *Internet Encyclopedia of Philosophy*. URL = https://iep.utm.edu/epis-mem/#SSH3ai

SEMINAL PRESENTATION

Harman, G. 1986. *Change in View*. Cambridge, MA: MIT Press.

ADDITIONAL IMPORTANT DISCUSSIONS

Conee, E. and Feldman, R. 2001. Internalism Defended. *American Philosophical Quarterly* 38: 1–18.

Conee, E. and Feldman, R. 2011. Replies. In T. Dougherty (ed), *Evidentialism and Its Discontents*. New York: Oxford University Press, 428–501.

Goldman, A. 1999. Internalism Exposed. *Journal of Philosophy* 96: 271–293.

Goldman, A. 2011. Toward a Synthesis of Reliabilism and Evidentialism? Or: Evidentialism's Troubles, Reliabilism's Rescue Package. In T. Dougherty (ed), *Evidentialism and Its Discontents*. New York: Oxford University Press, 393–426.

Huemer, M. 1999. The Problem of Memory Knowledge. *Pacific Philosophical Quarterly* 80: 346–357.

McCain, K. 2015. Is Forgotten Evidence A Problem for Evidentialism? *Southern Journal of Philosophy* 53: 471–480.

McGrath, M. 2007. Memory and Epistemic Conservatism. *Synthese* 157: 1–24.

Poston, T. 2014. *Reason and Explanation: A Defense of Explanatory Coherentism*. New York: Palgrave Macmillan.

Smithies, D. 2019. *The Epistemic Role of Consciousness*. Oxford: Oxford University Press.

26

THE SLEEPY STUDENT (PROBLEM OF STORED BELIEFS)

Background: There are three important distinctions when it comes to beliefs that it can be helpful to make clear. First, there are what are often called "occurrent beliefs". These are beliefs that are present before your consciousness, i.e. you're thinking about them right now. For instance, think about your belief that Canada is north of the United States. Right now, the belief "Canada is north of the United States" is occurrent for you. Second, there are "dispositional beliefs". These are beliefs that you have stored in memory. For instance, before you started consciously thinking about the fact that Canada is north of the United States, it's plausible that you already believed it. This belief was stored in your memory, and in fact it still is. Any belief that you have in memory is dispositional. Some of them are occurrent, such as your belief that Canada is north of the United States, when you are thinking about them, and others are dispositional but non-occurrent (they are stored in memory, but you aren't currently thinking about them). The third distinction isn't really a kind of belief, but it is definitely related to beliefs. It is the "disposition to believe" something. For example, right now (prior to looking) you have a disposition to believe that there is a car parked outside. You don't currently believe this, but were you to look out the window (and see a car, of course) you would form the belief. So, you are disposed to believe this given the right stimulus.

EPISTEMOLOGICAL ISSUES: EPISTEMIC JUSTIFICATION: EXTERNALISM VS. INTERNALISM; STORED BELIEFS

Kai is a good student. He is naturally curious, does his work, he pays attention in class, and he carefully thinks about things that his philosophy professor tells him. However, Kai is also very tired many days because he spends so much time staying up late thinking about philosophy. One day, the professor presents the class (including Kai) a logical principle L. She doesn't tell them whether the principle is true or not, but instead she asks them to reflect upon it to see if it is knowable *a priori* (i.e. by reflection alone). Kai has never thought of this principle before, but he dutifully sets to thinking long and hard about the principle and whether it is true. After several minutes of focused attention on L, it strikes Kai that the principle seems clearly true. As a result of this intellectual seeming (what we might call an "intuition"), Kai believes that L is true. For the sake of simplicity, let's assume that such an intellectual seeming is sufficiently good evidence to justify Kai in believing that L is true, and let's assume that L is true and Kai is not in some sort of strange Gettier-style situation. So, Kai justifiedly believes that L, in fact he knows it. He tells his professor that L is true and how he can see that it is so. Unfortunately, before he can receive the praise he rightly deserves, he falls into a deep sleep. The hard work that Kai put in to thinking about L coupled with his exhaustion from another long night philosophizing was just too much for him. His sleep is so deep that he is not even dreaming. While Kai is asleep, his professor tells another professor (pointing at the sleeping Kai), "he knows that L is true."

It seems pretty intuitive that the professor speaks truly when she says of Kai that he knows L while he's sleeping. However, it's not clear what evidence Kai has for his belief that L in this case. If Kai really does know L while in a dreamless sleep and he doesn't have evidence for L while in this state, then evidentialism and other theories that require evidence for justification are in deep trouble. After all, such theories claim that one cannot have justification or knowledge that p unless one's evidence provides sufficiently strong support for believing that p.

RESPONSES

Although this case is importantly different from a case of forgotten evidence (see *Avocados Are Healthy, But I Forgot Why* pp. 129–133), the two are similar in that they arise from the consideration of the role that memory plays in justification. In light of their similarities, it is not surprising that some of the responses that are used to respond to the problem of forgotten evidence are often appealed to as a way to handle this sort of case as well. For example, some respond to this sort of case by insisting that it's not one's present evidence that matters for determining justification, instead what matters is the evidence that one had when originally forming a belief (Huemer 1999). If the belief is justified when initially formed, then it will be justified later (assuming that one hasn't gained new evidence that undermines the belief). So, on this response one might claim that the reason Kai knows (and so, has a justified belief) now is that he had good evidence for believing L when he formed the belief and he obviously hasn't gained any defeating evidence while in a dreamless sleep.

Another response to forgotten evidence that may be appealed to here is that of coherentism (Poston 2014). Recall that coherentism is the view that a particular belief is justified just in case it coheres sufficiently well with one's other beliefs. A coherentist might say that Kai's belief that L is justified when he forms it because the belief coheres sufficiently well with his other beliefs. Additionally, the coherentist could insist that while Kai dreamlessly sleeps, the coherence among his beliefs isn't affected, i.e. they cohere just as well as they did when he was awake. Hence, the coherentist may be able to respond by claiming that Kai's belief remains justified while he sleeps because of its coherence.

Yet another response to forgotten evidence that may be applicable to the problem of stored beliefs is epistemic conservatism (McGrath 2007, Smithies 2019). Since epistemic conservatism says that having a belief confers some positive epistemic status on the content of the belief, one might appeal to it in order to say that all that matters for Kai's belief that L to be justified while he sleeps is that he has the belief.

An additional response here is similar to, but importantly different from, yet another response to the problem of forgotten evidence. Some respond to the problem of forgotten evidence by claiming that the belief in question seems to the person to be something that they remember (Conee and Feldman 2011, McCain 2014). A similar move might apply here. One might argue that the reason that Kai's belief that L is justified is because he has a disposition to recall L as something he remembers. A somewhat related response is to argue that just as we can distinguish between occurrent and dispositional beliefs, we can distinguish between occurrent and dispositional evidence (Piazza 2009). This response then claims that insofar as it is reasonable to accept that Kai's dispositional belief that L is justified while he dreamlessly sleeps, it is equally reasonable to assume that he has dispositional evidence in support of his belief.

A final sort of response involves arguing that there are in fact no stored beliefs at all (Frise 2018). This somewhat radical response argues that the cognitive science of memory teaches us that memory simply doesn't function in the way that is necessary for it to be true that there really are stored beliefs rather than simply dispositions to believe. Hence, on this response there is no problem here because Kai doesn't actually believe that L while he is asleep.

RECOMMENDED READING

GENERAL OVERVIEWS

Memory. *Stanford Encyclopedia of Philosophy.* URL = https://plato.stanford.edu/entries/memory/
Epistemology of Memory. *Internet Encyclopedia of Philosophy.* URL = https://iep.utm.edu/epis-mem/#SSH3ai

SEMINAL PRESENTATIONS

Pappas, G. 1980. Lost Justification. *Midwest Studies in Philosophy* 5: 127–134.
Moon, A. 2012. Knowing without Evidence. *Mind* 121: 309–331.

ADDITIONAL IMPORTANT DISCUSSIONS

Audi, R. 1994. Dispositional Belief and Dispositions to Believe. *Noûs* 28: 419–434.
Conee, E. and Feldman, R. 2011. Replies. In T. Dougherty (ed), *Evidentialism and Its Discontents.* New York: Oxford University Press, 428–501.
Goldman, A. 2011. Toward a Synthesis of Reliabilism and Evidentialism? Or: Evidentialism's Troubles, Reliabilism's Rescue Package. In T. Dougherty (ed), *Evidentialism and Its Discontents.* New York: Oxford University Press, 393–426.

Frise, M. 2018. Eliminating the Problem of Stored Beliefs. *American Philosophical Quarterly* 55: 63–79.

Huemer, M. 1999. The Problem of Memory Knowledge. *Pacific Philosophical Quarterly* 80: 346–357.

McCain, K. 2014. *Evidentialism and Epistemic Justification*. New York: Routledge.

McGrath, M. 2007. Memory and Epistemic Conservatism. *Synthese* 157: 1–24.

Piazza, T. 2009. Evidentialism and the Problem of Stored Beliefs. *Philosophical Studies* 145: 311–324.

Poston, T. 2014. *Reason and Explanation: A Defense of Explanatory Coherentism*. New York: Palgrave Macmillan.

Smithies, D. 2019. *The Epistemic Role of Consciousness*. Oxford: Oxford University Press.

27

A VISITOR FROM THE SWAMP (SWAMPMAN OBJECTION TO PROPER FUNCTIONALISM)

Background: Proper functionalism is a specific externalist theory that, as we've seen (see Psychic Powers pp. 125–128), some appeal to in order to avoid problems facing simple reliabilist views. Although the view is most famously formulated as a theory of "warrant" (this term is used to stand for whatever turns true belief into knowledge, i.e. it encompasses both justification and the condition required to solve the Gettier Problem), versions of proper functionalism have been generated for various epistemic goods such as justification, epistemic probability, and so on. Here we will focus on the "warrant" formulation because it is central to proper functionalism and because it is close enough to justification to fit with this section of the book. According to proper functionalism, S's belief that p is warranted when and only when: (1) S's belief that p is produced by a properly functioning cognitive faculty, (2) the cognitive faculty that produces S's belief is aimed at truth, (3) S forms the belief that p in the sort of environment for which the relevant cognitive faculty was designed, and (4) the design plan of the cognitive faculty is reliable (in the appropriate environment, it is highly probable that beliefs formed by the proper functioning of that cognitive faculty are true). A key question about proper functionalism is: what exactly is a "design plan"? One prominent way of understanding proper functionalism takes the idea of a design plan literally—God is the creator and designer of one's cognitive faculties. God designed one's cognitive faculties to function properly in certain environments. The other prominent way of understanding proper functionalism takes the idea of a design plan less literally. On this way of construing proper functionalism, the design plan of a cognitive faculty concerns how the faculty has developed to function over the course of generations of that sort of creature via the process of natural selection. That said, the end result for both versions of proper functionalism is the same—to have warrant, it is necessary that one's belief be formed by a cognitive faculty that is functioning according to its design plan in the appropriate environment.

EPISTEMOLOGICAL ISSUES: EPISTEMIC JUSTIFICATION: EXTERNALISM VS. INTERNALISM; PROPER FUNCTIONALISM; SWAMPMAN

One beautiful spring day, Al is out for a stroll. Thoroughly enjoying himself he continues to walk until he finds himself at the edge of a swamp. It's early afternoon and a pleasant sunny day, so Al stands by the swamp for a while and enjoys gazing at the trees, watching some birds flying around, and hearing the occasional flop of a fish in the water. While Al is standing there enjoying the scenery, the swamp is struck by a bolt of lightning! Luckily, Al is far enough away to not be injured in any way. "Wow!" he thinks, "I've always heard of instances where lightning strikes on a clear day, but this is the first time I've seen it happen." Not seeing storm clouds or any other signs that there may be more lightning, he decides to continue to enjoy the view. He is so caught up in gazing over the swamp that he doesn't notice the person who is standing a few feet from him also gazing at the swamp. This person is Sal. Sal is a molecule for molecule duplicate of Al. Somehow Sal was created when the lightning struck the swamp.

Since Sal is a molecule for molecule duplicate of Al, he looks like Al, talks like Al, walks like Al, and thinks like Al. In fact, Sal has all of the same beliefs as Al, and he reasons exactly the same way as Al. Right now, Al believes that there is a bird flying not far from where he is because he sees it. Sal also believes that there is a bird flying not far from where he is standing because, like Al, he sees it. Clearly, Al's belief that there's a bird flying is warranted. After all, he is a normal adult with good vision looking at a bird that is nearby in good viewing conditions and there's no strange Gettier-case generating things happening. Proper functionalism agrees with this assessment because Al's faculty of vision is properly functioning, in this case in an environment (good viewing conditions) for which it was designed. What about Sal though? Intuitively, Sal's belief that there is a bird flying nearby is also warranted. Sal is looking at the same bird with just as clear a view as Al. Sal's vision works exactly as well as Al's, after all he's Al's exact molecule for molecule duplicate! Here, it seems that proper functionalism faces a problem. Sal was created just moments ago by a random lightning strike. Consequently, Sal's cognitive faculties don't have a design plan—they were neither designed by a conscious designer nor by the process of natural selection. Since Sal's cognitive faculties lack a design plan, his belief cannot satisfy proper functionalism's requirements for warrant. Hence, proper functionalism is committed to Sal's belief being unwarranted. But, intuitively, Sal's belief is warranted. After all, how could Al's belief be warranted and yet Sal, who is a molecule for molecule duplicate of him, not be warranted in holding the same belief when looking at the same thing under the same conditions?

RESPONSES

As we know, examples don't have to be realistic in order to be effective when it comes to evaluating epistemological theories, but they do have to be possible. Some have responded to this sort of case by arguing that it isn't actually possible (Graham 2012). The thought here is that if there were a creature such as Sal he wouldn't actually have beliefs at all because he would lack the representational content to form them (this is what the earliest form of a swampman example was thought to show in philosophy of mind).

Another response is to allow that the example is possible but insist that perhaps there are other ways for a cognitive faculty to meet the design requirement aside from intentional design or the process of natural selection (Plantinga 1991, Graham 2014). Thus, this response is an attempt for proper functionalism to yield the intuitive result that Sal's belief is warranted just like Al's by claiming that his faculties count as functioning properly for some reason or other despite lacking design.

A different response also allows that this sort of case is possible; but rather than trying to present a way that proper functionalism can allow that Sal's belief is warranted, it involves arguing that we actually have good reason to think it isn't warranted (Boyce and Plantinga 2012). The general idea here is that given the way that Sal was created, in an important sense, Sal's belief is correct as a matter of luck. Hence, this response claims that Sal's belief really isn't warranted because he, unlike Al, is in a situation analogous to Gettier cases.

A final sort of response seeks to attack the intuition that we rely upon in judging that Sal's belief is warranted (Boyce and Moon 2016). Roughly, this response insists that the reason that we tend to think that Sal's belief is warranted is that we are relying on an intuition that says that if two subjects hold the same belief and they came to hold it in the same way in relevantly similar environments, then if one is warranted so is the other. This response argues that although this intuition seems plausible, there are a number of examples that illustrate that it is false. Once it is shown that this intuition is false, we no longer have good reason to think that Sal's belief is warranted.

RECOMMENDED READING

GENERAL OVERVIEWS

Proper Functionalism. *Internet Encyclopedia of Philosophy*. URL = https://iep. utm.edu/prop-fun/#:~:text='Proper%20Functionalism'%20refers%20to%20a, item%20of%20knowledge%2C%20or%20a

Boyce, K. and Plantinga, A. 2012. Proper Functionalism. In A. Cullison (ed), *The Continuum Companion to Epistemology*. New York: Continuum Press, 124–140.

SEMINAL PRESENTATIONS

Millikan, R. 1984. Naturalist Reflections on Knowledge. *Pacific Philosophical Quarterly* 4: 315–334.

Plantinga, A. 1993. *Warrant and Proper Function*. Oxford: Oxford University Press.

ADDITIONAL IMPORTANT DISCUSSIONS

Bergmann, M. 2006. *Justification without Awareness: A Defense of Epistemic Externalism*. New York: Oxford University Press.

Boyce, K. and Moon, A. 2016. In Defense of Proper Functionalism: Cognitive Science Takes on Swampman. *Synthese* 193: 2897–3001.

Feldman, R. 1993. Proper Functionalism. *Nous* 27: 34–50.

Graham, P. 2012. Epistemic Entitlement. *Nous* 46: 449–482.

Graham, P. 2014. Warrant, Functions, History. In A. Fairweather and O. Flanagan (eds), *Naturalizing Epistemic Virtue*. Cambridge: Cambridge University Press, 15–35.

Plantinga, A. 1991. Warrant and Designing Agents: A Reply to James Taylor. *Philosophical Studies* 64: 203–215.

Sosa, E. 1993. Proper Functionalism and Virtue Epistemology. *Nous* 27: 51–65.

Taylor, J. 1991. Plantinga's Proper Functioning Analysis of Epistemic Warrant. *Philosophical Studies* 64: 185–202.

MISSING THE SHOW
(UNPOSSESSED EVIDENCE)

Background: Recall from General Background: The Nature of Justifica-
tion (pp. 113–119) that evidentialism, a prominent internalist theory of
justification, claims that justification is a matter of the evidence that one
has. Importantly, evidentialism claims that S's justification with respect to
any proposition supervenes upon the evidence that she has at that time.
(When X supervenes upon Y that means that there cannot be differences in
X without differences in Y.) So, according to evidentialism whether or not
S is justified in believing that p at a particular time is determined by the
evidence that S has at that time. Evidence that S once had but has now for-
gotten makes no difference to what S is justified in believing now. Similarly,
evidence that S doesn't have yet, but will come to possess, doesn't make a
difference to what S is justified in believing now. Simply put, evidentialism
says that evidence is all that matters when it comes to justification, and the
only evidence that matters is the evidence one has right now.

EPISTEMOLOGICAL ISSUES: EPISTEMIC
JUSTIFICATION: EXTERNALISM VS.
INTERNALISM; UNPOSSESSED EVIDENCE

Andrea and Rich are planning to see a show later tonight. They are
currently trying to decide whether they should get on the waitlist at

a particular restaurant because they have been told it's a fairly long wait. Given the wait time and how long it will take them to finish the meal, they wouldn't be able to make it to the venue for the show until 8:30pm. They both really want to see the show and would hate to miss any of it. Andrea asks Rich, "Do you think we have enough time to eat here and still make it to the show?" Rich responds, "We'll be fine. I checked the showtime earlier today, and it doesn't start until 9pm." Since they both know that the showtimes at this venue almost never change and dinner wouldn't interfere with a 9pm start time, they decide to get on the waitlist and enjoy a meal at the restaurant.

Later, Andrea and Rich arrive at the venue. They make it at 8:45pm because they decided to have dessert, since they'd still have plenty of time to make it to the show before 9pm. When they arrive, they are informed that they can't go in because the show is in progress—it started at 7pm! When they complain that the show wasn't supposed to start until 9pm, they are informed that it had to be moved to 7pm to allow for a different show to run afterward. The person at the ticket booth tells them that they not only posted this change on their website, but they also emailed and messaged ticket holders. When Rich looks at his phone, sure enough, there's both a text and an email from the venue informing him that the show would start at 7pm instead of 9pm. On their way home, Andrea says:

> Why didn't you check your phone at the restaurant? You didn't know they sent emails or messages, but you could have at least checked the website. If you would've checked, we wouldn't have eaten there, and we would have made it to the show.

In this case, Rich had good evidence for believing that the show would start at 9pm; so evidentialism says that his belief was justified. Nevertheless, had he simply looked at the phone in his pocket he would have had additional evidence that would have not only made believing that the show starts at 9pm unjustified, it would have justified believing that it starts at 7pm. It seems that Andrea's criticism of Rich for not checking his phone is appropriate. However, evidentialism says that there is nothing epistemically wrong with Rich's belief. But, if that is true, how can it be that Andrea's criticism is appropriate?

RESPONSES

One response to this sort of case is to claim that Andrea's criticism is appropriate because Rich's belief wasn't justified. The thought here is that contrary to evidentialism, evidence that one doesn't currently possess but should have possessed affects whether or not one is justified. Since Rich could have easily checked and should have done so, the evidence that he could have had (but didn't) makes it so that his belief that the show starts at 9pm wasn't justified. Often this response is put forward by critics of evidentialism as a reason to look to other theories for the truth about justification. However, some evidentialists have proposed that while the judgment about this case is correct, it doesn't mean that evidentialism is false. Hence, a version of this response suggests that evidentialism should really be understood as saying that justification depends upon the evidence that S has *and* on S's gathering that evidence in a responsible way (Cloos 2015). Given this version of evidentialism, Rich's belief that the show starts at 9pm wouldn't count as justified. The reason for this is that although his evidence prior to arriving at the venue supported believing that the show starts at 9pm, his evidence gathering wasn't conducted responsibly.

A similar response insists that there are two senses of justification. There is what we normally call "justification", which this response claims is necessary for knowledge and accurately described by evidentialism, and there is "robust justification" (Matheson 2020). Robust justification requires that one's evidence gathering be responsible in addition to the requirement that the evidence support believing the proposition in question. According to this response, cases like that of Andrea and Rich don't show that evidentialism is false, but instead reveal that there is another sort of justification—the robust kind—that isn't necessary for knowledge yet still important.

A further response put forward by a number of evidentialists claims that while it is correct that Andrea's criticism is appropriate, it isn't because of any lack of justification on Rich's part (Conee and Feldman 2011, McCain 2014, Stapleford and McCain 2020). The idea here is that evidentialism is correct in maintaining that Rich's justification for believing that the show starts at a particular time depends solely upon the evidence that he has, i.e. it doesn't matter that he could easily have had additional evidence. All that matters is that Rich has evidence that supports believing that the show starts at 9pm. That said, this response goes on to claim that Rich can still be criticized for being a poor epistemic agent. He would be much better off as an epistemic agent were he to gather evidence that is readily at hand in such situations. Nonetheless, this response contends that Rich's general failings as an epistemic agent do not bear on what he has justification to believe at any particular time.

RECOMMENDED READING

SEMINAL PRESENTATIONS

DeRose, K. 2000. Ought We To Follow Our Evidence? *Philosophy and Phenomenological Research* 60: 697–706.

Kornblith, H. 1983. Justified Belief and Epistemically Responsible Action. *Philosophical Review* 92: 33–48.

ADDITIONAL IMPORTANT DISCUSSIONS

Baehr, J. 2011. *The Inquiring Mind: On Intellectual Virtues and Virtue Epistemology.* Oxford: Oxford University Press.

Ballantyne, N. 2015. The Significance of Unpossessed Evidence. *Philosophical Quarterly* 63: 315–335.

Cloos, C. 2015. Responsibilist Evidentialism. *Philosophical Studies* 172: 2999–3016.

Conee, E. and Feldman, R. 2011. Replies. In T. Dougherty (ed), *Evidentialism and Its Discontents.* New York: Oxford University Press, 428–501.

Feldman, R. 2000. The Ethics of Belief. *Philosophy and Phenomenological Research* 60: 667–695.

Feldman, R. 2003. *Epistemology.* Upper Saddle River, NJ: Prentice Hall.

Matheson, J. 2020. Robust Justification. In K. McCain and S. Stapleford (eds), *Epistemic Duties: New Arguments, New Angles.* New York: Routledge, 146–160.

McCain, K. 2014. *Evidentialism and Epistemic Justification.* New York: Routledge.

Miracchi, L. 2019. When Evidence Isn't Enough: Suspension, Evidentialism, and Knowledge-first Virtue Epistemology. *Episteme* 16: 413–437.

Stapleford, S. and McCain, K. 2020. Bound by the Evidence. In K. McCain and S. Stapleford (eds), *Epistemic Duties: New Arguments, New Angles.* New York: Routledge, 113–124.

29

A PAIR OF HENS
(SPECKLED HEN PROBLEM)

Background: It will be helpful here to distinguish between two forms of foundationalism. The first is what is often called "classical foundationalism" because it places the sort of very stringent requirements on basic beliefs that Descartes proposed. The second is often referred to as "moderate foundationalism" because its requirements on basic beliefs are more moderate. A prominent version of classical foundationalism (others are similar) says that in order to have non-inferential (i.e. not based upon other beliefs) justification for believing that p, three conditions must be satisfied: (1) S must be directly acquainted with the thought that p, (2) S must be directly acquainted with a truthmaker for p (the feature of the world that makes p true), and (3) S must be directly acquainted with the correspondence between the thought that p and the truthmaker for p. What exactly is direct acquaintance? It's very difficult to spell it out precisely, so classical foundationalists tend to explain it by way of examples. Consider a situation where you are in severe pain. The relationship that you bear to your sensation of pain is one of direct acquaintance. As might be guessed from the stringent nature of these requirements, classical foundationalists hold that you can't have non-inferentially justified beliefs about the world around you. You can only have non-inferentially justified beliefs about the contents of your own mind (and perhaps some truths of logic). Classical foundationalism is one of the most extreme forms of internalism. By contrast, moderate foundationalism, which comes in both internalist and externalist varieties, is much less stringent when it comes to the requirements for non-inferential justification. Many forms of moderate foundationalism allow, for instance, that if one has an experience as of p, then one has non-inferential justification for believing p.

EPISTEMOLOGICAL ISSUES: EPISTEMIC JUSTIFICATION: EXTERNALISM VS. INTERNALISM; SPECKLED HEN PROBLEM

Gilbert has decided that he would like to have a chicken for a pet. So, Gilbert is looking at some hens in a pen. He sees two hens in good lighting and from a pretty close distance. Both hens have white feathers with black speckles. One of them has just a few speckles, but the other has many. But oddly enough, in both cases all of the hen's speckles are on one side of its body. So when Gilbert looks, he sees all of the speckles on each hen. The first hen has exactly three speckles and the second has exactly 48 speckles. Gilbert, however, hasn't taken the time to count the speckles on either of the hens.

This case sounds rather mundane and uninteresting. And yet, it poses a widely discussed challenge for classical foundationalism. Additionally, the challenge has been argued to apply to moderate forms of foundationalism as well. What's the problem? Well, it seems that Gilbert's visual experience presents him with the image of a three-speckled hen when he looks at the first hen and with a 48-speckled hen when he looks at the second. However intuitively, when it comes to what Gilbert is justified in believing, it seems that while he is justified in believing that it looks like the first hen has three speckles, he isn't justified in believing that it looks like the other hen has 48 speckles. But how can the classical foundationalist account for this difference? Similarly, it seems that Gilbert is justified in believing that the first hen has three speckles but not that the other has 48 speckles. How can the moderate foundationalist account for this difference?

RESPONSES

As we noted, the speckled hen problem is most widely posed as a problem for classical foundationalism. Consequently, it isn't surprising that some respond to it by arguing that it shows that classical foundationalism is mistaken. In particular, externalist versions of moderate foundationalism appear to have an easy time with this sort of case. Why is Gilbert justified in believing that the hen with three speckles has three speckles but not that the other hen has 48 speckles? Externalists claim that the answer is that Gilbert is reliable when it comes to forming beliefs about three speckles when looking and not reliable when it comes to similar beliefs about 48 speckles. That said, internalists (both classical foundationalists and moderate foundationalists) have put forward a number of responses to the problem that don't appeal to reliability.

One response claims that the difference when it comes to Gilbert's justification in this case results from the fact that he has a phenomenal concept of looking three-speckled but lacks such a concept when it comes to looking 48-speckled (see *Mary Sees an Apple* pp. 109–112 for more on phenomenal concepts) (BonJour and Sosa 2003). This is why it is correct to say that Gilbert can recognize the three-speckled hen as having three speckles but can't recognize the 48-speckled hen as having 48 speckles.

Another sort of response involves arguing that one can be directly acquainted with a determinable property without being directly acquainted with the underlying determinate property (Fumerton 2009). "Red" is an example of a determinable property, whereas "crimson" is an example of a determinate property. So, for example, a shirt has the determinable property of being red because it has the determinate property of being a particular shade of red—crimson. In the case of the hens, the idea is that Gilbert might be directly acquainted with the second hen being many speckled without being directly acquainted with its being 48-speckled. This lack of acquaintance with the hen being 48-speckled explains why Gilbert isn't justified in believing that the hen looks 48-speckled.

Alternatively, a different response says that Gilbert is directly acquainted with the hen looking 48-speckled, but insists that he isn't directly acquainted with the correspondence between the hen looking this way and the thought that the hen is 48-speckled (Fumerton 2009). Again, on the classical foundationalist picture, this would mean that Gilbert isn't justified in believing that the hen looks to be 48-speckled.

When it comes to moderate foundationalism, one response is to insist that in order to have justification of this sort, one has to be justified in believing that 48-speckled hens look a certain way, but Gilbert isn't justified in this looks proposition (McGrath 2018). The general idea here is that in order to be justified in believing that something is an F, based on a visual experience, one has to be justified in believing that Fs look like *this*—without justification for this looks proposition, one can't have justification for thinking that something is an F just because one has a particular visual experience.

Yet another response involves distinguishing between seemings and sensations (Tucker 2010). Roughly, on this response, seemings are experiences that present a particular content as true, and sensations are more like mental pictures. A way to get a handle on this distinction, at least according to proponents of this response, is by thinking about the psychological phenomenon of associative agnosia. People suffering from associative agnosia cannot recognize familiar objects by sight, though they seem to remember them (i.e. they know what pencils are in general, for example, but can't recognize one when they see it). What's more, although such individuals cannot recognize a pencil, for instance, when they are looking at one, they can accurately draw the pencil that they see. Reflecting on this phenomenon leads some to insist that what is going on is that the person has visual sensations of the pencil (they see what it looks like), but they lack the normally associated seeming (it doesn't seem to them that the object is a pencil). This response contends that it is seemings—not sensations—that provide justification. Applied to the speckled hens, this response claims that when it comes to the first hen, Gilbert has both sensations of its three speckles and the seeming that the hen is three-speckled; so he is justified in believing that the hen has three speckles. When it comes to the 48-speckled hen, Gilbert has the sensations of it, but he lacks the seeming that the hen is 48-speckled. And so Gilbert isn't justified in believing that the hen has 48 speckles.

A final sort of response claims that Gilbert experiences each speckle of the 48-speckled hen without experiencing the hen *as* 48-speckled (Chudnoff and DiDomenico 2015). The thought here is that Gilbert's experience represents that $speckle_1$, that $speckle_2$, that $speckle_3$, and so on, but it doesn't represent that there are 48 speckles. So, Gilbert isn't justified in believing that the hen has 48 speckles. However, in the case of the hen with three speckles, Gilbert's experience represents the individual speckles, and it represents that the hen is three-speckled.

RECOMMENDED READING

SEMINAL PRESENTATIONS

Ayer, A.J. 1940. *The Foundations of Empirical Knowledge*. London: Macmillan.
Chisholm, R. 1942. The Problem of the Speckled Hen. *Mind* 51: 368–373.

ADDITIONAL IMPORTANT DISCUSSIONS

BonJour, L. and Sosa, E. 2003. *Epistemic Justification: Internalism vs. Externalism, Foundations vs. Virtues*. Malden, MA: Blackwell Publishing.

Chudnoff, E. and DiDomenico, D. 2015. The Epistemic Unity of Perception. *Pacific Philosophical Quarterly* 96: 535–549.

Feldman, R. 2004. The Justification of Introspective Belief. In E. Conee and R. Feldman, *Evidentialism*. New York: Oxford University Press, 199–218.

Fumerton, R. 1995. *Metaepistemology and Skepticism*. Lanham, MD: Rowman & Littlefield.

Fumerton, R. 2009. Markie, Speckles, and Classical Foundationalism. *Philosophy and Phenomenological Research* 79: 207–212.

Markie, P. 2009. Classical Foundationalism and Speckled Hens. *Philosophy and Phenomenological Research* 79: 190–206.

McGrath, M. 2018. Looks and Perceptual Justification. *Philosophy and Phenomenological Research* 96: 110–133.

Pace, M. 2017. Experiences, Seemings, and Perceptual Justification. *Australasian Journal of Philosophy* 95: 226–241.

Poston, T. 2007. Acquaintance and the Problem of the Speckled Hen. *Philosophical Studies* 132: 331–346.

Tucker, C. 2010. Why Open-Minded People Should Endorse Dogmatism. *Philosophical Perspectives* 24: 529–545.

30

BIRDWATCHING (PROBLEM OF BACKGROUND BELIEFS; EXPERT/NOVICE)

Background: A particular form of moderate foundationalism that has become increasingly popular is what is known as "phenomenal conservatism". Phenomenal conservatism in general claims that appearances or seemings— ways things appear to be—are the source of non-inferential justification. More precisely, phenomenal conservatism says that if it clearly and firmly seems to S that p, then (assuming that S doesn't have undefeated defeaters) S is justified in believing that p. A couple questions need to be answered so that we can firmly grasp what phenomenal conservatism is saying. The first question is: what is a seeming? While there is disagreement on this point, most agree (in fact just about every supporter of phenomenal conservatism thinks this) that seemings are a kind of experience. Seemings are experiences with three distinctive features. First, seemings have propositional content. This means that they represent the world as being a particular way. It is this feature that accounts for why seemings are always seemings that something is the case. Second, seemings can be accurate/inaccurate. Since seemings represent the world as being a particular way, they are accurate when the world really is that way and inaccurate when the world isn't that way. Third, seemings have a particular phenomenology. They have what is sometimes called "phenomenal force". They present their content in a way that makes the content feel true. For example, think about imagining that there is a tree in the yard versus actually seeing that there is a tree in the yard. In both cases, the experience (the imagining and the visual experience) has propositional content—namely that there is a tree in the yard. However, only your visual experience has phenomenal force. The visual experience presents its content in a way that the content feels true, but the imagining doesn't.

With the concept of seemings in hand, let's turn to the second question: what is an undefeated defeater? A defeater is something that takes away justification. Commonly, two kinds are distinguished: rebutting defeaters and undercutting defeaters. Let's think of an example. Imagine that someone you trust tells you that p. Now imagine that someone you trust just as much tells you that not p. In this case, the second person's testimony is a rebutting defeater for the first person's testimony. It gives you a reason to think that what the first person told you is false. Now imagine that rather than someone giving you contradictory testimony, you learn that the person who told you p is not trustworthy like you thought but is prone to lie about things like p. It seems in this case you also lose the justification for p that the person's testimony provided. However, you don't gain reasons for thinking that p is false. Instead, in this case the justification provided by that person's testimony is undercut by learning that the person isn't trustworthy. We've just seen examples of rebutting and undercutting defeaters. Importantly, such defeaters are themselves subject to defeaters. Let's take again the first version of the example. The first person tells you p, and then you gain a defeater because a second person tells you not p. Imagine that you now learn that while the first person is trustworthy, the second person is completely unreliable. In this case, the defeater that the second person's testimony provided you is now itself defeated, so you are left with the justification that the first person's testimony provided. You start with justification (because the first person tells you p), that justification is defeated (you get a defeater from what the second person tells you), and then your original justification is restored (the defeater you gained from the second person's testimony is itself defeated). That all said, the general idea of phenomenal conservatism is that its seeming to you that p gives you justification to believe that p as long as that justification isn't defeated by other information that you have.

EPISTEMOLOGICAL ISSUE: THE CHALLENGE OF BACKGROUND BELIEFS (EXPERT/NOVICE)

John and DeShawn have decided to spend the afternoon birdwatching. DeShawn is an expert when it comes to birdwatching, but John is a complete novice. At one point, they both see a fairly large bird with brownish feathers and a distinctive red tail. DeShawn immediately recognizes because of these and other features that the bird is a Red-Tailed Hawk. John thinks it is a Red-Tailed Hawk too. Neither DeShawn nor John specifically call to mind particular beliefs or information about the distinctive features of this particular kind of bird. Rather, they both simply see the bird and form the belief that it is a Red-Tailed Hawk.

It seems clear in this case that DeShawn's belief is justified, but John's isn't. Although it is immediately clear what a theory of justification *should* say in this case, it isn't immediately clear how a theory like phenomenal conservatism can yield the intuitively correct result. After all, DeShawn and John are seeing the same bird in the same conditions. Doesn't this mean that they are having the same appearance/seeming? And, if they both have the same seeming and it provides justification for one of them, shouldn't it provide justification for the other?

RESPONSES

There are a number of responses to this sort of case. One way that phenomenal conservatives may go is to distinguish between seemings and sensations (see *A Pair of Hens* pp. 148–152) (Tucker 2010). The thought here is that while it is true that DeShawn and John have the same visual sensations, they don't actually have the same seemings. It seems to DeShawn that the bird is a Red-Tailed Hawk, but it doesn't seem so to John. This difference in their seemings explains why one is justified in his belief but the other isn't.

Another response doesn't separate seemings from sensations, but instead insists that through training, an expert's appearances present different content to them than a novice's experiences do (Chudnoff 2021). The idea here is that because of his expert training, DeShawn's visual experiences offers him more information than John's does, and it is this additional richness of DeShawn's experiences that explain the difference in justification between them.

Yet another response simply appeals to justified background beliefs to explain the difference between DeShawn's and John's justification (McCain and Moretti forthcoming). DeShawn has a number of justified background beliefs that support trusting his seeming in this case, whereas John has justified background beliefs that serve as defeaters for his seeming. For instance, John plausibly has justified background beliefs such as that he is a novice and that he can't identify most birds by sight. Such justified background beliefs provide undercutting defeaters. Hence, the justification that John's seeming that the bird is a Red-Tailed Hawk would normally provide is defeated.

One final sort of response is to insist that such cases pose a serious problem for phenomenal conservatism, and so maintain that phenomenal conservatism needs to be revised or that some other theory should be accepted instead. Some externalists accept a version of phenomenal conservatism where seemings provide justification, but only when those seemings reliably indicate the truth of their content (Bergmann 2013). Such an externalist version of phenomenal conservatism could avoid this problem by claiming that only DeShawn's seeming is reliable, so only his seeming provides justification. Of course, an externalist might deny phenomenal conservatism altogether and claim that the difference here is simply that DeShawn's belief is formed by a reliable belief-forming process and John's isn't. Internalists might insist that for any seeming to provide justification, one must have justification for believing that that sort of seeming is reliable. Alternatively, internalists might opt for the sort of looks view discussed in the previous entry (see *A Pair of Hens* pp. 148–152) rather than phenomenal conservatism (McGrath 2018). The idea being that rather than the seeming providing justification on its own, what justifies DeShawn is that he has the seeming *and* that he knows what Red-Tailed Hawks look like, whereas John doesn't know what they look like.

RECOMMENDED READING

SEMINAL PRESENTATION

Austin, J.L. 1946. Symposium: Other Minds II. *Proceedings of the Aristotelian Society, Supplementary Volume* 20: 148–187.

ADDITIONAL IMPORTANT DISCUSSIONS

Bergmann, M. 2013. Externalist Justification and the Role of Seemings. *Philosophical Studies* 166: 163–184.

Chudnoff, E. 2021. *Forming Impressions: Expertise in Perception and Intuition*. Oxford: Oxford University Press.

Huemer, M. 2001. *Skepticism and the Veil of Perception*. Lanham, MD: Rowman & Littlefield.

Huemer, M. 2007. Compassionate Phenomenal Conservatism. *Philosophy and Phenomenological Research* 74: 30–55.

McCain, K. and Moretti, L. Forthcoming. *Appearance and Explanation: Phenomenal Explanationism in Epistemology*. Oxford: Oxford University Press.

McGrath, M. 2018. Looks and Perceptual Justification. *Philosophy and Phenomenological Research* 96: 110–133.

Moretti, L. 2020. *Seemings and Epistemic Justification*. Cham: Springer.

Pryor, J. 2000. The Skeptic and the Dogmatist. *Nous* 34: 517–549.

Tucker, C. 2010. Why Open-Minded People Should Endorse Dogmatism. *Philosophical Perspectives* 24: 529–545.

Tucker, C. (ed) 2013. *Seemings and Justification: New Essays on Dogmatism and Phenomenal Conservatism*. Oxford: Oxford University Press.

Smithies, D. 2019. *The Epistemic Role of Consciousness.* Oxford: Oxford University Press.

31

GOLD RUSH
(COGNITIVE PENETRATION)

Background: Another challenge to phenomenal conservatism concerns what is known as "cognitive penetration". The general idea is that it seems that various non-evidential factors can change how things seem to us. For instance, if we are really angry, someone's facial expression might seem hostile, whereas if we weren't angry, that same expression might seem neutral. Some argue that the possibility of cognitive penetration poses a serious problem for phenomenal conservatism because it suggests that not all seemings provide justification.

EPISTEMOLOGICAL ISSUE: COGNITIVE PENETRATION

Patricia and Peter have decided to try their hands at panning for gold in a particular stream together. Patricia is an expert at panning for gold. She has trained for many years to be able to identify gold even in very small quantities by sight, she knows proper panning techniques, and so on. Peter, on the other hand, is completely new to all of this. He has never learned to distinguish gold from other things, such as fool's gold, by sight, he doesn't know proper panning techniques, etc. However, Peter is extremely keen to find some gold on his first outing. After getting everything set up, Patricia and Peter start scooping up soil from the streambed and sifting through it. This goes on for quite some time. At this point Peter is getting a bit anxious—he worries that he won't find any gold. Nevertheless, he really wants to do so. Finally, as they are sifting through the hundredth panful, Patricia and Peter both see something that catches their eyes. As a result of her training, a pebble in their pan seems to Patricia to be gold. That same pebble also seems to be gold to Peter, but not because of training—after all he's had none—instead, it seems that way to Peter because he really wants to find gold.

What are we to think about Patricia's and Peter's seemings in this case? It seems intuitive that Patricia's seeming that the pebble is gold gives her justification for believing that the pebble is gold. But what about Peter's? Some claim that since his seeming is the result of his wishful thinking, it doesn't give him justification for believing that the pebble is gold. Why does this matter? Recall that phenomenal conservatism says that if it clearly and firmly seems to S that p, then (assuming that S doesn't have undefeated defeaters) S is justified in believing that p. In this case, it clearly and firmly seems to Patricia that the pebble is gold, and it clearly and firmly seems to Peter that the pebble is gold. So, assuming that they don't have undefeated defeaters, phenomenal conservatism is committed to claiming that both of them are justified in believing that the pebble is gold. Yet, it may seem that Peter shouldn't believe that the pebble is gold. If Peter shouldn't believe that the pebble is gold, it appears that phenomenal conservatism may be in serious trouble.

RESPONSES

One response to this sort of case is to accept that both Patricia and Peter are justified in believing that the pebble is gold (Huemer 2013b). The thought here is that it doesn't matter what causes a seeming, all that matters is that one has the seeming. That said, one way of fleshing out this sort of response yields the result that even though each of their seemings provide justification, only Patricia is ultimately justified in believing that the pebble is gold. This way of taking the response argues that although Peter's seeming provides justification, his justification is defeated by other things he knows (Huemer 2013a). For example, Peter knows that he isn't an expert and that he can't tell whether something is gold rather than fool's gold simply by looking. As a result of these undefeated defeaters, this response insists, the justification, which Peter's seeming really does supply, is defeated. Hence, Patricia has justification for believing that the pebble is gold and Peter doesn't—but this isn't a problem for phenomenal conservatism.

Another response is to contend that while both Patricia and Peter are justified in believing that the pebble is gold, only Patricia is warranted in doing so (Tucker 2011, Huemer 2013a). Recall from *A Visitor from the Swamp* (pp. 139–143) that warrant is stipulated to be the property that turns true belief into knowledge. In other words, warrant encompasses both justification and whatever is necessary to solve the Gettier Problem. The thinking with this response is that although both Patricia and Peter are justified in believing that the pebble is gold, only Patricia would know that it is (assuming that it is true that the pebble is gold). The reason for this is that given the way Peter's seeming is caused, it would be a matter of luck (similar to a Gettier-style case) if he managed to believe the truth about the pebble being gold. One way to explain why Peter would be lucky in this sense is that, unlike Patricia, his seeming that the pebble is gold isn't produced by a properly functioning cognitive faculty of gold detection, but instead by his wishful thinking (Moretti 2020, McCain and Moretti forthcoming). Hence, even if correct, Peter wouldn't be able to know that the pebble is gold on the basis of his seeming. Thus, Peter's belief lacks warrant.

There are also responses to this sort of case that yield the result that Patricia, but not Peter, has justification that are not friendly to phenomenal conservatism. One such response is that offered by reliabilism. A reliabilist can insist that what makes it the case that Patricia, but not Peter, is justified is that only Patricia is reliable at distinguishing gold from other things (Lyons 2016). Another sort of response is to insist that contrary to phenomenal conservatism, whether or not a seeming is caused in the right way determines whether the seeming provides justification (Siegel 2017). On this response, Peter's cognitive process, which leads to his seeming, is irrational because it's simply wishful thinking. This response contends that irrational processes can only generate seemings that fail to provide justification.

RECOMMENDED READING

SEMINAL PRESENTATIONS

Markie, P. 2005. The Mystery of Direct Perceptual Justification. *Philosophical Studies* 126: 347–373.

Siegel, S. 2012. Cognitive Penetrability and Perceptual Justification. *Noûs* 46: 201–222.

ADDITIONAL IMPORTANT DISCUSSIONS

Huemer, M. 2013a. Epistemological Asymmetries between Belief and Experience. *Philosophical Studies* 162: 741–748.

Huemer, M. 2013b. Phenomenal Conservatism Über Alles. In C. Tucker (ed), *Seemings and Justification: New Essays on Dogmatism and Phenomenal Conservatism.* Oxford: Oxford University Press, 328–350.

Lyons, J. 2016. Inferentialism and Cognitive Penetration of Perception. *Episteme* 13: 1–28.

McCain, K. and Moretti, L. Forthcoming. *Appearance and Explanation: Phenomenal Explanationism in Epistemology.* Oxford: Oxford University Press.

McGrath, M. 2013. Siegel and the Impact for Epistemological Internalism. *Philosophical Studies* 162: 723–732.

Moretti, L. 2020. *Seemings and Epistemic Justification.* Cham: Springer.

Tucker, C. 2010. Why Open-Minded People Should Endorse Dogmatism. *Philosophical Perspectives* 24: 529–545.

Siegel, S. 2017. *The Rationality of Experience.* Oxford: Oxford University Press.

Tucker, C. 2011. Phenomenal Conservatism and Evidentialism in Religious Epistemology. In K.J. Clark and R.J. Van Arragon (eds), *Evidence and Religious Belief.* Oxford: Oxford University Press, 52–73.

Tucker, C. (ed) 2013. *Seemings and Justification: New Essays on Dogmatism and Phenomenal Conservatism.* Oxford: Oxford University Press.

32

ARMCHAIR QUARTERBACK (ISOLATION/INPUT OBJECTION TO COHERENTISM)

Background: As we saw in the General Background: The Nature of Justification (pp. 113–119), coherentism holds that the structure of justification is weblike. Importantly, on coherentism whether a belief is justified depends upon how well it fits with the other beliefs that one has. In other words, coherentism (at least in its pure sense) contends that coherence among one's beliefs is necessary and sufficient for those beliefs to be justified.

EPISTEMOLOGICAL ISSUES: COHERENTISM; ISOLATION/INPUT OBJECTION

David is a big fan of professional football. In particular, he's a Cheesehead (i.e. he's a fan of the Green Bay Packers). One summer afternoon, David is wishing it was time for football season, so he decides to watch an old game. He picks one of his favorites because it has his favorite quarterback, Brett Favre. Oddly enough, while David is watching this game, he is struck by an imperceptible burst of cosmic radiation. Unfortunately, unlike what happens in the comic books David doesn't gain any superpowers from this burst of radiation. However, on the bright side David doesn't suffer any negative consequences either, aside from one curious thing. While watching the game from his armchair, David suddenly has all of the same beliefs that Brett Favre had while playing the game. David believes that he is over six feet tall (although he's not), that his name is Brett Favre, that he is currently playing football, that it's third down, that the linebacker looks like he's going to blitz, and so on. David has exactly the same beliefs that Favre did while playing the game, and he no longer has any of his own beliefs prior to the burst of radiation striking him. Despite this, David's sensory organs haven't been negatively affected in any way. So, David still has perceptual experiences as of watching TV, sitting in his chair, and so on.

Clearly, in this situation there is a terrible disconnect between David's beliefs and his experiences of the world around him. Nevertheless, David's beliefs are coherent. After all, Favre's beliefs while he was actually playing the football game were coherent, and David has all the same beliefs as Favre. This appears to be a major problem for coherentism. Coherentism claims that coherence among one's beliefs is necessary and sufficient for those beliefs to be justified. Hence, since, intuitively, Favre's beliefs were justified while he was playing the football game, they must have been coherent. But if those beliefs were coherent then, they seem to be coherent now when David has them. After all, they are the exact same beliefs! And yet, it seems clear that David isn't justified in believing the things that Favre believed. David isn't playing football; he's sitting in an armchair. What's more, David isn't even being deceived about what's going on like in some skeptical scenarios—he still has all of the experiences he would normally have while sitting in his chair watching TV. David's beliefs are simply out of touch with his experiences. Nonetheless, those beliefs cohere with one another, so coherentism seems to yield the result that David's beliefs are justified despite their obvious conflict with his experiences.

RESPONSES

One early pure coherentist response to this problem looked for a way out by adding further required beliefs for coherence. The general idea here is that in order for one's set of beliefs to really be coherent, one had to have beliefs that some of one's beliefs occur spontaneously and believe that such spontaneous beliefs are reliable (BonJour 1985). This is supposed to secure the role of experience in justification because beliefs caused by experiences are spontaneous and one would believe that such beliefs are reliable. Even the original supporter of this sort of response, Laurence BonJour, later abandoned it though, likely because it doesn't seem to actually address the problem. Even if it is true that such beliefs are required for coherence, and so for justification, it's plausible that Favre had these beliefs. After all, Favre was a normal human, forming beliefs in the ways that normal humans do. And David, therefore, has the same required beliefs because he has all of the same beliefs as Favre. Hence, it's not clear how this additional requirement could actually block this problem for coherentism.

A different sort of pure coherentist response involves arguing that the case envisioned here is actually impossible. Importantly, the impossibility isn't because it's somehow impossible that cosmic radiation could cause someone to have beliefs like this. That is likely impossible in our universe, but not impossible in the broader sense that matters for philosophy. Instead, the reason that this sort of case is impossible, according to this response, is that perceptual states themselves involve (or at least entail) believing (Armstrong 1968). The thought being that when David has experiences of sitting in his armchair and watching TV, those experiences themselves are partly constituted by (or entail) beliefs. Hence, the response insists that it's impossible for David to have the exact same beliefs as Favre and at the same time have experiences as of sitting at home in his chair. This response contends that if David has experiences as of sitting at home in his chair, then these experiences bring with them beliefs. So, David could have Favre's beliefs plus the beliefs constituting (or entailed by) his experiences of sitting at home, but he couldn't have just Favre's beliefs in this situation. If this view of perceptual experience is correct, then in this situation David wouldn't really have coherent beliefs at all. So, coherentism wouldn't be committed to the counterintuitive result that David's beliefs are justified.

Finally, there is another response to this problem that is more common among contemporary theorists that are supportive of coherentism. This response abandons pure coherentism (where the only objects that need to be in coherence relations are beliefs) for a view that requires coherence among one's beliefs and the contents of one's experiences (Kvanvig and Riggs 1992, Poston 2014). On this version of coherentism, David's beliefs wouldn't count as coherent. The reason for this is that although the beliefs cohere with one another, they don't cohere with the contents of his experiences. And since both beliefs and the contents of experiences belong in the web, David's web of beliefs fails to meet the requirements for justification.

RECOMMENDED READING

GENERAL OVERVIEWS

Coherentist Theories of Epistemic Justification. *Stanford Encyclopedia of Philosophy.* URL = https://plato.stanford.edu/entries/justep-coherence/
Coherentism in Epistemology. *Internet Encyclopedia of Philosophy.* URL = https://iep.utm.edu/coherent/#SH5a

SEMINAL PRESENTATIONS

BonJour, L. 1985. *The Structure of Empirical Knowledge.* Cambridge, MA: Harvard University Press.
Pollock, J. 1974. *Knowledge and Justification.* Princeton, NJ: Princeton University Press.

ADDITIONAL IMPORTANT DISCUSSIONS

Armstrong, D.M. 1968. *A Materialist Theory of the Mind.* New York: Routledge.
Conee, E. 1988. The Basic Nature of Epistemic Justification. *The Monist* 71: 389–404.
Conee, E. 1995. Isolation and Beyond. *Philosophical Topics* 23: 129–146.
Feldman, R. 2003. *Epistemology.* Upper Saddle River, NJ: Prentice Hall.
Haack, S. 1993. *Evidence and Inquiry: Toward Reconstruction in Epistemology.* Oxford: Blackwell Publishing.
Kvanvig, J. 2012. Coherentism. In A. Cullison (ed), *The Continuum Companion to Epistemology.* New York: Continuum Press, 57–72.
Kvanvig, J. and W. Riggs. 1992. Can a Coherence Theory Appeal to Appearance States? *Philosophical Studies* 67: 197–217.
Lehrer, K. 1990. *Theory of Knowledge.* Boulder, CO: Westview Press.
Plantinga, A. 1993. *Warrant: The Current Debate.* New York: Oxford University Press.
Poston, T. 2014. *Reason & explanation: A Defense of Explanatory Coherentism.* New York: Palgrave-MacMillan.

PART IV

SOCIAL EPISTEMOLOGY

GENERAL BACKGROUND: SOCIAL EPISTEMOLOGY

For most of its history epistemology has been focused on individuals. Epistemologists have long been preoccupied with determining what it takes for an individual person to have knowledge, whether an individual can adequately respond to the threat of skepticism, and so on. While answering epistemological questions pertaining to the knowledge of individuals is still very important, recently many epistemologists have turned their attention to social epistemology. Social epistemology looks beyond just individual agents and their mental states to groups of people and how knowledge is shared among members of groups or even how groups themselves have (or lack) knowledge or justification. More specifically, social epistemology concerns issues related to testimony, disagreement, determining who is an expert on a topic, and epistemological questions concerning groups.

It is important to note a mistake that may be tempting to make when first considering the idea of social epistemology. One might think that there's no need for social epistemology at all because one may believe that once we have settled the epistemological issues pertaining to individuals, there's no more work to be done. The gist of this line of thinking is that once we understand how individuals come to have knowledge or justification, all we have to do is apply this understanding to all of the members of the relevant group. Although this line of thought might seem plausible at first glance, reflection reveals that it is mistaken for a variety of reasons, two of which we'll highlight here. For one thing, individuals gain a significant amount (perhaps most!) of their knowledge from others via testimony. Consequently, we can't really understand the knowledge of individuals apart from the social epistemological issue of testimony. For another thing, as we'll see in discussing some entries to come, the epistemic statuses of various states of groups can diverge in important ways from the epistemic statuses of the relevant states of the individuals composing those groups. In light of this, we can't simply solve the epistemological problems of individual epistemology and thereby solve the problems of social epistemology. So let's take a look at some of the key issues and thought experiments to arise from the social epistemology literature.

33

THE UNBELIEVING TEACHER (TRANSMISSION VIEW OF TESTIMONY—NECESSITY)

Background: Testimony is a vital source of knowledge and justified beliefs. It is not an understatement to say that a very large portion of the things we know are known on the basis of testimony. For example, you know your birthdate. How? You don't remember being born. You can't deduce your birthdate from a priori principles via reasoning alone. You know your birthdate because of testimony. People have told you when you were born. If you haven't been to China, how do you know that China exists? Testimony again. If you know how far it is from your home to campus, odds are very good that you haven't measured the distance yourself but instead know this via testimony. Perhaps you used an app on your phone or Googled the distance. Any time you learn something from reading or being told, you are gaining knowledge via testimony. Hence, a whole lot of our knowledge (and, of course, our justified beliefs; see General Background: The Traditional Account of Knowledge pp. 1–5) comes by way of testimony.

When can we get knowledge or justified beliefs via testimony? One prominent answer to this question is that we can only get knowledge or justified beliefs from someone's testimony when that person knows or justifiedly believes what they are telling us. The thought behind this so-called "transmission" view of testimony is that in order for you to come to know (or justifiedly believe) that p on the basis of someone telling you that p that person must herself know (or justifiedly believe) that p. The general idea is that someone cannot give you what they don't have. A very helpful analogy for understanding the transmission view of testimony is that it is like a bucket brigade. In the past when there were fires, people would try to combat them by forming a bucket brigade. This is when one person is at a water source and fills up a bucket of water, which they pass along to the next person, who then passes it to the next person, and so on until it reaches a person who is standing near the fire and this person tosses the water on the fire. If you are standing near the fire and the person next to you hands you an empty bucket, you're not going to have any water to toss on the fire. Those who favor the transmission view of testimony think that testimony is like this. If the person who tells you that p doesn't have knowledge or a justified belief that p, then they're passing you an empty bucket. You can't come to know or justifiedly believe that p on the basis of their testimony.

EPISTEMOLOGICAL ISSUES: TESTIMONY; TRANSMISSION; NORMS OF ASSERTION

Let's explore a challenge for the transmission view of testimony by considering the case of a particular schoolteacher: Mr. Flat. Not only is Mr. Flat a schoolteacher, he is also an active member of the Flat Earth Society (an actual group of people who believe that the earth is flat; here's their website: https://www.tfes.org/). Unfortunately (from his perspective), Mr. Flat has been tasked with teaching his class about the spherical shape of the Earth. And, even worse in his mind, he has been strictly forbidden from "teaching the controversy" on this issue. Mr. Flat is an especially diligent teacher, so he is well acquainted with the facts of the actual shape of the Earth—its circumference, how if you were to travel in a straight line for long enough you would end up back where you started, and so on. Furthermore, Mr. Flat takes his duty as a teacher very seriously. So, although it goes against his own beliefs, he tells his class the facts about the planet being spherical and never betrays that he has any doubts about this at all. As a result of Mr. Flat's testimony, his students come to believe the facts concerning Earth's shape. They have no clue that Mr. Flat is a flat earther and doesn't believe any of the facts that he has taught them.

The particular subject matter in this case isn't all that important. What matters is that it seems that Mr. Flat's students come to know/ justifiedly believe facts about the shape of the Earth on the basis of his testimony. However, Mr. Flat neither knows nor justifiedly believes the facts he tells them—he doesn't believe these facts at all! Cases like this seem to suggest that testimonial knowledge can be *generated* by someone who doesn't actually have the knowledge in question. If this is correct, it seems to be a serious problem for the transmission view of testimony. This is exactly what Jennifer Lackey and Peter Graham each claim that this sort of case shows in their seminal discussions of such cases. Lackey also claims that this kind of case poses a problem for what is called the "knowledge norm of assertion". This is the idea that it is proper to assert some claim when and only when you know that the claim is true. So, according to the knowledge norm of assertion, we can legitimately criticize someone for asserting things that they don't know to be true. Lackey claims that there's nothing wrong with Mr. Flat's assertions about the Earth's shape even though he lacks knowledge of these facts. After all, it doesn't seem that we could legitimately criticize Mr. Flat for teaching his students these facts about the shape of our planet.

RESPONSES

One might respond to this sort of case, as some fans of the transmission view of testimony do, by maintaining that it is not really intuitive that Mr. Flat's students come to know the shape of Earth on the basis of his testimony. One way that this sort of response might be developed is by arguing that the students' beliefs in this sort of case are analogous to beliefs that one forms in a fake barn scenario (see *A Strange County* pp. 16–20) (Audi 2006). If this is correct, this would mean that the students' beliefs are not really knowledge. However, appealing to fake barns isn't sufficient for showing that Mr. Flat's students fail to have *justified beliefs* on the basis of his testimony. So, if supporters of the transmission view want to protect their view when it comes to justification, more would need to be done.

A different response that some supporters of the transmission view of testimony take is to allow that Mr. Flat's students really do come to have knowledge from his testimony, but argue that this is because transmission of knowledge is actually occurring in this case. The thought is that while Mr. Flat doesn't himself have knowledge, he is connected via earlier testimony to others who do (Faulkner 2000, 2011, Graham 2006). When it comes to his students, Mr. Flat is essentially serving as a link between his students and others who do have knowledge of the Earth's shape. However, some argue that cases like that involving Mr. Flat can be slightly modified so that it still seems that the students come to have knowledge, but with Mr. Flat being the first link in the testimonial chain. This would arise in a case where Mr. Flat discovers, on his own, strong evidence for thinking that the Earth is spherical and teaches his students this evidence.

A final response to these sorts of cases on behalf of the transmission view of testimony is to argue that what these cases actually show is that the transmission view of testimony should be focused on propositional justification (see *General Background: The Nature of Justification* pp. 113–119) rather than knowledge or justified beliefs (Wright 2016). The thought here is that in cases like the one above, Mr. Flat isn't transmitting knowledge or justified belief (because he has neither), but he is transmitting propositional justification. He is sharing good reasons to accept that the Earth is spherical that he himself possesses. Hence, this response takes onboard the main claims of those who use this sort of case as an objection to the transmission view of testimony, and then uses these insights to refine the theory rather than abandon it.

RECOMMENDED READING

GENERAL OVERVIEWS

Epistemological Problems of Testimony, *Stanford Encyclopedia of Philosophy*. URL = https://plato.stanford.edu/archives/win2017/entries/testimony-episprob/

Graham, P. and Bachman, Z. 2019. Counterexamples to Testimonial Transmission. In M. Fricker, P. Graham, D. Henderson, and N. Pedersen (eds), *The Routledge Handbook of Social Epistemology*. New York: Routledge, 61–77.

SEMINAL PRESENTATIONS

Graham, P. 2000. Conveying Information. *Synthese* 123: 365–392.

Lackey, J. 1999. Testimonial Knowledge and Transmission. *Philosophical Quarterly* 49: 471–490.

ADDITIONAL IMPORTANT DISCUSSIONS

Audi, R. 2006. Testimony, Credulity, and Veracity. In J. Lackey and E. Sosa (eds), *The Epistemology of Testimony*. Oxford: Oxford University Press, 25–49.

Burge, T. 1993. Content Preservation. *Philosophical Review* 102: 457–488.

Coady, C.A.J. 1992. *Testimony: A Philosophical Study*. Oxford: Oxford University Press.

Faulkner, P. 2000. On the Social Character of Testimonial Knowledge. *Journal of Philosophy* 97: 581–601.

Faulkner, P. 2011. *Knowledge on Trust*. Oxford: Oxford University Press.

Goldberg, S. 2005. Testimonial Knowledge through Unsafe Testimony. *Analysis* 65: 302–311.

Graham, P. 2006. Can Testimony Generate Knowledge? *Philosophica* 78: 105–127.

Lackey, J. 2008. *Learning from Words: Testimony as a Source of Knowledge*. Oxford: Oxford University Press.

Williamson, T. 2000. *Knowledge and Its Limits*. Oxford: Oxford University Press.

Wright, S. 2016. The Transmission of Knowledge and Justification. *Synthese* 193: 293–311.

34

A CONSPIRACY (TRANSMISSION VIEW OF TESTIMONY—SUFFICIENCY)

Background: In the background to the previous entry, we discussed the transmission view of testimony. In particular, we examined the idea that we can only get knowledge or justified beliefs from someone's testimony when that person knows or justifiedly believes what they are telling us. This is the idea that in order for knowledge or justified belief to transmit from one person to the other, it is necessary that the testifier has knowledge/justified belief. Another aspect of the transmission view of testimony is that having a particular epistemic good is sufficient for transmitting that epistemic good to others. In other words, if a testifier actually does know/justifiedly believe that p, then that is sufficient to make it so that someone who believes that p on the basis of the testifier's testimony will also thereby come to know/justifiedly believe that p. In terms of the bucket brigade metaphor from the previous entry, the idea is that as long as the testifier has water in their bucket that is sufficient for the next person in line to receive a bucket full of water.

EPISTEMOLOGICAL ISSUES: TESTIMONY; TRANSMISSION

A presidential candidate collapsed while being escorted to her vehicle after giving a stirring campaign speech. The paramedics arrive and pronounce that she has had a massive heartache, then rush her off to the hospital. One reporter for a local news outlet happens to be within earshot of the paramedics when they tell this news to the candidate's campaign manager. Unfortunately, the reporter wasn't recording the exchange, but he does immediately pull out his phone and call his editor to give her the scoop. So *Small Town News* starts working up the story to release on their website and to put in their print newspaper. At the same time, the quick-thinking campaign manager immediately makes an announcement on social media that the candidate is in perfect health and taking a bit of a vacation from the campaign trail. He even posts pictures of the candidate and her family on a beach—pictures that he has had saved on his phone in the case of just such an emergency. Afterward, the candidate's political party exerts a tremendous amount of energy and resources to keep the real story out of the hands of any of the major media outlets. After all, fears about a candidate's health can sink a presidential campaign, even though it is very likely that the candidate in this case will make a full and speedy recovery. So, instead of the actual story of the candidate's heart attack, the major media outlets are told the vacation story. And it is the vacation story that is all over the internet and newspapers.

Liz happens to be staying at a hotel when the story comes out. As she heads to breakfast, she picks up a newspaper from the selection that the hotel staff has set out. She happens to grab the latest copy of *Small Town News* rather than one of the national papers. Liz reads the paper as she enjoys her breakfast. When she reads about the incident with the candidate, she comes to justifiedly believe that the candidate suffered from a major heart attack. Of course, this belief is true. So Liz comes to have a justified true belief on the basis of the testimony provided by *Small Town News*. But some insist that Liz's justified true belief fails to amount to knowledge because she could have so easily believed the story about the candidate being on vacation. After all, every other newspaper published the vacation story, and it is the story that is all over TV and the internet. If this is correct, it is a problem for the transmission view of testimony because the folks at the *Small Town News* do know that the candidate has had a heart attack and they have provided this testimony to Liz via the newspaper article, but Liz fails to come to know this after forming the belief. Hence, this case appears to be an instance where a testifier's knowledge is not sufficient for transmitting knowledge to another person.

RESPONSES

One response is to insist that Liz really does have knowledge (Lycan 1977). The thought here is roughly that this sort of case is analogous to fake barn cases (see *A Strange County* pp. 16–20). This response involves denying that fake barn cases are genuine threats to knowledge and says the same is true in this case. As we saw in our discussion of such cases, there is a sizeable number of epistemologists who deny the intuition that the presence of many fake barns undermines one's ability to know that the real barn one is looking at is a barn. Additionally, empirical research suggests that nonphilosophers are inclined to deny this as well. This response makes a similar claim here—it insists that the intuition that Liz fails to know is simply a version of the fake barn intuition, and the response denies that intuition. Put simply, this response claims that the presence of the misleading news stories in Liz's environment do not undermine her knowledge.

There are ways of modifying the case in an attempt to undercut the plausibility of the response that contends that Liz has knowledge, though. These modifications seek to make it even more likely that Liz could've gone wrong in what she believes about the candidate's situation. If any such modification is successful in showing that Liz has a justified true belief without knowledge, the idea that knowledge is sufficient for transmitting knowledge is undermined.

RECOMMENDED READING

GENERAL OVERVIEWS

Epistemological Problems of Testimony, *Stanford Encyclopedia of Philosophy.* URL = https://plato.stanford.edu/archives/win2017/entries/testimony-episprob/

Graham, P. and Bachman, Z. 2019. Counterexamples to Testimonial Transmission. In M. Fricker, P. Graham, D. Henderson, and N. Pedersen (eds), *The Routledge Handbook of Social Epistemology*, New York: Routledge, 61–77.

SEMINAL PRESENTATION

Harman, G. 1973. *Thought*. Princeton, NJ: Princeton University Press.

ADDITIONAL IMPORTANT DISCUSSIONS

Adler, J. 1996. Transmitting Knowledge. *Nous* 30: 99–111.

Audi, R. 1997. The Place of Testimony in the Fabric of Knowledge and Justification. *American Philosophical Quarterly* 34: 405–422.

Burge, T. 1993. Content Preservation. *Philosophical* Review 102: 457–488.

Coady, C.A.J. 1992. *Testimony: A Philosophical Study*. Oxford: Oxford University Press.

Fricker, E. 1987. The Epistemology of Testimony. *Proceedings of the Aristotelian Society* 61: 57–84.

Graham, P. 2000. Transferring Knowledge. *Nous* 34: 131–152.

Graham, P. 2016. Testimonial Knowledge: A Unified Account. *Philosophical Issues* 26: 172–186.

Lycan, W. 1977. Evidence One Does Not Possess. *Australasian Journal of Philosophy* 55: 114–126.

35

HE CAN'T POSSIBLY KNOW (EPISTEMIC INJUSTICE—TESTIMONIAL)

Background: It is obvious that there are many ways in which someone might be wronged or treated unjustly. Often we think of unjust treatment as strictly a moral matter. However, many epistemologists argue that a person might be subject to epistemic injustice in various ways. Roughly, the idea is that a person might be wronged specifically in their capacity as an epistemic agent—they may not be treated as a source of information, denied access to epistemic goods, and so on.

EPISTEMOLOGICAL ISSUE: EPISTEMIC INJUSTICE—TESTIMONIAL

Martin is a talented and very accomplished scientist. He is currently involved in a joint project with several other scientists. Martin also happens to be an African American man. One day George, a financial investor in the project, visits the lab where Martin and the rest of the team are conducting their research. George has asked for an explanation of how things are progressing and how soon concrete results will materialize. Martin carefully and thoroughly answers George's questions. After Martin finishes, George nods and then immediately asks one of Martin's white colleagues the same questions. When the white colleague tells George the same things that Martin did, he is satisfied with the answers. George didn't ask the colleague because he was going to ask two of the team members no matter what. He asked the other colleague because he is a racist and thinks that Martin, an African American man, can't possibly know the answers to his questions.

Clearly, there are many things wrong with this situation. Most obviously is that George deserves moral criticism because he is a racist. Also obvious is that Martin has been wronged by George's actions. George has disregarded what Martin told him simply because Martin is African American. Everyone can agree that *moral* wrongs have occurred in this situation. However, in the contemporary epistemology literature, it has been noted that there is a specifically *epistemic* factor involved in this sort of case. In addition to other ways, it seems that Martin has been wronged as an epistemic agent. As a result of racial prejudice, Martin's capacity to engage in testimonial exchange has been impeded.

Miranda Fricker, in her seminal discussion of epistemic injustice, argued that various prejudices, such as the racial prejudice in this case, generate what we might call "credibility deficits". Martin has a credibility deficit in this case because he is being treated as a far less credible testifier than he in fact is. The thought here is that such inappropriate credibility deficits produce a particularly epistemic kind of testimonial injustice. Although most everyone has agreed with Fricker that there can be epistemic injustice and that credibility deficits are one of them, much of the literature that followed Fricker has been focused on identifying additional sources of epistemic injustice.

RESPONSES

One response to this sort of case contends that it is not just credibility deficits that lead to this sort of testimonial injustice, but rather, there are also credibility excesses (Medina 2011, 2013). The thought is that in a given context, credibility isn't something that one person has in isolation. Instead, one's credibility in a given context is determined by comparisons between that person and others. Hence, Martin is wrongly given a credibility deficit in part because George affords Martin's colleagues a credibility excess. Some have argued that the way to remedy situations like the one described in the case above is by way of large-scale structural changes. The idea is that in order to correct for the sort of prejudice that leads to this sort of epistemic injustice, it is necessary to change the way various institutions function when it comes to the sharing of information.

A further insight that consideration of this sort of case has yielded is the recognition that there may be different kinds of testimonial injustice (Dotson 2011). The first kind is the sort that earlier responses discussed, what might be called "testimonial quieting". This is what happens to Martin when George fails to treat him as knowledgeable, and so doesn't accept his testimony. A different sort of testimonial injustice would occur if Martin, realizing that George wouldn't be open to accepting him as knowledgeable, were to change what he says so that it is limited to things that George would be likely to believe given that Martin is the speaker. This latter sort of testimonial injustice has been called "testimonial smothering". It is where a speaker, like Martin, is pressured to limit their testimony because they will be ignored otherwise.

RECOMMENDED READING

GENERAL OVERVIEWS

Feminist Social Epistemology. *Stanford Encyclopedia of Philosophy*. URL = https://plato.stanford.edu/entries/feminist-social-epistemology/#EpiInj
McKinnon, R. 2016. Epistemic Injustice. *Philosophy Compass* 11: 437–446.

SEMINAL PRESENTATION

Fricker, M. 2007. *Epistemic Injustice: Power and the Ethics of Knowing*. Oxford: Oxford University Press.

ADDITIONAL IMPORTANT DISCUSSIONS

Anderson, E. 2012. Epistemic Justice as a Virtue of Social Institutions. *Social Epistemology* 26: 163–173.
Daukas, N. 2006. Epistemic Trust and Social Location. *Episteme* 3: 109–124.
Daukas, N. 2011. A Virtue-Theoretic Approach to Pluralism in Feminist Epistemology. In H. Grasswick (ed), *Feminist Epistemology and Philosophy of Science: Power in Knowledge*. Dordrecht: Springer, 45–67.

Dotson, K. 2011. Tracking Epistemic Violence, Tracking Practices of Silencing. *Hypatia* 26: 236–257.

Fricker, M. 1999. Epistemic Oppression and Epistemic Privilege. *Canadian Journal of Philosophy* 29: 191–210.

Kidd, I.J., Medina, J., and Pohlhaus Jr., G. 2017. *The Routledge Handbook of Epistemic Injustice*. New York: Routledge.

Medina, J. 2011. The Relevance of Credibility Excess in a Proportional View of Epistemic Injustice: Differential Epistemic Authority and the Social Imaginary. *Social Epistemology* 25: 15–35.

Medina, J. 2013. *The Epistemology of Ignorance: Gender and Racial Oppression, Epistemic Injustice, and Resistant Imaginations*. Oxford: Oxford University Press.

36

WHAT'S HARASSMENT?
(EPISTEMIC INJUSTICE—
HERMENEUTICAL)

Background: The previous entry discussed how one can be harmed by not receiving appropriate treatment as an epistemic agent. It seems that there are other ways for someone to suffer epistemic injustice though. One of these ways is for the person to be in a situation where the tools necessary for expressing the wrongness of their situation aren't available. In other words, it seems that someone can be harmed epistemically by being in a position where the knowledge of how to express harm isn't available.

EPISTEMOLOGICAL ISSUE: EPISTEMIC INJUSTICE—HERMENEUTICAL

Unfortunately, imagining a case like the following isn't difficult to do. It's 1950 and Pam works in the office of a local paper company. Pam has overheard a number of lewd comments about her figure while at work. She has noticed some of her colleagues staring at her while she tries to work. Some have even told her inappropriate things to her face. And more than once she has had to fend off attempts by colleagues to give her "pats" or "squeezes" in inappropriate places. Pam feels that in addition to being rude, these behaviors by her colleagues are downright wrong; they aren't simply in "good fun" like some of them have told her. While she doesn't want to be branded as someone who is difficult to work with, she knows that what's going on isn't right. Yet, Pam doesn't quite know how to put into words what's wrong about the conditions in which she finds herself.

Regrettably, Pam's situation wasn't all that uncommon in the past, and it still exists today. Like the previous entry, it is clear that moral wrongs are occurring in this case; however, the idea that epistemic wrongs are also occurring has recently emerged in the epistemological literature. Since it's 1950, Pam hasn't heard of workplace harassment or sexual harassment in general, and as a result it seems that she doesn't really have the requisite concepts to fully understand and express her situation and what's wrong about it. She doesn't have the concept of *sexual harassment* because it isn't yet a concept that is widely used or understood. It seems that Pam's being unable to express her situation to others, or even fully understand it herself, is a kind of epistemic injustice. In this situation, Pam is experiencing a kind of epistemic injustice that has been termed "hermeneutical injustice".

RESPONSES

Once the idea of hermeneutical injustice arose in epistemology, a number of new insights started to emerge. One such insight is that there may in fact be (at least) two important kinds of ignorance that arise from hermeneutical injustice (Fricker 2007). The first is the sort we have discussed by thinking about Pam. The sort of ignorance where the person who has been/is being marginalized can't understand their own situation or express it to others. The second sort is where people in other social groups may remain ignorant of the situation because those in marginalized groups aren't able to give expression to the problem. For instance, Pam's coworker Jim, a member of the dominant male social group, doesn't harass Pam, and he would be apt to try to help Pam if he knew there was a problem. Nevertheless, given that the conceptual framework isn't in place for Pam to express her experiences or for others to realize that something is wrong, Jim is ignorant that Pam is suffering as a result of what she experiences at work.

Another insight that has arisen is that there may be hermeneutical injustice even when a marginalized group does have the concepts and hermeneutical tools necessary to express their experiences. Dominant social groups can perpetuate hermeneutical injustice by failing to accept the conceptual resources that marginalized groups have developed to express their experiences (Dotson 2012). For instance, imagine that Pam comes up with an idea about how to express what she is going through—she calls her experiences "sexual harassment". Her coworkers can commit hermeneutical injustice by refusing to accept this concept. If they tell her there's no such thing, or they don't know what she's talking about, and so on, they are failing to accept the resources that she's developed for sharing her experiences in addition to ignoring what she is trying to tell them is clearly wrong.

Relatedly, some have argued that there is an additional sort of hermeneutical injustice that is a kind of "epistemic exploitation" (Berenstain 2016). The idea here is that dominant groups may wrongly pass the buck when it comes to understanding the situation of oppressed groups. That is to say, this sort of epistemic exploitation occurs when oppressed groups are expected to educate dominant groups about their plight rather than dominant groups taking on the responsibility to learn about the oppression of other groups.

RECOMMENDED READING

GENERAL OVERVIEWS

Feminist Social Epistemology. *Stanford Encyclopedia of Philosophy*. URL = https://plato.stanford.edu/entries/feminist-social-epistemology/#EpiInj

McKinnon, R. 2016. Epistemic Injustice. *Philosophy Compass* 11: 437–446.

SEMINAL PRESENTATION

Fricker, M. 2007. *Epistemic Injustice: Power and the Ethics of Knowing*. Oxford: Oxford University Press.

ADDITIONAL IMPORTANT DISCUSSIONS

Berenstain, N. 2016. Epistemic Exploitation. *Ergo* 3: 569–590.

Collins, P.H. 2000. *Black Feminist Thought: Knowledge, Consciousness, and the Politics of Empowerment*. New York: Routledge.

Dotson, K. 2012. A Cautionary Tale: On Limiting Epistemic Oppression. *Frontiers* 33: 24–47.

Dotson, K. 2014. Conceptualizing Epistemic Oppression. *Social Epistemology* 28: 115–138.

Kidd, I.J., Medina, J., and Pohlhaus Jr., G. 2017. *The Routledge Handbook of Epistemic Injustice*. New York: Routledge.

Mason, R. 2011. Two Kinds of Unknowing. *Hypatia* 26: 294–307.

Pohlhaus Jr., G. 2012. Relational Knowing and Epistemic Injustice: Toward a Theory of *Willful Hermeneutical Ignorance*. *Hypatia* 27: 715–735.

37

EXPECTING A BAD TIP (MORAL ENCROACHMENT)

Background: Recall that evidentialism says justification is strictly a matter of the evidence that one has at a particular time. In its traditional "pure" form, evidentialism holds that any two people with the same evidence have the same justification regardless of other differences in their circumstances. As we have seen (Going to the Bank pp. 48–52 and Winning the Lottery pp. 80–84), some views such as contextualism and pragmatic encroachment deny this though. This doesn't mean however that such views are entirely anti-evidentialist. It is possible for these views to be constructed in ways that are weakly evidentialist. For example, one might be a contextualist and yet maintain that evidence is what provides justification. Hence, one might think that evidence is what justifies, but whether it is correct to attribute knowledge or justified belief to someone depends both upon the evidence the person has and upon the context in which the attributor finds herself. Similarly, one might accept pragmatic encroachment and also accept that only evidence justifies. The thought here is that evidence is the only thing that provides justification, but one's pragmatic concerns affect how much evidence is required for knowledge or for believing to be justified. Interestingly, both of these "impure" versions of evidentialism hold that it is the stakes for the person (either the believer or the attributor of knowledge/justification) that matter. However, some argue that the stakes for others also affect what is justified.

EPISTEMOLOGICAL ISSUE: MORAL ENCROACHMENT

Karen has been a server at a local restaurant for a couple of years now. During that time, she has developed the impression that people from a particular minority group tend to be bad tippers—on average they leave much lower tips than other groups of people. Karen decides to research her impression to see if there is evidence for this or if she has just formed a mistaken impression. After diligently searching the internet and consulting reliable studies about this, Karen discovers that there is strong evidence that people from this particular minority group on average tip less than people from other groups. In fact, according to the research, the odds that people from this group will tip lower than average are around 80–95%.

One day after her research has been conducted, Karen is working at the restaurant. She notices a customer eating lunch by himself that has been assigned to a different server. The customer is a member of the particular minority group that Karen has researched. Karen believes "he's not going to leave a good tip." It turns out that Karen was correct, and this person left a tip that is below the average for the restaurant.

Many insist that Karen's belief is morally wrong despite being well supported by evidence. And a number claim that this isn't simply a moral matter—they claim that Karen's belief isn't epistemically justified because the moral import of the belief makes a difference to what is required for justification. As the case is constructed, it seems that Karen has good evidence for thinking that the customer isn't going to leave a good tip—the statistics suggest that it is 80–95% likely that he won't. Nevertheless, some argue that Karen's belief isn't justified despite this good evidence. Assuming that the evidence is strong enough in general to believe (that is, assuming that 80–95% probability that p is generally sufficient for making one justified in believing that p), this case is a counterexample to evidentialism if Karen's belief isn't justified. After all, evidentialism holds that all that matters when it comes to justification is the evidence that one has. But, if Karen's belief isn't justified in spite of her having very good evidence, then evidentialism gets this case wrong. Similar to pragmatic encroachment, "moral encroachment" contends that the moral implications of one's beliefs affect how much evidence is necessary for a belief to be justified. Hence, moral encroachment says that Karen's evidence would be good enough to make her belief justified *if* the evidence concerned something without moral import, but since this belief is harmful to the group to which the customer belongs, more evidence is required for justification. Some insist that these sorts of cases as well as arguments that support pragmatic encroachment (see *Going to the Bank* pp. 48–52 *and Winning the Lottery* pp. 80–84) equally support moral encroachment (of course, others contend that the arguments *against* pragmatic encroachment are equally arguments against moral encroachment) (Fritz 2017).

RESPONSES

Many who accept moral encroachment insist that while moral concerns affect whether someone should believe that *p* outright, they don't affect what credence it is rational to have. Basically, the idea here is that many supporters of moral encroachment think that Karen is rational in holding that it is 80–95% likely that the customer will leave a bad tip, but she isn't justified in believing that he will leave a bad tip. Hence, the moral import of her belief affects whether or not that credence is high enough to justify outright belief that the person is going to leave a bad tip, but moral concerns don't affect what credence one should have. However, some contend that if the arguments for moral encroachment work in the case of outright belief, they also work when it comes to rational credence (Fritz and Jackson forthcoming). In other words, if Karen shouldn't believe in this case, she also shouldn't have the high credence normally supported by the evidence she has.

As we have been discussing, one response to this sort of case is to accept moral encroachment, i.e. accept that Karen's belief (and perhaps her credence) isn't justified because of the moral importance of the belief. There are differences of opinion among those who accept moral encroachment as to where exactly the problem lies with Karen's belief though. Some argue that while statistical information like what she has is good evidence in some cases, it fails to justify when it is demographic evidence, such as when we're thinking about an entire people group (Munton 2019). Others claim that the moral reasons for her not to form this belief themselves provide defeaters for her belief. Yet others claim that the risks involved with getting a morally charged belief wrong make it so that more evidence is required for justification. Regardless, all of these ways of cashing out moral encroachment yield the result that evidentialism gets things wrong because moral concerns affect what is justified.

Another sort of response to these cases is to insist that while Karen has a moral obligation to treat this person like she would anyone else the moral facts simply don't affect what is epistemically justified for her. The thought here is that the intuition that there is something wrong with Karen's belief is really tracking facts about how she should treat this person, not facts about what she should believe (Osborne 2021). Of course, this sort of response defends evidentialism because it is consistent with this response to claim that evidentialism is correct about what Karen should believe.

A different sort of response attempts to get the result that Karen shouldn't believe as she does without impugning evidentialism in the process. One route those offering this response go is to argue that in this sort of situation, Karen has additional evidence that makes it so that her belief isn't justified (Gardiner 2018). She might have evidence concerning how this person is dressed, for instance in an expensive suit, that would counteract the statistical evidence that she has. Alternatively, one might argue that Karen's belief, while justified, might easily become unjustified because statistical evidence is precarious, in the sense that it is easily undermined by other evidence. And so, insist that it is this feature of her belief that leads us to mistakenly think that it isn't justified in the case as described.

RECOMMENDED READING

SEMINAL PRESENTATIONS

Gendler, 2011. On the Epistemic Costs of Implicit Bias. *Philosophical Studies* 156: 33–63.
Pace, M. 2011. The Epistemic Value of Moral Considerations: Justification, Moral Encroachment, and James' 'Will To Believe'. *Nous* 45: 239–268.
Stroud, S. 2006. Epistemic Partiality in Friendship. *Ethics* 116: 498–524.

ADDITIONAL IMPORTANT DISCUSSIONS

Basu, R. 2019. What We Epistemically Owe to Each Other. *Philosophical Studies* 176: 915–931.

Basu, R. 2019. The Wrong of Racist Beliefs. *Philosophical Studies* 176: 2497–2515.

Basu, R. and Schroeder, M. 2018. Doxastic Wrongings. In B. Kim and M. McGrath (eds), *Pragmatic Encroachment in Epistemology* (pp. 181–205). New York: Routledge.

Bolinger, R.J. 2020. The Rational Impermissibilty of Accepting (Some) Racial Generalizations. *Synthese* 197: 2415–2431.

Buchak, L. 2014. Belief, Credence and Norms. *Philosophical Studies* 169: 285–311.

Fritz, J. 2017. Pragmatic Encroachment and Moral Encroachment. *Pacific Philosophical Quarterly* 98: 643–661.

Fritz, J. and Jackson, E. Forthcoming. Belief, Credence, and Moral Encroachment. *Synthese*.

Gardiner, G. 2018. Evidentialism and Moral Encroachment. In K. McCain (ed), *Believing in Accordance with the Evidence: New Essays on Evidentialism*. Cham: Springer, 169–195.

Moss, S. 2018. *Probabilistic Knowledge*. Oxford: Oxford University Press.

Munton, J. 2019. Beyond Accuracy: Epistemic Flaws with Statistical Generalizations. *Philosophical Issues* 29: 228–240.

Osborne, R.C. 2021. What Do We Epistemically Owe to Each Other? A Reply to Basu. *Philosophical Studies* 178: 1005–1022.

Schroeder, M. 2018. Rational Stability under Pragmatic Encroachment. *Episteme* 15: 297–312.

38

SPLITTING THE CHECK (DISAGREEMENT—IN FAVOR OF EQUAL WEIGHT)

Background: Disagreement is something that we face in most areas of thought. For instance, as we have seen time and time again, there is disagreement about what we should think about, and how we should respond to, pretty much every thought experiment, puzzle, and paradox in this book. People disagree about politics, religion, philosophy, you name it. Relatively recently, the epistemology of disagreement has become a major topic of discussion. The central concern of this literature is how disagreement affects what is epistemically justified for us. The focus here is on genuine disagreements—where the parties aren't simply miscommunicating, but instead they are talking about the same thing and hold different views. The simplest sort of disagreement is when one person believes p and another believes not p—such as when one person believes that God exists and another believes that God does not exist. Additionally, it's not the mere fact that there is a disagreement that is thought to be important. After all, someone might disagree with S about p, but S may be completely oblivious to the fact that anyone disagrees. So, the interesting issues surround recognized disagreement, i.e. situations where one knows that other people disagree. That is to say, the cases that epistemologists are interested in are cases where S believes that p and S learns that someone else doesn't believe that p (either they believe not p or they suspend judgment, neither believing nor disbelieving p). What should one believe in this sort of case? Of course, there are some kinds of disagreement where the epistemically appropriate response is easy to discern. For example, most everyone agrees that if you find yourself in a disagreement with an expert on a topic on which you are not an expert, you should simply accept what the expert says and give up on your position. Hence, if you go to the doctor (and you're not a medical expert yourself) and the doctor tells you that you don't have the flu, even if you thought you had the flu when you went to the doctor, you should believe what the doctor tells you; you don't have the flu. Similarly, if you find yourself in a disagreement with someone who clearly doesn't know as much as you, you should simply stick with your own opinion. For instance, if a young child informs you that the moon is made of cheese, you shouldn't suddenly change your mind about the composition of the moon! You should simply disregard the disagreement with the child when it comes to your beliefs. Those disagreements are easy to adjudicate, but others aren't so easy. What should be done when you find yourself disagreeing with a peer—someone who isn't superior or inferior to you epistemically? That is, what does it do to your justification for believing that p when you learn that an epistemic peer (someone who you justifiedly believe is just as likely to be correct about things like p as you are) disagrees with you about p?

EPISTEMOLOGICAL ISSUE: DISAGREEMENT

Asa and Pedro are out to dinner with a large group. After the meal, they decide that they will each calculate everyone's share of the tip. Asa and Pedro each justifiedly believe that they are equally good at math. They both look at the bill and round the total up to the same whole number. They both also agree that the tip should be 20%. After a few minutes, Asa concludes that everyone owes $20. Pedro concludes that everyone owes $22. Puzzled they double check if they both started with the same total for the bill; they did. They check that they both agree that the tip should be 20%; they do. And, they each assure one another that they're not kidding about what they think each person owes—Asa sincerely believes each person owes $20 and Pedro sincerely believes that each person owes $22. So, they each discover that their friend, whom they take to be their epistemic peer about this sort of thing (they are each just as good at math, after all), disagrees with them. Clearly, someone has made a mistake; but who?

When it comes to the epistemology of disagreement, the key issue is what should Asa and Pedro do with respect to their beliefs about what that everyone owes when they discover their disagreement. Of course, everyone can agree that they should recalculate (perhaps using a calculator this time) to figure out what each person actually owes. But what about their beliefs before those new calculations are completed? The issue when it comes to the epistemology of disagreement is whether Asa or Pedro (or both) should change their belief at the time they first learn of the disagreement—have they lost (or, no one holds this view, gained) justification by learning that their epistemic peer disagrees with them?

RESPONSES

There have been a number of positions defended in the epistemology of disagreement literature. One position, what is called the *equal weight view*, was proposed as a response to exactly this sort of case (Christensen 2007, Feldman 2007, Matheson 2015). According to the equal weight view, you should give equal weight to your epistemic peer's thinking as you do to your own. In particular, the equal weight view says that learning that an epistemic peer disagrees gives Asa good reasons for thinking that she is mistaken that are *equal* to the reasons she has for thinking she is correct based on her own assessment of the check. And, the same is true of Pedro. The equal weight view says that unless Asa (or Pedro) has some independent evidence for thinking that it is her peer who has made a mistake (evidence that is independent of the fact that Pedro disagrees about the check), her belief that everyone owes $20 each is defeated. Hence, according to the equal weight view in this situation, Asa and Pedro should give up their beliefs because they are no longer epistemically justified. Instead of believing, they should now suspend judgment about how much each person owes until they get new evidence—such as they would get when they recalculate.

Another position on disagreement is what is called the *steadfast view* (Kelly 2005). As the name suggests, this view claims that you should remain steadfast in your belief in the face of peer disagreement. This position on disagreement is often motivated by criticizing the equal weight view. One ground for denying the equal weight view is that there is something special about the evidence that a person has (Huemer 2011). For instance, the evidence Asa has for thinking that everyone owes $20 is on stronger grounds for her than the evidence she gains from learning that Pedro disagrees with her. The reason for this is that Asa has direct access to her evidence in a way that she doesn't to the evidence that Pedro provides.

Others object to the equal weight view on the basis of the rationality of self-trust (Enoch 2010, Zagzebski 2012). They maintain that trust in your own reasoning and cognitive faculties is of fundamental importance for rationality. They go on to insist that trusting yourself amounts to remaining steadfast in your belief when it is discovered that an epistemic peer disagrees. Thus, Asa and Pedro should remain steadfast in their beliefs because they are rational to trust themselves.

Yet another ground for objecting to the equal weight view has to do with what is known as the *uniqueness thesis* (see *You Only Believe that Because…* pp. 85–89). The uniqueness thesis is the idea that given a set of evidence, E, there is only one uniquely justified position to take with respect to p. In other words, uniqueness holds that for anyone who has E, the same attitude toward p is justified. Some, however, deny uniqueness. Instead, they accept *permissivism*, which allows that the same set of evidence can support different justified attitudes toward p (Kelly 2014). Given permissivism, it may be that in at least some cases of peer disagreement, both peers are rational in continuing to hold their beliefs in spite of their disagreement. There are other views that lie between the extremes of the equal weight view, which basically says that whenever you discover disagreement with a peer that gives you a defeater for your justification, and the steadfast view, which basically says that in general, discovering disagreement doesn't give you a defeater for your justification. The most important of these middle-ground views will be discussed in the next entry.

RECOMMENDED READING

GENERAL OVERVIEWS

Disagreement. *Stanford Encyclopedia of Philosophy*. URL = https://plato.stanford.edu/entries/disagreement/#RespDisaVsSubsLeveConf

Christensen, D. 2009. Disagreement as Evidence: The Epistemology of Controversy. *Philosophy Compass* 4: 756–767.

SEMINAL PRESENTATIONS

Christensen, D. 2007. Epistemology of Disagreement: The Good News. *Philosophical Review* 116: 187–217.

Elga, A. 2007. Reflection and Disagreement. *Nous* 41: 478–502.

Feldman, R. 2007. Reasonable Religious Disagreements. In L. Antony (ed), *Philosophers without Gods*. Oxford: Oxford Universty Press, 194–214.

ADDITIONAL IMPORTANT DISCUSSIONS

Bogardus, T. 2009. A Vindication of the Equal Weight View. *Episteme* 6: 324–335.

Christensen, D. and Lackey, J. (ed). 2013. *The Epistemology of Disagreement: New Essays*. New York: Oxford University Press.

Conee, E. 2009. Peerage. *Episteme* 6: 313–323.

Enoch, D. 2010. Not Just a Truthometer: Taking Oneself Seriously (but not Too Seriously) in Cases of Peer Disagreement. *Mind* 119: 953–997.

Feldman, R. and Warfield, T. (ed) 2010. *Disagreement*. Oxford: Oxford University Press.

Frances, B. 2014. *Disagreement*. Cambridge: Polity Press.

Huemer, M. 2011. Epistemological Egoism and Agent-Centered Norms. In T. Dougherty (ed), *Evidentialism and Its Discontents*. New York: Oxford University Press, 17–33.

Kelly, T. 2005. The Epistemic Significance of Disagreement. *Oxford Studies in Epistemology* 1: 167–196.

Kelly, T. 2014. Evidence Can Be Permissive. In M. Steup, J. Turri, and E. Sosa (eds), *Contemporary Debates in Epistemology Second Edition*. Malden, MA: Blackwell Publishing, 298–311.

Matheson, J. 2015. *The Epistemic Significance of Disagreement*. London: Palgrave Macmillan.

Zagzebski, L. 2012. *Epistemic Authority: A Theory of Trust, Authority, and Autonomy in Belief*. New York: Oxford University Press.

39

BAD MATH (DISAGREEMENT—AGAINST EQUAL WEIGHT)

Background: As we saw in the previous entry, some cases of disagreement seem to support giving equal weight to the beliefs of one's epistemic peer. There are other cases however that challenge this view. In these cases, it seems that we should think that it is our epistemic peer who is mistaken rather than ourselves when we disagree.

EPISTEMOLOGICAL ISSUE: DISAGREEMENT

Let's reimagine the restaurant case that we discussed in the previous entry. Again, Asa and Pedro are out to dinner, but this time it's with a small group of people. And again they are going to calculate the check. However, this time they first decide they need to figure out how many people to split the check between. Asa says, "well there's me and you, that's two. And, there's Jill, Jamal, and Jose; that's three. So, we need to split the check between five." Pedro disagrees. At first, Asa thinks he's kidding. But he assures her that he's not. Puzzled Asa says, "Wait, there's you and me; that's two." He replies, "right." "Okay," Asa says, "and there's Jill, Jamal, and Jose—that's three." "Correct," Pedro responds. "Alright, am I missing anyone?" Asa asks. "Nope," Pedro assures her. "Okay, then. That makes five," she responds. "Wrong," Pedro says. Again, Asa makes sure that he's not kidding. In exasperation, Asa says, "Look, me and you, that's two. Jill, Jamal, and Jose, that's three. 2 + 3 = 5!" To which Pedro replies, "No, it doesn't." Noticing Asa's puzzled expression, Pedro explains that two plus three doesn't equal five. After making sure that they are using their words in the same way, Asa realizes that Pedro is literally disagreeing with her about "2 + 3 = 5". Asa thinks that this is true, and Pedro believes that it isn't.

What makes this case a particularly interesting variation of the previous restaurant case is that the intuitions that people usually have in these two versions of the case are very different. Many people have the intuition that in the previous case, Asa should think that it is equally likely that she made a mistake as it is that Pedro did. It is this sort of intuition that provides powerful support for the equal weight view. However, things look different in this variation of the case. Most have the intuition that Asa should think that it is clearly Pedro that has made a mistake, not her. Pedro's answer is so obviously wrong. What's particularly important about this case is that it seems that, contrary to the equal weight view, Asa's evidence for thinking that it is Pedro who has made the mistake rather than her is *not independent* of the disagreement at hand. It is because Pedro disagrees in such an extreme way that Asa has good reason to think that it is Pedro who is making the mistake.

Jennifer Lackey presented this sort of case to motivate a view that lies between the equal weight view and the steadfast view, what is called the *justificationist view*. According to the justificationist view, in cases of disagreement where you are very justified in believing the proposition in question before discovering the disagreement (like Asa's belief that 2 + 3 = 5, for instance), the personal access that you have to your evidence makes it clear to you that it is your friend (rather than you) who is messing up when you disagree. Notice though if this is correct, then you are able to use evidence from the disagreement itself to justifiedly disregard your peer's opinion. This is counter to the equal weight view.

RESPONSES

A similar view to the justificationist view is what is known as the *total evidence view* (Kelly 2005). According to this position, in cases of disagreement, what you are justified in believing depends upon both your original evidence and the evidence that you gain from discovering the disagreement. The thought is that in cases like *Bad Math*, Asa's initial evidence is so strong that the evidence from the disagreement doesn't make it so that her original belief loses justification.

Some respond to positions like the justificationist view and the total evidence view by arguing that merely having a very high degree of justification for the disagreed upon proposition doesn't make it justified for Asa to think that Pedro is more likely to be wrong in this case. One of the key ways of arguing for this position is to appeal to the following sort of situation (Christensen 2007). Your friend has purchased a lottery ticket in an extremely large, but fair, lottery. You have very good justification for thinking that your friend's ticket lost the lottery—the odds against winning are incredibly low. However, you add up the numbers (we assume that the lottery is won by adding up one's numbers and the total matching the winning number) and realize that her ticket's number doesn't match. Now, imagine that your friend adds up the numbers and says they match. In this case, opponents of the justificationist view claim that although you have a very high degree of justification for believing that your friend's number doesn't match the winning number, this doesn't give you sufficiently good reason to think that it is she who has made the mistake in adding the numbers.

There are many additional moves in the debates concerning the various positions about how we should respond to disagreement with epistemic peers; far too many to discuss here. It is, however, worth keeping in mind one thing about these debates. The reason that they are taken to be significant is that if we are honest with ourselves, we will recognize that we disagree with people who are our epistemic peers when it comes to many of the things that are most important to us: religion, politics, philosophy, and so on. As a result, what we are justified in doing in the face of disagreement impacts the rationality of many of our most cherished beliefs.

RECOMMENDED READING

GENERAL OVERVIEWS

Disagreement. *Stanford Encyclopedia of Philosophy*. URL = https://plato.stanford. edu/entries/disagreement/#RespDisaVsSubsLeveConf

Christensen, D. 2009. Disagreement as Evidence: The Epistemology of Controversy. *Philosophy Compass* 4: 756–767.

SEMINAL PRESENTATION

Lackey, J. 2010. What Should We Do When We Disagree? *Oxford Studies in Epistemology* 3: 274–293.

ADDITIONAL IMPORTANT DISCUSSIONS

Benjamin, S. 2015. Questionable Peers and Spinelessness. *Canadian Journal of Philosophy* 45: 425–444.

Christensen, D. 2007. Epistemology of Disagreement: The Good News. *Philosophical Review* 116: 187–217.

Christensen, D. and Lackey, J. (eds). 2013. *The Epistemology of Disagreement: New Essays*. New York: Oxford University Press.

Feldman, R. and Warfield, T. (eds) 2010. *Disagreement*. Oxford: Oxford University Press.

Frances, B. 2014. *Disagreement*. Cambridge: Polity Press.

Kelly, T. 2005. The Epistemic Significance of Disagreement. *Oxford Studies in Epistemology* 1: 167–196.

Kelly, T. 2010. Peer Disagreement and Higher-Order Evidence. In D. Christensen and J. Lackey (eds), *The Epistemology of Disagreement: New Essays*. New York: Oxford University Press, 31–53.

Lackey, J. 2010. A Justificationist View of Disagreement's Epistemic Significance. In A. Haddock, A. Millar, and D. Pritchard (eds), *Social Epistemology*. Oxford: Oxford University Press, 145–154.

Matheson, J. 2015. *The Epistemic Significance of Disagreement*. London: Palgrave Macmillan.

Vavova, K. 2014. Confidence, Evidence, and Disagreement. *Erkenntnis* 79: 173–183.

Vavova, K. 2014. Moral Disagreement and Moral Skepticism. *Philosophical Perspectives* 28: 302–333.

MAJORITY RULES? (GROUP BELIEF AGGREGATION)

Background: It is fairly commonplace to talk about groups performing actions and even having beliefs. For example, we say things like "the team believed they could win" or "that company knew full well what would happen if they dumped there." There are numerous interesting philosophical questions concerning groups and group behaviors. Many of these are metaphysical questions such as how does a group have a belief?—is this because each member of the group believes the proposition in question or only some of the group? There are interesting epistemological questions as well. Particularly interesting are questions of how groups can be rational and how group rationality can interact with individual rationality.

EPISTEMOLOGICAL ISSUE: JUDGMENT AGGREGATION

Ted is a philosophy professor, and he is eligible for a promotion. As with most things in an academic setting, it is decided that the best way to determine whether Ted is deserving of the promotion is to form a committee to make the decision. Jorge, Christine, and Kenji are selected by the Dean to be on the committee. The Dean informs Jorge, Christine, and Kenji that the two criteria for this promotion are research and teaching. Ted must have demonstrated excellence in both in order to get the promotion. And, if Ted has demonstrated excellence in both areas, then he is to be promoted. The Dean also informs them that they are to follow the rule of accepting the majority opinion when making their decision as a committee, i.e. if two or more of them vote in favor of something, then that is the committee's position. Just to be clear they will each decide (and vote) on whether Ted has demonstrated excellence in research and teaching, and so whether he should be promoted. As is also pretty common, Jorge, Christine, and Kenji will be voting via secret ballot and the Dean's assistant will tally the votes to determine the committee's decision.

Here's how the voting goes. Jorge votes that Ted demonstrated excellence in both research and teaching, so he votes that Ted be promoted. Christine votes that Ted demonstrated excellence in research but not in teaching, so she votes that Ted not be promoted. And Kenji votes that Ted failed to demonstrate excellence in research but did in teaching, so he votes that Ted not be promoted. Putting this all in a table can help make things clearer:

	Jorge	Christine	Kenji	Committee
Excellent Research	Yes	Yes	No	Yes
Excellent Teaching	Yes	No	Yes	Yes
Promote	Yes	No	No	No

When we consider the committee's position, we notice something strange—the committee's decision violates the rules. The committee's position is that Ted demonstrated both excellence in research and excellence in teaching, but he shouldn't be promoted. That's an irrational position. To see this more clearly, the idea is that excellent research and excellent teaching entail that Ted deserves a promotion. So, in essence, the committee is committed to accepting claims that entail a conclusion while at the same time denying that conclusion—that's irrational. Notice though that none of the individual members of the committee voted irrationally. Jorge voted that Ted satisfied both criteria and deserves the promotion, which is rational. Christine and Kenji each voted that Ted satisfied one criterion, but not the other, so they each voted that he shouldn't be promoted. Again, their combination of votes is rational. Hence, what this case seems to show is that the individual members of a group can all believe/vote rationally; yet when following the seemingly rational rule of majority rule, the group's beliefs/votes can end up irrational. As this is sometimes expressed, when we aggregate rational individual positions following seemingly rational rules, we can end up with an irrational aggregation.

RESPONSES

One of the major responses to this sort of case is the proof of an impossibility theorem (List and Pettit 2011). That is to say, it has been proven that it is impossible to satisfy certain seemingly rational constraints on judgment aggregation at the same time. Here are the conditions that it has been proven are impossible to jointly satisfy when there are multiple claims to evaluate and multiple individuals evaluating them:

1) Give each individual member an equal say in the group's position.
2) The group's position on any particular claim depends upon the individual members' positions toward that claim.
3) Any set of individual attitudes that are logically consistent are used in determining the group's position.
4) Aggregating all of the individual positions yields a group position on all of the claims that is logically consistent.

Given the practical importance of these sorts of group decision processes (the seminal presentation of this sort of problem was written because of how juries are to deliberate in courts of law, after all), there is definitely pressure to figure out ways to best navigate the tension between individual rationality and group rationality. Since it is impossible to jointly satisfy all four of these conditions, various responses involve giving up at least one of these conditions. For instance, some argue that it is too stringent of a requirement that each of a group's positions be logically consistent (this amounts to giving up on 4) (Briggs et al. 2014). Instead, they propose that we should hold group rationality in these sorts of cases to require something weaker than logical consistency. Roughly, the idea here is that in order to be rational, groups don't have to have positions that are logically consistent;

instead, they must have positions that are coherent (in a sense where coherence is weaker than logical consistency). At first, this might seem to not be genuine rationality until we reflect on the fact that each of us likely has some beliefs that are inconsistent with one another. Likely, we aren't conscious of these inconsistent beliefs at the same time, but there is a good chance that somewhere in the vast collection of beliefs that we each have, there are some beliefs that are inconsistent with each other—perhaps we couldn't even recognize their inconsistency if we were to think about both of them at the same time. At any rate, the thinking here is that we can still count as rational, even though we have some inconsistent beliefs, so we should think of groups in the same way. Of course, other responses might seek to retain (4) but give up on some of the other conditions leading to various forms of aggregating. Interestingly, (4) seems to be the only condition that can be relaxed while still holding onto majority rule though.

RECOMMENDED READING

GENERAL OVERVIEW

Social Epistemology. *Stanford Encyclopedia of Philosophy*. URL = https://plato.stanford.edu/entries/epistemology-social/#JudgAggr

SEMINAL PRESENTATION

Kornhauser, L. and Sager, L. 1986. Unpacking the Court. *The Yale Law Journal* 96: 82–117.

ADDITIONAL IMPORTANT DISCUSSIONS

Briggs, R., Cariani, F., Easwaran, K. and Fitelson, B. 2014. Individual Coherence and Group Coherence. In J. Lackey (ed), *Essays in Collective Epistemology*. Oxford: Oxford University Press, 215–239.

Bright, L., Dang, H., and Heesen, R. 2018. A Role for Judgment Aggregation in Coauthoring Scientific Papers. *Erkenntnis* 83: 231–252.

Goldman, A. 2011. A Guide to Social Epistemology. In A. Goldman and D. Whitcomb (eds), *Social Epistemology: Essential Readings*. New York: Oxford University Press, 11–37.

Lackey, J. 2016. What Is Justified Group Belief? *Philosophical Review* 125: 341–396.

List, C. and Pettit, P. 2011. *Group Agency: The Possibility, Design, and Status of Corporate Agents*. Oxford: Oxford University Press.

McCain, K. 2016. *The Nature of Scientific Knowledge: An Explanatory Approach.* Cham: Springer.

Solomon, M. 2006. *Groupthink* versus *The Wisdom of Crowds:* The Social Epistemology of Deliberation and Dissent. *Southern Journal of Philosophy* 44: 28–42.

Wray, B. 2014. Collaborative Research, Deliberation, and Innovation. *Episteme* 11: 291–333.

PART V

PUZZLES AND PARADOXES

GENERAL BACKGROUND: PUZZLES AND PARADOXES

The entries up to this point have all been thought experiments. And, as we've seen, many of these thought experiments are designed to be counterexamples to particular theories or claims. Even those that aren't specifically designed to be counterexamples are intended to motivate a particular argument or claim. The puzzles and paradoxes presented in the remaining entries are different. Rather than imaginative thought experiments, these entries include more abstract presentations of features that generate puzzles or paradoxes. When it comes to the entries in this section, they differ from the earlier entries because they typically aren't presented with the aim of motivating a particular epistemological view. Instead, they are genuinely raising puzzles and paradoxes to be solved.

Before moving on, it's worth taking a brief moment to explain the general structure of puzzles and paradoxes. The two are similar in some ways (that's why they're in the same section of the book!), but they are also importantly different. Puzzles and paradoxes are similar to one another, in that they both present us with problems that don't have obvious solutions. And, in many cases, it is really difficult to figure out what the correct solutions to these puzzles and paradoxes are. Despite their similarities, puzzles and paradoxes are different in at least one very important way. A puzzle can arise when we find ourselves facing an unexpected result or a challenge to something that we take for granted (this is why, for example, the challenge of external world skepticism is sometimes referred to as a puzzle). However, a paradox requires more than this. Typically, a paradox will only arise when we realize that two or more things that each seem clearly true are inconsistent with one another. As we will see, in many cases each response to a given paradox involves giving up on or drastically revising a seemingly obvious truth.

A GRUESOME RIDDLE (NEW RIDDLE OF INDUCTION/GRUE)

Background: In order to appreciate this puzzle it is helpful to remind our-
selves of the nature of inductive inference. A helpful way to do this is to first
start with deductive inferences by way of a contrast. Deductive inferences are
such that if they are valid, the truth of the premises entails the truth of the
conclusion. Hence, if you make a valid deductive inference starting from true
premises, there is no way that your conclusion can be false. Inductive infer-
ences are different. Even if they are very good inferences and they start with
all true premises, it is still possible for the conclusion to be false. Broadly
speaking, inductive inferences are where we infer things about unobserved
cases from things we have observed. An example will help (the abstract form
is in parentheses):

- *Ravens have been observed in a variety of situations. (F's have been*
  observed in a variety of situations.)
- *All the observed ravens have been black. (All observed F's are G's.)*
- *Therefore, the next raven will be black. (Therefore, the next F will*
  be a G.)

In this case, we are drawing an inductive inference about the next raven
based on the ravens that have been previously observed. It is also common
to draw general conclusions from observed cases:

- *Ravens have been observed in a variety of situations. (F's have been observed in a variety of situations.)*
- *All the observed ravens have been black. (All observed F's are G's.)*
- *Therefore, all ravens are black. (Therefore, all F's are G's.)*

Although neither of these inferences are such that their conclusions must be true, it is clear that they are good ways to reason. And it is clear that as long as one has good reason to accept the premises of the inferences, one has good reason to accept the conclusions as well.

EPISTEMOLOGICAL ISSUE: GRUE/NEW RIDDLE OF INDUCTION

Let's consider a case of what appears to be a good inductive inference. There have been many emeralds observed in a wide variety of situations. All of the observed emeralds have been green. Therefore, all emeralds are green. This is such a clear example of a good inductive inference that it is often used in textbooks to illustrate induction and inductive inferences. So far so good.

But, now let us think about a strange sort of predicate, *grue*. An object is grue just in case it is examined before the year 2100 and green or examined at 2100 or later and blue. All of our observations of emeralds have supported both the claim that they are green and the claim that they are grue (after all, all of the emeralds that we've observed have been green and observed before the year 2100). So, it is true to say that all observed emeralds have been grue. If this is correct, it seems that we could infer that all emeralds are grue rather than inferring that they are all green.

What are we to make of this? It might be tempting at first to say that we should just infer both that all emeralds are green and that all emeralds are grue. This would be a mistake though. After all, being green and being grue are very different. As a result, the proposition that *all emeralds are green* yields very different predictions than the proposition that *all emeralds are grue* does. The first predicts that when emeralds are observed after 2100 they will be green, but the second predicts that those emeralds will be blue.

The heart of the problem of grue (which is also known as the "New Riddle of Induction"—the "old" riddle is skepticism about the reasonability of inductive inference in general) is this question: what makes it so that we can project some properties from observed cases to unobserved cases but not others? That is to say, why is it that we can infer that all emeralds are green, but we can't legitimately infer that all emeralds are grue?

A response that may immediately jump to mind is that the difference is that grue is defined in terms of when objects are observed, and this makes it illegitimate, whereas green doesn't have this problem. So, we can legitimately project green from observed cases to unobserved cases, but we can't do so with grue. Unfortunately, this response fails because we can introduce another predicate, *bleen*, and see that green (and blue) can likewise be defined in terms of when something is observed. Let's start with bleen. An object is bleen just in case it is examined before the year 2100 and blue or examined at 2100 or later and green. With grue and bleen in hand, we can define our more familiar "green" and "blue" in ways that makes them dependent upon when something is observed. After all, an object is green just in case it is examined before the year 2100 and grue or examined at 2100 or later and bleen. Similarly, an object is blue just in case it is examined before the year 2100 and bleen or examined at 2100 or later and grue. Hence, this seemingly obvious response doesn't get off the ground. The answer to this gruesome riddle must lie elsewhere.

RESPONSES

All responses to this puzzle have one common feature: they all seek to find some sort of asymmetry between green and grue with the hopes that the asymmetry will explain why it is legitimate to project the former but not the latter. The earliest attempt to come up with such an asymmetry came from Nelson Goodman (the person who came up with this New Riddle of Induction) (1954). He proposed that what makes a predicate projectable comes down to our actual inductive practices. "Green" is much more entrenched in our practices than "grue" is. In other words, we have used "green" in a number of our past inductive inferences, but we haven't used "grue." So, the thought is that the difference between what is projectible and what isn't is simply a matter of what we have projected in the past when making such inferences.

Another sort of response involves arguing that "green" picks out a natural kind, whereas "grue" doesn't (Quine 1969). The general idea here is that green is in some sense a feature of the world that is independent of us and our interests, but grue isn't. The response contends that it is only natural kind properties that can be projected.

A different way of responding insists that "green" is an observable predicate but "grue" is not (Thomson 1966a, 1966b). The gist of this response is that you can tell simply by looking whether something is green or not—if you're in the right lighting conditions, you simply look and can tell if it is green. However, the same isn't true when it comes to telling whether something is grue. In order to know if an object is grue, you must not only look at it, but you must also know *when* you are observing it.

Yet another response contends that hypotheses employing "green" are simpler than those employing "grue" because the former involve stable laws of nature, whereas the latter involve those that change. The thought here is that if in fact all emeralds are green, then whether we observe an emerald or not has no effect on its color. But if all emeralds are grue, then the actual appearance of the emerald will change depending upon whether it is observed before a particular time or not (Rheinwald 1993).

A different sort of explanatory response argues that in some sense, "all emeralds are green" better explains our observations than "all emeralds are grue" does (White 2005, Ward 2012). One way of cashing out this kind of response is to point out that any hypothesis, such as that all emeralds are grue, which holds that unobserved emeralds aren't green will have to include some condition that accounts for why we, for some reason, have only observed the emeralds that look green. This is a seemingly ad hoc addition that the hypothesis that all emeralds are green doesn't need in order to account for our observations. As a result, the hypothesis that all emeralds are green offers a better explanation of the many observations of green (and only green) emeralds than the hypothesis that all emeralds are grue does.

RECOMMENDED READING

GENERAL OVERVIEW

Nelson Goodman. *Stanford Encyclopedia of Philosophy*. URL = https://plato.stanford.edu/entries/goodman/#OldNewRidIndTheSol

SEMINAL PRESENTATION

Goodman, N. 1954. *Fact, Fiction, and Forecast*. London: Athlone Press.

ADDITIONAL IMPORTANT DISCUSSIONS

Elgin, C. (ed) 1997. *The Philosophy of Nelson Goodman Vol. 2: Nelson Goodman's New Riddle of Induction*. New York: Garland.

Hesse, M. 1969. Ramifications of 'Grue'. *British Journal for the Philosophy of Science* 20: 13–25.

Jackson, F. 1975. Grue. *Journal of Philosophy* 72: 113–131.

Quine, W.V.O. 1969. *Ontological Relativity and Other Essays*. New York: Columbia University Press.

Rheinwald, R. 1993. An Epistemic Solution to Goodman's New Riddle of Induction. *Synthese* 95: 55–76.

Stalker, D. (ed) 1994. *Grue! The New Riddle of Induction*. Chicago, IL: Open Court.

Thomson, J.J. 1966a. Grue. *Journal of Philosophy* 63: 289–309.

Thomson, J.J. 1966b. More Grue. *Journal of Philosophy* 63: 528–534.

Ward, B. 2012. Explanation and the New Riddle of Induction. *Philosophical Quarterly* 62: 365–385.

White, R. 2005. Explanation as a Guide to Induction. *Philosophers' Imprint* 5: 1–29.

RAVENS PARADOX

Background: Confirmation concerns how likely some evidence makes a hypothesis. For instance, observing a black raven confirms (to at least some degree) the hypothesis that all ravens are black. Although there are various principles of confirmation that seem obviously true, when they are combined apparent paradoxes arise.

EPISTEMOLOGICAL ISSUE: RAVENS PARADOX/ CONFIRMATION PARADOX

Here's something that seems true. If some evidence confirms (i.e. supports/makes more likely to be true) a particular hypothesis, H_1, then that evidence equally confirms any hypothesis, H_2, that is logically equivalent to H_1. For instance, seeing a book on the shelf in the library confirms/provides support for thinking "there are many books in the library". It seems that seeing a book on the shelf in the library equally confirms/provides support for thinking "hay muchos libros en la biblioteca". Why? Because these statements mean the same thing. They are logically equivalent to one another. Similarly, evidence that confirms "if today is Saturday, then there's no class" equally confirms "if there's class, then today isn't Saturday". Again, the reason is that these statements are logically equivalent. The idea that logically equivalent statements are confirmed to the same degree by the same evidence is known as the "Equivalence condition."

Here's something else that seems true. Universal claims are confirmed/supported by their positive instances. In other words, observing a green emerald confirms (at least to some degree) the claim that all emeralds are green. This principle is known as the "Nicod condition" (it is called this because French philosopher Jean Nicod was the first to explicitly endorse the principle in print).

Although both the Equivalence condition and the Nicod condition are intuitively plausible conditions on confirmation, together they generate what is known as the Ravens Paradox. Let's take a look at this. First, we start with the Nicod condition. Observing a black raven provides confirmation for the claim that all ravens are black. So far, so good. According to the Equivalence condition, any evidence for "all ravens are black" is equally good evidence for "all nonblack things are non-ravens" because these two claims are logically equivalent. Hence, observing a black raven is evidence for "all nonblack things are non-ravens". There doesn't appear to be a problem.

But what about when we look at the other side of things? Let's consider another observation that confirms "all nonblack things are non-ravens"—observing a white piece of chalk. Since a white piece of chalk is a nonblack non-raven, the Nicod condition holds that it confirms (to some degree) that all nonblack things are non-ravens. However, the Equivalence condition yields that observing the white piece of chalk also confirms "all ravens are black" because this is logically equivalent to "all nonblack things are non-ravens". But what does a white piece of chalk have to do with the color of ravens?! Intuitively, it seems that observing pieces of chalk (regardless of their colors) tells us nothing about the color of ravens. And yet, if the Equivalence condition and the Nicod condition are true, it seems that observing white chalk can give us evidence for thinking that all ravens are black. This is the Ravens Paradox (sometimes called the "Confirmation Paradox").

RESPONSES

One response is to simply accept that there is no problem here. In fact, when Carl Hempel originally presented the Ravens Paradox, he took it to simply show that observing a white piece of chalk confirms "all ravens are black" (1937, 1945). Many have been uncomfortable with following Hempel's acceptance of this conclusion, however.

Before considering other responses, it is worth noting that it has been argued that the Ravens Paradox and the New Riddle of Induction/Grue Problem (see *A Gruesome Riddle* pp. 207–211) are logically equivalent (Boyce 2014). This is important because if it is correct and the two really are logically equivalent, then any solution to one is automatically a solution to the other. Hence, if this line of reasoning is right, any of the responses to the New Riddle of Induction considered in the previous entry have the potential to be a response to the Ravens Paradox as well. That said, most respond to these two problems differently.

There is a notable exception to the general trend to respond to the Ravens Paradox and the New Riddle of Induction differently though. As we saw in the previous entry, one way of responding to the New Riddle of Induction involves arguing that "green" picks out a natural kind, whereas "grue" doesn't. The general idea with this response is that green is in some sense a feature of the world that is independent of us and our interests, but grue isn't. The response contends that it is only natural kind properties that can be projected. This same "natural kinds" response has been put forward as a solution to the Ravens Paradox as well (Quine 1969). According to this way of responding to the Ravens Paradox, the Nicod Condition is false. The response contends that it is only universal statements about natural kinds that are confirmed by their instances. Thus, this response yields the result that observing a black raven confirms "all ravens are black" (because ravens and blackness are natural kinds), but a white piece of chalk doesn't confirm "all nonblack things are non-ravens" (because nonblack and non-ravens aren't natural kinds). This move allows supporters of this response to deny the conclusion that observing a white piece of chalk confirms "all ravens are black".

Perhaps the most common response to the Ravens Paradox is the Bayesian response (Maher 1999, Fitelson and Hawthorne 2010, Rinard 2014). This sort of response makes use of Bayesian confirmation theory to make the conditions of confirmation more precise (we won't worry about the details of Bayesianism here). What is perhaps most interesting about this response is that, like the previous response, it involves a denial of the Nicod condition (though for different reasons than the natural kind response), but it embraces the conclusion that observing a white piece of chalk confirms "all ravens are black". In order to make this conclusion less troubling, the Bayesian response insists that observing a white piece of chalk doesn't support "all ravens are black" nearly as strongly as observing a black raven does. In fact, many Bayesians insist that the support that observing a white piece of chalk provides for "all ravens are black" is extremely miniscule. It does, they contend, nevertheless provide some small amount of confirmation for "all ravens are black".

A final sort of response to the Ravens Paradox, which purports to be at least consistent with the Bayesian framework, denies the Equivalence condition. According to this way of responding, the accuracy of formal representations of hypotheses varies with contexts of inquiry (Clarke 2010). In other words, in some contexts "all nonblack things are non-ravens" will be an accurate way of formulating "all ravens are black", i.e. there are contexts where the two are equivalent. However, in other contexts, such as the context where we are looking at ravens or pieces of chalk, "all nonblack things are non-ravens" misrepresents the hypothesis that all ravens are black. The general idea is that we are not stuck with the counterintuitive conclusion that observing a white piece of chalk confirms that all ravens are black because the Equivalence condition is false as a general principle, and it fails to hold in this particular instance.

RECOMMENDED READING

GENERAL OVERVIEWS

Confirmation. *Stanford Encyclopedia of Philosophy*. URL = https://plato.stanford.edu/entries/confirmation/#TwoParOthDif

Fitelson, B. 2006. The Paradox of Confirmation. *Philosophy Compass* 1: 95–113.

SEMINAL PRESENTATIONS

Hempel, C.G. 1937. Le problème de la verité. *Theoria* 3: 206–246.

Hempel, C.G. 1945. Studies in the Logic of Confirmation I & II. *Mind* 54: 1–26 & 97–121.

ADDITIONAL IMPORTANT DISCUSSIONS

Boyce, K. 2014. On the Equivalence of Goodman's and Hempel's Paradoxes. *Studies in History and Philosophy of Science* 45: 32–42.

Clarke, R. 2010. "The Ravens Paradox" is a Misnomer. *Synthese* 175: 427–440.

Cohen, Y. 1987. Ravens and Relevance. *Erkenntnis* 26: 153–179.

Fitelson, B. and Hawthorne, J. 2010. How Bayesian Confirmation Theory Handles the Paradox of the Ravens. In E. Eells and J. Fetzer (eds), *The Place of Probability in Science* (pp. 247–275). Chicago, IL: Open Court.

Good, I.J. 1960. The Paradox of Confirmation. *British Journal for the Philosophy of Science* 11: 145–149.

Good, I.J. 1961. The Paradox of Confirmation (II). *British Journal for the Philosophy of Science* 12: 63–64.

Maher, P. 1999. Inductive Logic and the Ravens Paradox. *Philosophy of Science* 66: 50–70.

Quine, W.V.O. 1969. *Ontological Relativity and Other Essays.* New York: Columbia University Press.

Rinard, S. 2014. A New Bayesian Solution to the Paradox of the Ravens. *Philosophy of Science* 81: 81–100.

Sylvan, R. and Nola, R. 1991. Confirmation without Paradoxes. In G. Schurz and G.J.W. Dorn (eds), *Advances in Scientific Philosophy: Essays in Honour of Paul Weingartner.* Amsterdam: Rodopi, 5–44.

Vranas, P. 2004. Hempel's Raven Paradox: A Lacuna in the Standard Bayesian Solution. *British Journal for the Philosophy of Science* 55: 545–560.

THE DOGMATISM PUZZLE

Background: Generally, we think that one shouldn't be dogmatic. Even when it comes to things that we know to be true; it is widely agreed that we should keep an open mind when it comes to the opinions of others and be willing to consider new evidence. Nevertheless, it seems that some intuitively plausible principles about knowledge and evidence lead to the conclusion that we should sometimes be dogmatic.

EPISTEMOLOGICAL ISSUES: DEFEAT; MISLEADING EVIDENCE

Here's something that is clearly true: if a proposition, p, is true, then any evidence that p is false is misleading evidence. After all, it is evidence that wrongly suggests that something true is not true. For example, the Chicago Bears won Super Bowl XX in 1986. If you come across an article that says that some other team won the Super Bowl in 1986, that article is mistaken and the evidence it provides is misleading.

Here's something else that seems clearly true: if you know that some bit of evidence is misleading, you can (and should) disregard it. Take Super Bowl XX again. If you know that an article which says the New England Patriots won Super Bowl XX is mistaken, it seems that you should disregard what that article says about the game. The evidence that this article would provide about Super Bowl XX is misleading, and you know that it is misleading. So far so good, but we are getting close to something puzzling. Let's consider one more thing that seems clearly true: we shouldn't be dogmatic in our beliefs. In other words, we should be open to changing our minds about things, and we should believe in accordance with the evidence that we have rather than believing things because we want them to be true.

These seemingly obvious principles along with some uncontroversial points about the nature of knowledge yield a challenging puzzle. Let's say that you know some particular proposition, p. Since you know that p, any evidence against p is misleading. Why? Well, it is uncontroversial that if you know that p, then p is true. In fact, to say that "you know that p is true" is just another way of saying "you know that p." So, you know that p, and this means that p is true. Now let's assume that you gain some evidence, E, that provides reason for thinking that p is false. What should you do? Given that your knowing that p entails that p is true and given the truth of the principles we mentioned above, it seems that you should simply disregard E altogether. This may not seem to be much of a puzzle until we consider that this applies to *anything* you know and *any* evidence that you *ever* gain against something that you know. It seems that you should always simply ignore any evidence that goes against things that you know. But if you do this, it seems that you are being extremely dogmatic.

In order to better appreciate the puzzling nature of what seems to be going on here, let's think about a concrete case. Imagine you have just read and learned for the first time that the Chicago Bears won Super Bowl XX by reading a highly reliable epistemology book (this very book, in fact). Since you trust what you read in this highly reliable epistemology book, you believe and even know that the Chicago Bears won Super Bowl XX. Now let's imagine that tomorrow you come across another highly reliable book that says that some other team won Super Bowl XX. What should you do? Given that you should disregard evidence that goes against what you know because it is misleading, it seems that you shouldn't pay any attention to what this new book says. Imagine that after reading this other book you decide to google "Super Bowl XX" and the first five hits that come up all say that the Chicago Bears didn't win Super Bowl XX. What should you do now? Well, since you know that the Chicago Bears *did* win the Super Bowl, it seems that again you shouldn't pay any attention to this evidence either. The story is the same, no matter how much additional evidence you come across saying that the Chicago Bears didn't win Super Bowl XX. But it seems crazy to think that you should ignore all of this evidence! Imagine that someone else were to tell you that they learned about the Chicago Bears winning Super Bowl XX in the way that you did and that they are now simply ignoring any evidence that they encounter that goes against this claim. Wouldn't you think that they are being unreasonably dogmatic?

On the one hand, it seems that we should disregard evidence that we know to be misleading, and we know that evidence that goes against the things we know to be true is misleading evidence. On the other hand, it seems that ignoring evidence in this way amounts to being unreasonably dogmatic. That's the dogmatism puzzle. The challenge is to figure out where the seemingly correct reasoning that led us to being dogmatic went wrong.

RESPONSES

The most popular response to the dogmatism puzzle is to insist that an underlying assumption of the above reasoning is false (Harman 1973, Conee 2004). The underlying assumption is that knowledge is *indefeasible*. Claiming that knowledge is indefeasible amounts to claiming that when you currently know that *p* you also know that *p* at any later time when you believe *p* for the same reasons that you do now. In other words, your knowledge cannot be defeated by additional information as long as you believe for the same reasons as you do when you now have that knowledge. Many philosophers argue that knowledge is in fact *defeasible* though. So, they contend you might know that *p* now and believe it for the same reasons later, and yet fail to know that *p* at this later time. Take the Super Bowl example again. You know that the Chicago Bears won Super Bowl XX now because you read it in this book. However, this response claims that later when you gain evidence against this claim your knowledge will be defeated. Hence, you will no longer know that the Chicago Bears won Super Bowl XX. Of course, since at this later time you no longer know that the Chicago Bears won Super Bowl XX, you aren't in a position to reasonably ignore evidence for or against this claim.

While it may seem that accepting that knowledge is defeasible gets us out of the dogmatism puzzle, some argue that it doesn't fully succeed (Lasonen-Aarnio 2014). They worry about situations where you gain evidence that weakens your support for believing *p* without making it so that you fail to know *p*. It seems that in such cases, you will still be in a position to ignore this evidence, since you still know that *p*, and so, know that the evidence against *p* must be misleading. But this still seems problematically dogmatic—you shouldn't ignore this evidence. Thus, some philosophers argue that accepting that knowledge is defeasible isn't enough to solve the dogmatism puzzle.

Recognition of this concern about the defeasibility of knowledge not being enough to block the problematic dogmatism leads other philosophers to argue that in order to solve this puzzle, we have to acknowledge that knowledge is defeasible *and* realize that even if we know that some evidence is misleading it doesn't always mean that we can reasonably ignore it. Various reasons have been offered for accepting the claim that knowing that some evidence is misleading isn't sufficient for reasonably ignoring the evidence. One reason is that while we might know that some evidence is misleading, we may not know that we know this. This approach claims that we need this additional knowledge about what we know in order to reasonably disregard evidence. A related reason that has been given is simply that we are too likely to be mistaken about whether some evidence is misleading or not (Veber 2004). As a result of our fallibility, when it comes to determining whether evidence is misleading, we shouldn't ignore evidence. A final reason that some give is that misleading evidence concerning *p* might still be able to make it so that we should think that *p* is less likely to be true than we originally thought—even when we know that the evidence is misleading (Ye 2016).

RECOMMENDED READING

SEMINAL PRESENTATIONS

Harman, G. 1973. *Thought*. Princeton, NJ: Princeton University Press.
Kripke, S. 2011. Two Paradoxes of Knowledge. In S. Kripke (ed), *Philosophical Troubles: Collected Papers (Volume 1)*. New York: Oxford University Press, 27–51.

ADDITIONAL IMPORTANT DISCUSSIONS

Baumann, P. 2013. Knowledge and Dogmatism. *The Philosophical Quarterly* 63: 1–19.

Conee, E. 2004. Heeding Misleading Evidence. In E. Conee and R. Feldman, *Evidentialism*. New York: Oxford University Press, 259–276.

Fantl, J. 2018. *The Limitations of the Open Mind*. Oxford: Oxford University Press.

Ginet, C. 1980. Knowing Less by Knowing More. *Midwest Studies in Philosophy* 5: 151–162.

Hawthorne, J. 2004. *Knowledge and Lotteries*. Oxford: Oxford University Press.

Lasonen-Aarnio, M. 2014. The Dogmatism Puzzle. *Australasian Journal of Philosophy* 92: 417–432.

Neta, R. 2009. Defeating the Dogma of Defeasibility. In P. Greenough and Duncan Pritchard (eds), *Williamson on Knowledge*. Oxford: Oxford University Press, 161–182.

Sorell, T. 1981. Harman's Paradox. *Mind* 90: 557–575.

Sorensen, R. 1988. Dogmatism, Junk Knowledge, and Conditionals. *The Philosophical Quarterly* 38: 433–454.

Veber, M. 2004. What Do You Do with Misleading Evidence? *The Philosophical Quarterly* 54: 557–569.

Ye, R. 2016. Misleading Evidence and the Dogmatism Puzzle. *Australasian Journal of Philosophy* 94: 563–575.

SLEEPING BEAUTY

Background: When it comes to something simple like a fair toss of a coin, we tend to think that it is obvious how confident we should be of a given outcome. For example, if we know that a coin is fair and that it is fairly tossed, we are inclined to think that it is clear that one should think that it is 50% likely that the coin landed "heads" after the toss. There are situations that put pressure on this seemingly obvious thought though.

EPISTEMOLOGICAL ISSUES: SLEEPING BEAUTY PROBLEM; SELF-LOCATING BELIEF

Beauty has agreed to be a subject in a strange sleep experiment. Here's how the study is going to go. Beauty is going to be put to sleep on Sunday. The researchers are going to briefly wake her up either only once or they will wake her twice over the three days of the study. They're going to decide how many times to wake her by flipping a fair coin. If the coin lands "heads", they'll wake her only once. If the coin lands "tails", they'll wake her twice. When they put Beauty back to sleep, they'll do so with a drug that will make her forget that she woke up at all.

Let's explain the possibilities in detail to help make the case clear. Beauty is put to sleep on Sunday. The researchers definitely wake her up on Monday. Later that evening, they flip the coin. If it comes up "heads" they won't wake Beauty up again on Tuesday. Instead, they'll just let her rest until the experiment ends on Wednesday. If the coin lands "tails", the experimenters will briefly wake Beauty up on Tuesday and once again administer the drug that puts her to sleep and makes her forget waking up at all.

A couple more things to keep in mind about this situation. Beauty is absolutely certain that the coin is a fair coin, and she is absolutely certain that it will be tossed fairly. And so, Beauty is absolutely certain that when this coin is tossed the objective chance of it coming up heads is ½ (the same is true for tails). She is also absolutely certain that the researchers will abide by the results of the coin toss and run the experiment as promised.

Now things get interesting. When Beauty is awakened on Monday (before the experimenters tell her what day it is), what should she think about the results of the coin toss? In other words, what should she think about how likely it is that the coin lands heads or tails? What should Beauty think about the coin toss after the experimenters tell her that it is Monday? (What's going on here and why it's puzzling will become clearer as we look at responses to this puzzle.)

RESPONSES

There are three primary responses to the Sleeping Beauty problem, and they all have serious defenders. The positions are named in accordance with the credence (roughly how much confidence) that they think Beauty should assign to the coin coming up heads. The positions are "thirder" (Elga 2000), "halfer" (Lewis 2001), and "double halfer" (Bostrom 2007, Meacham 2008, Pust 2012).

Here's what they each claim. According to the thirder position, when Beauty first wakes up on Monday (before she knows what day it is) her credence that the coin lands heads should be 1/3 (this is why this is called the "thirder" position). The reason for this assessment is that when we look at the long run frequencies of this sort of experiment, we should expect Beauty to be awakened by the experimenters with a heads flip about 1/3 of the time. Here's why. The coin and its toss are absolutely fair. So, the odds of the coin landing heads are 1/2. If we imagine that this experiment were run 100 times, we should expect (roughly) that 50 times the coin lands heads and 50 times it lands tails. Recall that if the coin lands heads, Beauty is awakened only once, but if it lands tails, then she is awakened twice. So, this means that if the experiment were conducted 100 times, Beauty would be awakened 150 times (50 times when the coin came up heads and 100 times when it came up tails). The thirder position is that since Beauty understands these frequencies, when she wakes up Monday morning, she should think that the odds that the coin lands heads are 1/3. After the experimenters inform Beauty that it is Monday morning (and the coin actually hasn't been flipped yet), the thirder position contends that Beauty should revise her credence so that she now thinks that the odds of heads are 1/2. Why is this? Because Beauty knows that this is the first (and perhaps only) time that she will be awakened in this experiment. Additionally, she knows that the objective chance that the coin will come up heads is 1/2 (plausibly, she also knows that when it comes to long run frequencies, after being awakened on a Monday the coin lands heads half the time). To sum up, the thirder position is that when Beauty first wakes up her credence that the coin lands heads should be 1/3, and after she learns that it is Monday her credence that the coin lands heads should change to 1/2.

The halfer position contends that when Beauty is awakened Monday morning (before the researchers tell her what day it is), she should have a 1/2 credence that the coin lands heads. Why? The halfer position is that Beauty should have this credence because she is certain that the objective chance of the coin coming up heads (or tails) is 1/2, so she should think that on any given flip, the odds of heads are 1/2. After all, the halfer position insists that Beauty doesn't have any information about the results of the flip except for the fact that it is perfectly fair, which means that the objective chance of heads is 1/2. A difficulty facing this position though concerns what to say about Beauty's credence when she learns that it is Monday. It seems that before learning this there were three possibilities for her as to what has happened: it's Monday and heads, it's Monday and tails, or it's Tuesday and tails (remember that if the coin lands heads she'll only be awakened on Monday, so there's no Tuesday and heads possibility). When Beauty learns that today is Monday that information allows her to eliminate a possibility— it's definitely not Tuesday and tails. But this seems to suggest that after she learns that it is Monday, Beauty should become more confident (i.e. assign a higher credence) that the coin lands heads. However, this doesn't seem right because she knows the coin is fair. Assigning more than 1/2 credence to heads on the flip of a fair coin seems to be a mistake. Those defending the halfer position respond by insisting that somehow the new evidence that Beauty gains when she is told that it is Monday is inadmissible when it comes to updating her credence. And so they maintain that Beauty's credence should remain unchanged.

Of course, some are skeptical of the halfer move to claim that Beauty gains inadmissible evidence when she learns that it is Monday. However, a number of those who are skeptical of this move don't embrace the thirder position. Instead, they are double halfers. The "double" part comes from the fact that they contend that Beauty's credence that the coin lands heads is 1/2 both before and after she learns that it is Monday. They arrive at this double half position by claiming (as halfers do) that when Beauty first wakes on Monday she should have a 1/2 credence that the coin lands heads (for the same reasons that halfers do), but then they insist, unlike halfers, that Beauty's credences after learning it is Monday should not be generated by conditionalizing on her earlier credences. Conditionalization is a Bayesian (probability) norm of about how one should change one's credences over time. So, double halfers deny that this norm applies to Beauty's situation when she learns that it is Monday.

Each of the three positions has its advantages and disadvantages, so the Sleeping Beauty Problem remains a puzzle without a generally accepted solution.

RECOMMENDED READING

GENERAL OVERVIEW

Titelbaum, M. 2013. Ten Reasons to Care about the Sleeping Beauty Problem. *Philosophy Compass* 8: 1003–1017.

SEMINAL PRESENTATION

Elga, A. 2000. Self-Locating Belief and the Sleeping Beauty Problem. *Analysis* 60: 143–147.

ADDITIONAL IMPORTANT DISCUSSIONS

Bostrom, N. 2007. Sleeping Beauty and Self-Location: A Hybrid Model. *Synthese* 157: 59–78.

Huemer, M. 2018. *Paradox Lost: Logical Solutions to Ten Puzzles of Philosophy*. London: Palgrave Macmillan.

Lewis, D. 2001. Sleeping Beauty: Reply to Elga. *Analysis* 61: 171–176.

Luna, L. 2020. Sleeping Beauty: Exploring a Neglected Solution. *British Journal for the Philosophy of Science* 71: 1069–1092.

Meacham, C. 2008. Sleeping Beauty and the Dynamics of De Se Beliefs. *Philosophical Studies* 138: 245–269.

Pust, J. 2012. Conditionalization and Essentially Indexical Credence. *Journal of Philosophy* 109: 295–315.

White, R. 2006. The Generalized Sleeping Beauty Problem: A Challenge for Thirders. *Analysis* 66: 114–119.

Winkler, P. 2017. The Sleeping Beauty Controversy. *The American Mathematical Monthly* 124: 579–587.

Yamada, M. 2019. Beauty, Odds, and Credence. *Philosophical Studies* 176: 1247–1261.

45

THE SURPRISE QUIZ PARADOX

Background: It may seem obvious that one can know that a surprise quiz is coming next week when the professor announces that there will be one. Yet, a seemingly impeccable line of reasoning yields the conclusion that there cannot be such a quiz.

EPISTEMOLOGICAL ISSUE: SURPRISE QUIZ PARADOX

Aaliyah is a very clever student (as philosophy students tend to be) in an epistemology course that meets five days a week (Monday through Friday). One Friday, as class is finishing up Aaliyah's professor announces that there will be a surprise quiz someday next week. Aaliyah thinks for a few minutes; then right before class ends, she raises her hand. When the professor calls on her, Aaliyah tells the professor that there *cannot* be a surprise quiz next week. The professor knows that Aaliyah is a very conscientious student, but she can't think of anything that is coming next week so that class would need to be canceled or any other reason why the students couldn't have a quiz. So she asks Aaliyah to explain.

Here's Aaliyah's response. The quiz can't be on Friday because if the class makes it to Thursday without a quiz, a quiz on Friday wouldn't be a surprise. So, the quiz can't be Friday. However, it can't be on

Thursday either. Why not? Well, Aaliyah explains that she knows that it isn't on Friday, so if the quiz hadn't occurred by the end of class on Wednesday, then she would know that it was on Thursday. But again this would mean that the quiz isn't a surprise. So, the quiz can't be on Thursday. Now, Aaliyah knows that it's not on Thursday or Friday. She says it can't be on Wednesday either. After all, since she knows it's not on Thursday or Friday, if the quiz hasn't been given by the end of class on Tuesday, then it wouldn't be a surprise if it's on Wednesday. So the quiz can't be given on Wednesday. What about Tuesday? Well, Aaliyah knows that the quiz can't be Wednesday, Thursday, or Friday. Given this, if the quiz doesn't take place by the end of class Monday, then she would know that it is coming on Tuesday. But again that would mean that the quiz isn't a surprise. So, the quiz can't be on Tuesday. This only leaves Monday. The quiz can't be then either though, since Aaliyah knows that it isn't Tuesday, Wednesday, Thursday, or Friday, that only leaves Monday. But, of course, if there's only one day that the quiz can be, the quiz won't be a surprise. Thus, there is no day that a surprise quiz can be given next week.

After the cheers of Aaliyah's classmates end, the professor congratulates Aaliyah on her clever argument. But, she informs the class that there *will* be a surprise quiz next week so they had better prepare for it.

What makes this situation (at least seem) paradoxical is that on the one hand, it is commonsense that there can be a surprise quiz even when it is announced the week before that such a quiz is coming. Yet, on the other hand, Aaliyah's argument that there cannot be such a quiz appears sound.

RESPONSES

One response to the Surprise Quiz Paradox claims that the professor's announcement is self-defeating (O'Conner 1948). The idea here is that her very statement undercuts itself. For example, if someone says to you in English, "I speak absolutely no English," this statement is self-defeating because by speaking the sentence itself the speaker is making the statement false. This response says the same thing happens when the professor announces a surprise quiz.

Another response simply insists that although the professor's announcement about the quiz is true, the students (Aaliyah included) cannot know that it is true (Quine 1953). Since Aaliyah doesn't know that the announcement is true, her reasoning doesn't go through because it crucially relies upon her knowing this. Of course, one worry that immediately arises is why we should think that Aaliyah and the other students can't know that the professor's announcement is true. One way of insisting that the announcement cannot be known is by arguing that the announcement is a Moorean sentence (see *Moore's Paradox* pp. 235–238) (Wright and Sudbury 1977). Moorean sentences are things like "it's raining, but I don't believe that it's raining." Many think that even though such sentences express propositions that can be true, they can't be known to be true by the person uttering them. Similarly, some insist that the professor's announcement amounts to a Moorean sentence for the students. As a result, Aaliyah and her classmates cannot know that the announcement is true.

A related response doesn't claim that the professor's initial announcement is a Moorean sentence, but instead contends that it becomes one at the end of class on Thursday (Olin 2003). The thinking here is that if class ends on Thursday and there hasn't been a quiz yet, Aaliyah (as well as the other students) can no longer know that the professor's announcement of a surprise quiz is true. This stops the first step in Aaliyah's argument. Here's the idea. Aaliyah's knowledge that the professor's announcement is true is the basis for her knowing Thursday (after class ends) that there will be a surprise quiz on Friday. However, if Aaliyah were to know that there would be a surprise quiz on Friday, then the quiz wouldn't be a surprise. But this means that the professor's announcement is false—so, Aaliyah couldn't know the announcement is true. Hence, on this response, Aaliyah could know that the professor's announcement is true all week until the end of class on Thursday. At that point, Aaliyah would no longer know that the announcement is true. Consequently, this response maintains that Aaliyah's initial step in her argument doesn't work. She couldn't know that the announcement is true after class on Thursday, so she couldn't legitimately infer that the quiz will be on Friday.

RECOMMENDED READING

GENERAL OVERVIEW

Epistemic Paradoxes. *Stanford Encyclopedia of Philosophy*. URL = https://plato.
stanford.edu/entries/epistemic-paradoxes/#SurTesPar

SEMINAL PRESENTATIONS

O'Connor, D.J. 1948. Pragmatic Paradoxes. *Mind* 57: 358–359.
Scriven, M. 1951. Paradoxical Announcements. *Mind* 60: 403–407.

ADDITIONAL IMPORTANT DISCUSSIONS

Binkley, R. 1968. The Surprise Examination in Modal Logic. *Journal of Philosophy* 65: 127–136.
Chow, T.Y. 1998. The Surprise Examination or Unexpected Hanging Paradox. *American Mathematical Monthly* 105: 41–51.
Dodd, D. 2016. The Cookie Paradox. *Philosophy and Phenomenological Research* 92: 355–377.
Hall, N. 1999. How to Set a Surprise Exam. *Mind* 108: 647–703.
Kripke, S. 2011. On Two Paradoxes of Knowledge. In *Philosophical Troubles: Collected Papers vol. 1.* New York: Oxford University Press, 27–51.
Olin, D. 1983. The Prediction Paradox Resolved. *Philosophical Studies* 44: 225–233.
Olin, D. 2003. *Paradox.* Montreal: McGill-Queen's University Press.
Quine, W.V.O. 1953. On a So-Called Paradox. *Mind* 62: 65–68.
Ramachandran, M. 2016. Knowledge-to-Fact Arguments (Bootstrapping, Closure, Paradox, and KK). *Analysis* 76: 142–149.
Sorensen, R. 1988. *Blindspots.* New York: Oxford University Press.
Veber, M. 2016. On a So-Called Solution to a Paradox. *Pacific Philosophical Quarterly* 97: 283–297.
Wright, C. and Sudbury, A. 1977. The Paradox of the Unexpected Examination. *Australasian Journal of Philosophy* 55: 41–58.

46

KNOWABILITY PARADOX

Background: Various antirealist views are committed to the idea that all truths are knowable. For example, the pragmatic theory of truth is committed to this idea. Charles Sanders Peirce insisted that truth is a matter of what would be believed without doubt after concluding an ideal investigation. On this view, a proposition is true just in case it would be believed without doubt after learning all there is to know about the topic. Fellow pragmatist William James developed a different pragmatic theory of truth. According to James, a proposition is true when acting on the basis of accepting the proposition makes us successful at our endeavors. Of course, there are important differences between these theories, and there are serious problems with such accounts of truth aside from what we are going to discuss in this entry, but the key point to notice here is that they are both committed to all truths being knowable. For Peirce, something is true only if we would believe it after an ideal investigation; presumably, this means that the truth must be knowable. Similarly, for James, we can't act on the basis of accepting a proposition unless we are in a position to believe the proposition, which suggests that the proposition must be knowable. There are numerous other antirealist views (not just about the nature of truth) that are committed to the idea that in order for a proposition to be true, it must be knowable (note this doesn't mean that they are committed to all truths being known—only that all truths are in principle knowable).

EPISTEMOLOGICAL ISSUE: KNOWABILITY PARADOX

The Knowability Paradox yields a problem for any theory that is committed to the idea that all truths are knowable because it seems to show that this commitment forces one to accept that all truths are actually *known by someone*. Here's a simple expression of the Knowability Paradox. We start with an assumption that seems pretty safe—let's assume that there is some truth that no one knows. Let's call this truth (since we don't know its content—if we did know its content, it wouldn't be unknown, after all) "UNKNOWN". So, UNKNOWN is true, but no one knows it. Of course, this means that it is true that "UNKNOWN is true and not known".

Antirealist views, which claim that all truths are knowable, are committed to claiming that "UNKNOWN is true and not known" is knowable. In other words, antirealist views are committed to it being possible for someone to know that UNKNOWN is true and at the same time to know that UNKNOWN is not known to be true. This follows given a very plausible principle known as "single premise closure". Single premise closure says that if you know that "*p* and *q*", then you know that *p* and you know that *q*. For instance, if you know that the ball is red and the bat is blue, then you know that the ball is red and you know that the bat is blue. Thus, it seems clear that antirealists are committed to claiming that someone can know that UNKNOWN is true and at the same time know that UNKNOWN is not known to be true. But, knowledge is factive. In other words, if someone knows that *p*, then *p* is true. In this case, it means that if someone knows that no one knows that UNKNOWN is true, then no one knows that UNKNOWN is true. However, this means that the antirealist position has led to a contradiction—it is true that someone knows that UNKNOWN is true and at the same time it is true that *no one* knows that UNKNOWN is true. Clearly, this can't be correct. If someone knows UNKNOWN is true, then it can't be that no one knows this. And, if no one knows UNKNOWN is true, then it can't be that some knows UNKNOWN is true.

Let's take stock of things. We started with the assumption that there is something that is true but not known by anyone. We combined this assumption with the antirealist claim that all truths are knowable.

This combination along with single premise closure and the fact that knowledge entails truth led us straight to a contradiction. Thus, something along the way must be false. But what? Single premise closure and that knowledge entails truth are nonnegotiable for pretty much all epistemologists. So, this seems to leave only denying either (a) the antirealist position that all truths are knowable or (b) the assumption that there are some truths that are not known by anyone.

RESPONSES

One response to the Knowability Paradox is to insist that it isn't a paradox at all but instead an argument that shows antirealist positions of this sort are false (Williamson 2000). This response contends that it is clear that there can be some truths that are unknown, so the Knowability Paradox simply shows us that it is false that all truths are knowable.

Another response is to hang onto antirealism and simply accept that despite appearances to the contrary, all truths are in fact known. This may not be as troubling a consequence as it seems at first. After all, many people believe in God, and they believe that God is omniscient. One straightforward view of omniscience is that an omniscient being knows all truths. Hence, if one believes in an omniscient God, one is already committed to the idea that all truths are actually known. (It's worth noting that belief in God doesn't commit one to antirealism—the point here is simply that *if* one wants to save antirealism from the Knowability Paradox, the existence of an all-knowing God makes the seemingly problematic claim that all truths are known unproblematic.)

Another response argues that the logic of knowability is paraconsistent, i.e. there can be true contradictions in it (Priest 2009). Specifically, this response contends that it can be true that someone both knows that p and at the same time doesn't know that p. The challenge for this sort of response is to motivate this move without trivializing the logic of knowability—that is, making it so that one can't validly conclude anything on the basis of a purportedly true contradiction.

A final sort of response involves restricting the antirealist idea that all truths are knowable in some sense. One way of making this response contends that any true proposition that isn't provably inconsistent is knowable (Tennant 1997). Another way of making this response limits the idea that all truths are knowable to "basic" statements (Dummett 2001). Roughly, the idea is that compound propositions do not fall under the requirement of being knowable in order to be true; rather, only the simple propositions that make up these compounds do. Both of these options would rule out "UNKNOWN is true and not known" from counting as knowable.

RECOMMENDED READING

GENERAL OVERVIEWS

Epistemic Paradoxes. *Stanford Encyclopedia of Philosophy*. URL = https://plato. stanford.edu/entries/epistemic-paradoxes/#SurTesPar

Fitch's Paradox of Knowability. *Stanford Encyclopedia of Philosophy*. URL = https:// plato.stanford.edu/entries/fitch-paradox/#EpiRev

SEMINAL PRESENTATIONS

Church, A. 2009. Referee Reports on Fitch's 'A Definition of Value'. In J. Salerno (ed), *New Essays on the Knowability Paradox*. Oxford: Oxford University Press, 13–20.

Fitch, F. 1963. A Logical Analysis of Some Value Concepts. *The Journal of Symbolic Logic* 28: 135–142.

ADDITIONAL IMPORTANT DISCUSSIONS

Beall, J.C. 2000. Fitch's Proof, Verificationism, and the Knower Paradox. *Australasian Journal of Philosophy* 78: 241–247.

Brogaard, B. and Salerno, J. 2008. Knowability, Possibility and Paradox. In V. Hendricks and D. Pritchard (eds), *New Waves in Epistemology*. New York: Palgrave Macmillan, 270–299.

Dummett, M. 2001. Victor's Error. *Analysis* 61: 1–2.

Kvanvig, J. 2006. *The Knowability Paradox*. Oxford: Oxford University Press.

McCain, K. 2016. *The Nature of Scientific Knowledge: An Explanatory Approach*. Cham: Springer.

Priest, G. 2009. Beyond the Limits of Knowledge. In J. Salerno (ed.), *New Essays on the Knowability Paradox*. Oxford: Oxford University Press, 93–104.

Salerno, J. (ed) 2009. *New Essays on the Knowability Paradox*. Oxford: Oxford University Press.

Tennant, N. 1997. *The Taming of the True*. Oxford: Oxford University Press.

Williamson, T. 2000. *Knowledge and Its Limits*. Oxford: Oxford University Press.

47

MOORE'S PARADOX

Background: Saying something like "it's raining and it's not raining" (when referring to the same exact location at the same exact time) is absurd. Of course, in this sort of case the absurdity lies in the fact that what is said is contradictory. There are, however, other things that seem absurd to say that aren't contradictions. In fact, these other sorts of absurd claims might in fact be true! It can be challenging to explain exactly why it is that something that is true is nonetheless absurd to say or believe.

EPISTEMOLOGICAL ISSUE: MOORE'S PARADOX

Imagine that your friend George says to you "it's raining, but I don't believe it." Then, on another occasion he says, "it's raining, but I believe that it's not raining." After making sure that you heard him correctly, you're apt to conclude that he is talking nonsense. And this seems to be the right conclusion. What George said seems to be absurd. Nevertheless, he didn't utter a contradiction. That is, he didn't say something like "it's raining and it's not raining." In fact, what George said in both cases could be true. After all, it could be that it is raining and George doesn't believe that it is, and it could also be that it is raining and George believes that it's not raining. We can even assume that when George spoke to you on both of these occasions, he was telling the truth. Nonetheless, even if what George said was true, it still seems absurd for him to say it. But, it is challenging to explain what makes this absurd since it appears to have nothing to do with whether what George said is true. This is Moore's Paradox—it seems that what George says is absurd, but it's not clear why this should be so.

Until now, we've been discussing Moore's Paradox in terms of what's wrong with what George says; however, the paradox also applies to beliefs. In particular, it seems that the absurdity doesn't go away if George believes these things but keeps his mouth shut about them. In other words, it seems just as absurd to believe "it's raining, but I don't believe it" and "it's raining, but I believe that it's not raining" as it is to assert these claims to others. We will limit our focus to the belief version of this paradox because that is more clearly central to epistemology. That said, let's make sure that we are crystal clear on the general nature of Moore's Paradox. It seems that it is absurd to believe "p and I don't believe that p" or to believe "p and I believe that p is false". Nevertheless, neither of these Moorean sentences express obvious contradictions. In fact, it seems that they could both be true. So the challenge of Moore's Paradox is to explain why it is that believing such Moorean propositions is unreasonable.

RESPONSES

One response to Moore's Paradox contends that at least for one kind of Moorean proposition, it is impossible for you to believe its content. This response relies upon the idea that anytime you believe that p, you also believe that you believe that p (Hintikka 1962). Hence, this response insists that "p and I don't believe that p" cannot be rationally believed because it will land the believer in a contradiction. Here's how. According to this response, if you believe "p and I don't believe that p", that means that you believe p and you believe that "I don't believe that p". But since you believe that p, you must also believe that you believe that p. Thus, according to this response, what's absurd about believing a Moorean proposition is that in doing so, you would have to believe that you believe that p and (at the same time) believe that you don't believe that p, which is a contradiction. And, this response claims that it isn't possible for us to believe this sort of obvious contradiction.

Another response to this paradox is to argue that what makes believing a Moorean proposition absurd is that by believing it you thereby make the proposition false (Williams 1994). Here, the idea is that when George forms the belief "it's raining, but I don't believe it", his forming that belief makes it false. After all, when George forms this belief, he believes that it is raining (that's the first part of the proposition), but his believing that it's raining makes the second half of the proposition false. Thus, this response claims that the solution to Moore's Paradox is to realize that while Moorean propositions might be true, it is absurd to believe them because once you believe the proposition it becomes false.

A related way of responding to Moore's Paradox is to claim that rather than the believing making a Moorean proposition false, you can never be *justified* in believing a Moorean proposition whether or not it is true (Williams 2004). The thought here is that whatever justifies George in believing that it is raining also justifies him in believing that he believes that it is raining. So, the general idea here is that you can never justifiably believe a Moorean proposition. Either you will have justification for believing p, in which case you will also have justification for believing that you believe that p. Or you will have justification for believing that you don't believe that p, or that you believe that p is false, in which case you will lack justification for believing that p. In either scenario, you fail to have justification for the conjunction that is the Moorean proposition.

A final sort of response denies that there is actually a problem with believing Moorean propositions in general. This response insists that there are serious philosophical positions that one might hold that can make believing a Moorean proposition rational (Frances 2016). For example, you might be a nihilist about composition (this is a view in metaphysics that some philosophers accept which says that there are no compound objects, i.e. there are only fundamental particles) and accept that perceptual beliefs are not under our control. In such a case, you might reasonably believe "there's a book and I believe that it's false that there's a book" because your perceptual faculties spontaneously cause you to believe that there is a book, but you accept a philosophical theory on which there is no such thing as books. Similarly, this response holds that for the other sort of Moorean proposition, it is possible for one to believe "there's a book, but I don't believe that there is". In this case, it may be that you accept eliminative materialism (this is a view in philosophy of mind which holds that there are no beliefs—it claims that "belief" is simply an outdated folk concept). So, it might be true that there is a book and that you don't believe that there is because you don't believe that there are beliefs. Of course, the only way that *believing* Moorean propositions can actually be a problem is if eliminative materialism is false, so the assumption here is that this theory is false, even though one might believe it. Hence, it could be that you in fact believe that "there's a book, but I don't believe that there is" because you accept eliminative materialism, even though the theory is false. In sum, this way of responding to Moore's Paradox insists that there is no paradox because there's nothing irrational about believing Moorean propositions in at least some cases.

RECOMMENDED READING

GENERAL OVERVIEWS

Epistemic Paradoxes. *Stanford Encyclopedia of Philosophy*. URL = https://plato.stanford.edu/entries/epistemic-paradoxes/#SurTesPar

Williams, J.N. 2015. Moore's Paradox in Speech: A Critical Survey. *Philosophy Compass* 10: 10–23.

Williams, J.N. 2015. Moore's Paradox in Thought: A Critical Survey. *Philosophy Compass* 10: 24–37.

SEMINAL PRESENTATIONS

Moore, G.E. 1942. A Reply to My Critics. In P. Schilpp (ed), *The Philosophy of G.E. Moore*. La Salle: Open Court, 535–677.

Moore, G.E. 1944. Russell's Theory of Descriptions. In P. Schilpp (ed), *The Philosophy of Bertrand Russell*. La Salle: Open Court, 175–225.

ADDITIONAL IMPORTANT DISCUSSIONS

Brueckner, A. 2006. Justification and Moore's Paradox. *Analysis* 66: 264–266.

Frances, B. 2016. Rationally Held 'P, but I Fully Believe ~P and I am Not Equivocating. *Philosophical Studies* 173: 309–313.

Green, M.S. and Williams, J.N. (eds) 2007. *Moore's Paradox: New Essays on Belief, Rationality, and the First Person*. Oxford: Oxford University Press.

Hintikka, J. 1962. *Knowledge and Belief*. Ithaca, NY: Cornell University Press.

Smithies, D. 2012. Moore's Paradox and the Accessibility of Justification. *Philosophy and Phenomenological Research* 85: 273–300.

Williams, J.N. 1994. Moorean Absurdity and the Intentional 'Structure' of Assertion. *Analysis* 54: 160–166.

Williams, J.N. 2004. Moore's Paradoxes, Evans's Principle and Self-knowledge. *Analysis* 64: 348–353.

48

LOTTERY PARADOX

Background: Here are three principles that seem very plausible. First, what we might call "SUFFICIENCY". SUFFICIENCY says that it is rational to accept/believe that p, if the probability that p is sufficiently high (even if the probability isn't 1, i.e. even if it isn't absolutely certain that p is true). Many people accept this because it seems that if we require certainty (probability 1) before it is rational to believe something, we will be saddled with widespread skepticism. After all, very few things that we believe are absolutely certain for us. Second, there's what we might call "CONJUNCTION". CONJUNCTION says that if it is rational to believe p and rational to believe q, then it is rational to believe p and q. For example, it appears to be obviously true that if it is rational to believe that it is raining and it is rational to believe that you have your umbrella, then it is rational to believe it is raining and you have your umbrella. Third, there's what we might call "NO CONTRADICTION". NO CONTRADICTION is just that it isn't rational to believe a contradiction. In other words, it's not rational to believe p and not p at the same time. Although all three of these principles are plausible, the Lottery Paradox seems to show that they cannot all be true.

EPISTEMOLOGICAL ISSUE: LOTTERY PARADOX

Henry has recently purchased a ticket for a lottery with 100 tickets total. He knows that the lottery is fair, and it is guaranteed to have only one winning ticket. The drawing has just occurred, but Henry hasn't learned the results yet. What should he think about his ticket? While many claim that Henry doesn't *know* that his ticket lost, most people think that it would be *reasonable* for him to believe that it did. After all, it's 99% likely that Henry's ticket is a losing ticket. It seems that Henry is reasonable in thinking that his ticket, let's say that his is ticket #1, lost. Of course, if it is reasonable for Henry to think that ticket #1 (his ticket) lost, it seems equally reasonable for him to think that ticket #2 lost. It's just as likely that ticket #2 lost as it is that ticket #1 lost. The same is apparently true for ticket #3 as well, and it is true for each of the other tickets too. It is 99% likely that any given ticket in the lottery is a losing ticket. So, it seems that it is reasonable for Henry to believe of each ticket that it lost. But of course if it's reasonable for Henry to believe that ticket #1 lost and to believe that ticket #2 lost and that ticket #3 lost and so on, it seems that it is reasonable for him to believe "ticket #1 and ticket #2 and ticket #3 and… ticket #100 lost". But Henry knows that the lottery is fair and that one ticket is a winner! Thus, it seems that it is reasonable for Henry to believe that all the tickets lost and at the same time reasonable for him to believe that one of the tickets won. However, "all the tickets lost and one of the tickets won" is, of course, a contradiction. This is the lottery paradox.

It is important to keep in mind that there only appear to be three principles at play in the lottery paradox, what we have called SUF-FICIENCY, CONJUNCTION, and NO CONTRADICTION. Once we assume that one can know (and so rationally believe) that a particular lottery is fair, that it has one winning ticket, and that one knows how many tickets are in the lottery—exceedingly plausible assumptions—it is easy to come up with cases, like this one, that show that we can't reasonably accept all three principles. But, they are all at least initially very plausible. That is why this lottery problem is considered a paradox.

RESPONSES

As we have said, the lottery paradox seems to straightforwardly show that the three principles, SUFFICIENCY, CONJUNCTION, and NO CONTRADICTION, are jointly inconsistent. In other words, they cannot all be true. The challenge of the paradox lies in determining which principle we should think is false, since they are all plausible principles. Given that the paradox arises from three principles, there are three general ways of responding to it.

The first way of responding to the lottery paradox is to deny NO CONTRADICTION. This response involves accepting that it can actually be reasonable in some cases to believe something that you recognize is a contradiction (Priest 1998). This is by far the least popular option when it comes to responding to this sort of paradox, but it is not without a handful of serious defenders. The key to this sort of response is to delineate why it is reasonable to believe some contradictions but not others as well as explain how it is that a rational belief in a contradiction doesn't "explode" by allowing one to then reasonably infer anything else. (In classical systems of logic, every proposition is entailed by a contradiction. So the worry here is that supporters of this response need to give a principled reason for why one can rationally believe a contradiction but not then rationally infer every proposition from the rationally believed contradiction.)

A more popular response, which was what Henry Kyburg originally took the lottery paradox to show, is that CONJUNCTION is false (Kyburg 1961, 1970). The idea here is that while Henry can rationally believe that ticket #1 lost, that ticket #2 lost, that ticket #3 lost, and so on, he can't rationally believe the conjunction of all of these. In other words, Henry cannot rationally believe that "ticket #1 and ticket #2 and ticket #3… and ticket #100 lost". Proponents of this view often point out that risks add up, and once the risk of being wrong is high enough it is no longer rational to believe. To illustrate this idea, let's assume that in order for it to be rational to believe that p, it must be that your evidence makes p's truth higher than 95% (this is just an arbitrary assumption—the point here will be the same for any threshold that we set below 100%). Henry is rational in believing that ticket #1 lost because it is 99% likely that it lost. He is also rational in believing that ticket #2 lost because it is 99% likely that it lost. He is also rational in believing that ticket #3 lost because it is 99% likely that it lost. And so on. However, Henry isn't justified in believing the conjunction that all of the tickets lost because the little bit of risk that he is wrong about each individual ticket adds up. For example, it is 99% likely that ticket #1 lost and 99% likely that ticket #2 lost, but it is only 98.01% likely that both ticket #1 and ticket #2 lost. As we combine more of Henry's beliefs about the individual tickets together, the more likely it is that he is mistaken. Eventually, Henry's evidence will make the truth of the conjunction of beliefs about the tickets less likely than 95%. In fact, once he gets to the belief that "ticket #1 and ticket #2 and ticket #3 and ticket #4 and ticket #5 and ticket #6 lost" it is only 94.15% likely that he is correct. This response claims that because the risks of individual beliefs add up, it is false that when it is rational to believe p and rational to believe q, it must be rational to believe p and q. Thus, in this case Henry can rationally believe of each ticket that it lost, but he can't rationally put these beliefs together.

The final sort of response seeks to retain both NO CONTRA-DICTION and CONJUNCTION by denying SUFFICIENCY. The gist of this way of responding is that p having a sufficiently high probability isn't enough to make believing p rational (Smith 2010). In other words, there are cases where p has a high probability, but one shouldn't believe that p. According to this way of responding, Henry is in one of these situations. Although for any given ticket the probability that it lost is 99%, it isn't rational for Henry to believe that the ticket lost. There are various ways of cashing out this sort of response. One way of making this response is to simply add a principle that blocks this sort of case. For instance, one might insist that when the truth of a conjunction of otherwise rationally supported beliefs is called into question by a rational belief, then it is not rational to accept any of the beliefs of the conjunction (assuming that the belief that calls the conjunction into doubt doesn't target specific members of the conjunction) (Ryan 1996). Another route is to deny that purely statistical evidence, of the sort that Henry has, is sufficient to justify belief. Rather, one might contend that something like an explanatory connection between the belief and the fact in the world that makes the belief true is needed (Nelkin 2000). However exactly one spells out this response, the general idea is that it avoids the lottery paradox by claiming that Henry isn't rational in believing of any particular ticket that it lost. This allows one to continue to accept that it isn't rational to believe contradictions and to accept that it is rational to believe conjunctions of things that one rationally believes.

RECOMMENDED READING

GENERAL OVERVIEWS

Epistemic Paradoxes. *Stanford Encyclopedia of Philosophy*. URL = https://plato. stanford.edu/entries/epistemic-paradoxes/#SurTesPar

Wheeler, G. 2007. A Review of the Lottery Paradox. In W. Harper and G. Wheeler (eds), *Probability and Inference: Essays in Honour of Henry E. Kyburg, Jr.* London: College Publications, 1–31.

SEMINAL PRESENTATION

Kyburg, H. 1961. *Probability and the Logic of Rational Belief.* Middletown, CT: Wesleyan University Press.

ADDITIONAL IMPORTANT DISCUSSIONS

Douven, I. 2002. A New Solution to the Paradoxes of Rational Acceptability. *British Journal for the Philosophy of Science* 53: 391–410.

Douven, I. (ed) 2021. *Lotteries, Knowledge, and Rational Belief: Essays on the Lottery Paradox*. Cambridge: Cambridge University Press.

Douven, I. and Williamson, T. 2006. Generalizing the Lottery Paradox. *British Journal for the Philosophy of Science* 57: 755–779.

Foley, R. 1993. *Working without a Net*. Oxford: Oxford University Press.

Kroedel, T. 2012. The Lottery Paradox, Epistemic Justification and Permissibility. *Analysis* 72: 57–60.

Kyburg, H. 1970. Conjunctivitis. In M. Swain (ed), *Induction, Acceptance, and Rational Belief*. Dordrecht: D. Reidel, 55–82.

Nelkin, D. 2000. Paradox, Knowledge, and Rationality. *Philosophical Review* 109: 373–409.

Priest, G. 1998. What Is So Bad About Contradictions? *Journal of Philosophy* 95: 410–426.

Ryan, S. 1996. The Epistemic Virtues of Consistency. *Synthese* 109: 121–141.

Smith, M. 2010. What Else Justification Could Be. *Nous* 44: 10–31.

PREFACE PARADOX

Background: There is another paradox that is similar to the lottery paradox discussed in the previous entry. One of the things that makes this paradox seem importantly different is that it doesn't rely upon probabilistic evidence.

EPISTEMOLOGICAL ISSUE: PREFACE PARADOX

Sharon is a very careful scholar, and she has recently finished a meticulously researched book. Since the book is finished, she's putting the final touches on it. The last thing she has to write before sending the book in to her publisher is the preface, which she has almost completed. As she is concluding the preface, Sharon decides to include a statement that is typical of prefaces, and that expresses her genuine humility. Sharon acknowledges that:

> while I have done my utmost to carefully vet every claim made in this book, I am only human. So, surely there are errors that remain. Any such error is, of course, a failing on my part—not on the part of any of the many excellent colleagues who provided helpful feedback as I completed this project.

Sharon's remark at the end of the preface to her book is quite typical of academic books. It is very common for authors to remark that despite their best efforts, there are certainly errors remaining in their books. Not only is this commonplace, it seems to be something that any reasonable author would accept (even if not all authors explicitly acknowledge the point in their prefaces). Although such admissions are common and seem correct, they're also quite puzzling. In fact, they seem to suggest that authors tend to have inconsistent sets of beliefs. After all, Sharon believes every claim in her book—why would she make the claims if she didn't think they were true? In other words, she believes claim 1, claim 2, and so on. Importantly, because of her careful research, Sharon rationally/justifiedly believes each of these claims. So, for this large set of claims Sharon believes all of them. But she says (and presumably believes) that at least one of the members of the set of claims she makes in the book is mistaken. Again, this seems to be something that Sharon rationally/justifiedly believes on the basis of the fact that pretty much every book with as many claims as hers has at least some errors. However, this suggests that Sharon believes that each member of the set of claims made in her book is true and at the same time believes that the members of the set of claims in her book are not all true. It clearly cannot be the case that all of the claims in her book are true and some of them are false. It appears that Sharon's beliefs are inconsistent. What is more, Sharon seems perfectly aware of this apparent inconsistency in her beliefs. And yet, it seems that Sharon isn't being unreasonable, i.e. she seems to be rational/justified in believing the claims she made in her book and also believing that she has made some errors in the book. How can this be?

RESPONSES

Similar to the Lottery Paradox (see the previous entry), the Preface Paradox makes use of CONJUNCTION and NO CONTRADICTION (though, since the Preface Paradox isn't in terms of probabilities, it doesn't rely upon SUFFICIENCY). There is a problem with Sharon's beliefs because it seems that her belief that the conjunction is true contradicts her belief that she has made at least some errors, i.e. her belief that the conjunction is false. Given that the Preface Paradox, like the Lottery Paradox, assumes CONJUNCTION and NO CONTRADICTION, two of the ways of responding to the Preface Paradox are similar to responses to the Lottery Paradox. One way of responding is to deny NO CONTRADICTION by accepting that although Sharon's beliefs are inconsistent, they are still rational. Unlike the Lottery Paradox, a sizeable number of theorists have opted for claiming that the Preface Paradox shows exactly this—one can have inconsistent beliefs and yet all of those beliefs are justified (Klein 1985, Foley 1993, Priest 1998).

Another response is to deny CONJUNCTION. The idea here is that although Sharon justifiedly believes each of the claims in her book, she isn't justified in believing the conjunction of all of those claims. The thought here is that if she isn't justified in believing the conjunction, then her justified belief that the conjunction is false (that she has made some mistake somewhere in the book) doesn't contradict her other beliefs.

Two other kinds of responses remain—accept that Sharon has the beliefs mentioned in the case but deny that Sharon's beliefs are actually inconsistent in this case or deny that Sharon even has the justified beliefs that the Preface Paradox assumes that she does. Let's start with the latter. Some argue that Sharon doesn't have the justified beliefs that we have been assuming because she's not actually justified in believing that there is an error in her book (Ryan 1991, 1996). Instead, this response insists that at most Sharon is justified in believing something like the book *might* contain an error or that it *probably* contains an error. Hence, even if Sharon believes that her book contains an error, that belief isn't justified. Another way of cashing out this response is to contend that Sharon doesn't even have the beliefs that it appears that she does (Kim 2015). This response contends that saying the sort of thing that Sharon does in the preface of her book signals her acknowledgment of her own fallibility without implying that she actually believes that there is an error in her book. Of course, if Sharon doesn't actually have the beliefs that are claimed to be inconsistent, then there is no paradox here.

The final sort of response allows that Sharon has the justified beliefs that seem to generate the paradox but argues that those beliefs aren't inconsistent (Clarke 2017). One way to do this is to maintain that while Sharon believes the conjunction of the claims of her book and believes what she expressed in the preface, she doesn't have those beliefs in the same context. The idea is that whether or not someone has a belief is context sensitive. The thrust of this response is that in general, whether someone counts as believing something depends upon the particular context that the person is in. So, one might believe that *p* relative to one context but not relative to another. Consequently, this sort of response claims that Sharon counts as believing the claims of her book when she was writing the main part of her book, but not when she is writing the preface, and vice versa for the claim in the preface that she has made a mistake in the main part of the book. Thus, although Sharon has the justified beliefs that seem to generate the paradox, she doesn't actually have inconsistent beliefs because she doesn't count as believing each of these in the same context.

RECOMMENDED READING

GENERAL OVERVIEW

Epistemic Paradoxes. *Stanford Encyclopedia of Philosophy*. URL = https://plato.stanford.edu/entries/epistemic-paradoxes/#SurTesPar

SEMINAL PRESENTATION

Mackinson, D.C. 1965. The Paradox of the Preface. *Analysis* 25: 205–207.

ADDITIONAL IMPORTANT DISCUSSIONS

Clarke, R. 2017. Preface Writers are Consistent. *Pacific Philosophical Quarterly* 98: 363–381.

Douven, I. 2002. A New Solution to the Paradoxes of Rational Acceptability. *British Journal for the Philosophy of Science* 53: 391–410.

Foley, R. 1993. *Working without a Net*. Oxford: Oxford University Press.

Kim, B. 2015. This Paper Surely Contains Some Errors. *Philosophical Studies* 172: 1013–1029.

Klein, P. 1985. The Virtues of Inconsistency. *The Monist* 68: 105–135.

Olin, D. 2003. *Paradox*. Montreal: McGill-Queen's University Press.

Priest, G. 1998. What Is So Bad About Contradictions? *Journal of Philosophy* 95: 410–426.

Ryan, S. 1991. The Preface Paradox. *Philosophical Studies* 64: 293–307.

Ryan, S. 1996. The Epistemic Virtues of Consistency. *Synthese* 109: 121–141.

Smith, M. Forthcoming. The Hardest Paradox for Closure. *Erkenntnis*.

Worsnip, A. 2016. Belief, Credence, and the Preface Paradox. *Australasian Journal of Philosophy* 94: 549–562.

THE PROOF PARADOX

Background: The proof paradox is an epistemological puzzle that originally arose in the context of legal theory. It concerns how we are to think about statistical evidence (for example, 60% of Xs are Y) as compared to nonstatistical evidence (for example, eyewitness testimony). The issue arises because various legal standards seem to be quantifiable. Two of the most common legal standards are "preponderance of evidence", which is often the standard used in civil lawsuits, and "beyond reasonable doubt", which is often the standard employed in criminal proceedings. Preponderance of evidence is typically understood to mean anything more likely than 50%, and beyond reasonable doubt is typically taken to mean 90–95% odds that the person is guilty.

There is a broader view in epistemology that is also important to think about when considering the proof paradox. It is what is known as "probabilism". This is a view of epistemic justification that is commonly accepted by both internalists and externalists (see General Background: The Nature of Justification pp. 113–119). Roughly, probabilism is the idea that you have justification to believe that p when your evidence makes p's truth sufficiently probable. The connection between probabilism and legal standards of proof is especially clear in some theorists' views, e.g. evidentialists Earl Conee and Richard Feldman specifically suggest that having sufficient justification for knowing that p requires meeting the "criminal standard" of evidence, i.e. p's truth being beyond reasonable doubt.

EPISTEMOLOGICAL ISSUES: PROBABILISM; STATISTICAL EVIDENCE

Let's think about a couple scenarios.

> *BUSES*: Ginger is driving her car and hit by a reckless bus driver. Unfortunately, since Ginger was caught completely by surprise, she didn't get a good look at the bus or the driver. She could tell that it was clearly a bus that hit her, but she was so disoriented that she couldn't clearly make out whether the bus was black or blue. To make matters worse there were no eyewitnesses or security cameras nearby. However, Ginger learns that there are only two bus companies in town. One has all black buses and the other has all blue buses. And, the company with blue buses is considerably larger than its rival—85% of the buses operating in town are owned by this company.

> *TVs*: Fred was seen leaving a store with a new TV the same day the store was looted. That day 100 TVs were taken from the store, but only 1 of the 100 was actually purchased. Unfortunately, the TV that was purchased was a cash transaction and the customer left their receipt on the counter. And, as luck would have it there was no security footage showing the purchase being made.

When we think about situations like *BUSES* and *TVs* puzzles arise. For instance, suppose that Ginger decides to file a lawsuit against the company with the blue buses purely on the grounds that she was hit by a bus, and this company owns 85% of the buses in town. Intuitively, it doesn't seem like she should win this lawsuit. However, civil lawsuits like this one only require a preponderance of evidence (i.e. greater than 50% odds that one side is at fault). Similarly, think about Fred. Suppose Fred is picked up by the police and criminal charges are brought against him. The only evidence against Fred is that he left the store with a TV and 99% of the TVs taken from the store that day were stolen. If he were convicted of theft on those grounds and made to pay a stiff fine, it seems a grave injustice would have occurred. Yet, beyond reasonable doubt is typically taken to simply mean 90–95% odds that the person is guilty, and the odds that Fred is guilty are even better than that. It's 99% likely that he stole the TV.

The proof paradox becomes even more interesting when we consider slight variations of *BUSES* and *TVs*. Let's assume that in each case, there is actually an eyewitness who testifies about what happened. Let's further assume that the eyewitnesses aren't connected with Ginger or

Fred and don't seem to have any reason for giving false testimony. So, there's a neutral eyewitness who saw Ginger struck by a bus, and the witness says it was a blue bus. And there's a neutral eyewitness who says that Fred didn't pay for the TV, but instead he stole it. What should we think now? Most people think that now there are good grounds for awarding Ginger compensation in her lawsuit against the bus company, and there are good grounds for convicting Fred of theft. What is puzzling about this is that we know that eyewitness testimony is far from perfect. In fact, it is very likely that the odds that someone stole a TV, say, given that an eyewitness reports this is less than 99% (and depending on the details, the eyewitness report is likely to fail to make it more than 85% probable that a particular color bus was involved in a hit-and-run accident). So, we are left with a puzzle. Why is it that the statistical evidence, which makes it 99% likely that Fred stole the TV, is insufficient for convicting him of a crime, but the evidence from an eyewitness, which fails to make it even 99% likely that Fred stole the TV, is good enough for a conviction? This is the *proof paradox*.

As mentioned in the background above, beyond the applied epistemological challenge that the proof paradox raises in legal contexts, there is a broader challenge here. Probabilism suggests that solely on the basis of the statistical evidence, we should believe that Fred stole the TV (and in many forms, it also suggests that we should believe that a blue bus struck Ginger). But, intuitively, we shouldn't believe that Fred stole the TV. Nevertheless, once an eyewitness tells us that Fred stole the TV, it seems that we have sufficient evidence for believing he did so, even though this evidence doesn't make his theft as probable as the purely statistical evidence does.

RESPONSES

One response to the proof paradox is to insist that in order for evidence to be sufficient in a legal setting (and perhaps epistemically as well), there must be a causal connection between the evidence and the claim in question (Thomson 1986). For example, the reason that testimonial evidence is sufficient for ruling in Ginger's favor is that the bus's being blue is a cause of the eyewitness's testimony. The statistical evidence fails to meet this requirement because there isn't a causal connection between the color of the bus that hit Ginger and the statistical fact that 85% of the buses in town are blue. Hence, this response claims that the reason we have the intuitions that we do in *BUSES* and *TVs* is that the statistical evidence lacks the right sort of causal connection to the claim in question.

Another response is to appeal to sensitivity (see *A Strange County* pp. 16–20 and *Red Barns and Blue Façades* pp. 21–24 for more on sensitivity) (Enoch et al. 2012). The idea here is that in order for evidence to actually meet legal standards, it has to be the case that if the claim in question were false, the evidence wouldn't obtain. For instance, if Fred didn't steal the TV, the eyewitness wouldn't have said that he did. However, even if Fred didn't steal the TV, it would still be the case that it is 99% likely that he did given the number of TVs stolen on the day he walked out of the store with his TV.

Yet another response is to accept a view under which one's evidence consists of all and only what one knows (Williamson 2000). In this case, when the eyewitness tells us that Fred stole the TV we come to know that he did. So the evidence supports convicting him of a crime. However, when we learn that the odds are 99 to 1 that he stole the TV, we don't have that he stole the TV as evidence. Instead, we only have that it is 99% likely that he did.

Finally, there is a response to the proof paradox that, unlike the first three responses, gives up on probabilism. On this way of looking at things, we shouldn't think that evidence justifies believing that *p* whenever it makes *p* sufficiently probable. Instead, we should think that evidence supports *p* when it is the case that something abnormal would be going on if the evidence obtained but *p* were false (Smith 2016, 2018). For example, if the eyewitness says that a blue bus hit Ginger but a blue bus didn't hit Ginger something strange would have occurred and it would require explanation. Did the eyewitness make a mistake, were they paid by Ginger, or something else? However, if the statistical evidence is simply that 85% of the buses are blue, but a blue bus didn't hit Ginger nothing needs to be explained.

RECOMMENDED READING

GENERAL OVERVIEW

Ross, L.D. 2020. Recent Work on the Proof Paradox. *Philosophy Compass* 15: e12667.

SEMINAL PRESENTATIONS

Tribe, L. 1971. Trial by Mathematics: Precision and Ritual in the Legal Process. *Harvard Law Review* 84: 1329–1393.

Nesson, C. 1979. Reasonable Doubt and Permissive Inferences: The Value of Complexity. *Harvard Law Review* 92: 1187–1225.

Thomson, J.J. 1986. Liability and Individualized Evidence. *Law and Contemporary Problems* 49: 199–219.

ADDITIONAL IMPORTANT DISCUSSIONS

Blome-Tillmann, M. 2015. Sensitivity, Causality, and Statistical Evidence in Courts of Law. *Thought* 4: 102–112.

Conee, E. and Feldman, R. *Evidentialism*. New York: Oxford University Press.

Enoch, D., Spectre, L., and Fisher, T. 2012. Statistical Evidence, Sensitivity, and the Legal Value of Knowledge. *Philosophy and Public Affairs* 40: 197–224.

Gardiner, G. 2018. Legal Burdens of Proof and Statistical Evidence. In D. Coady and J. Chase (eds), *The Routledge Handbook of Applied Epistemology*. New York: Routledge, 175–195.

Moss, S. 2018. *Probabilistic Knowledge*. Oxford: Oxford University Press.

Pardo, M.S. and Allen, R.J. 2008. Juridical Proof and the Best Explanation. *Law and Philosophy* 27: 223–268.

Redmayne, M. 2008. Exploring the Proof Paradoxes. *Legal Theory* 14: 281–309.

Smith, M. 2016. *Between Probability and Certainty: What Justifies Belief*. Oxford: Oxford University Press.

Smith, M. 2018. When Does Evidence Suffice for Conviction? *Mind* 127: 1193–1218.

Williamson, T. 2000. *Knowledge and Its Limits*. Oxford: Oxford University Press.